The Concept of Conversation

Dedicated
With love,
to
Joshua Edward Randall

The Concept of Conversation

From Cicero's *Sermo* to the *Grand Siècle's Conversation*

David Randall

EDINBURGH
University Press

Edinburgh University Press is one of the leading university presses in the UK. We publish academic books and journals in our selected subject areas across the humanities and social sciences, combining cutting-edge scholarship with high editorial and production values to produce academic works of lasting importance. For more information visit our website: edinburghuniversitypress.com

Edinburgh University Press Ltd
The Tun – Holyrood Road,
12(2f) Jackson's Entry,
Edinburgh EH8 8PJ

Typeset in 11/13 Adobe Sabon by
IDSUK (DataConnection) Ltd, and
Printed and bound by CPI Group (UK) Ltd, Croydon, CR0 4YY

A CIP record for this book is available from the British Library

ISBN 978 1 4744 3010 4 (hardback)
ISBN 978 1 4744 3012 8 (webready PDF)
ISBN 978 1 4744 3013 5 (epub)

Contents

Acknowledgements

I am grateful to more people than I can possibly name – but among them are John Ackerman, Helen R. Andrews, Darin Barney, Michael Bristol, Marshall Brown, Samuel A. Chambers, Brooke Conti, Timothy Costelloe, Brian Cowan, Julie Cumming, Kyle Davis, Samuel Fleischacker, Bryan Garsten, Eugene Garver, John Guillory, Marc Hanvelt, Gerard Hauser, Torrance Kirby, Rita Koganzon, David Kopel, Jacob Levy, James Masschaele, Warren Moore, Kevin Pask, Mark Pennington, Adam Potkay, Ariane Randall, Francis Randall, Laura Randall, Eyvind Ronquist, Andrew Stevens, David Rosen, Samuel Chambers, Jeff Sypeck, Robert Tittler, William Walker, Christopher Welser, Ronald Witt, Peter Wong, Paul Yachnin, Leigh Yetter, the editors of *Past and Present* and several anonymous readers for their comments on different portions of this manuscript. I am also grateful to the Social Sciences and Humanities Research Council of Canada, the Making Publics project and Concordia University for their support while writing it.

Every book I have written has been inconceivable without the love and support of my wife, Laura H. Congleton, for which I am grateful every day, and which I will always try to make adequate recompense.

This book I dedicate to my son. I have been writing it all his life, and longer, but it has never been as important to me as he is.

Introduction

This book relates a story of the rebirth of conversation in Renaissance and early modern Europe. In the beginning, there was Cicero, who, in the midst of his strictures on the kinds of persuasive speech – the types of rhetoric – wrote scattered paragraphs on how conversation (*sermo*) should be conducted in the villas of noble Romans. Darkness fell on the land and the theory of conversation lay in ruins, until fourteen hundred years later Petrarch began to converse, so to speak, with the dead Cicero. This *so to speak* shifted the course of intellectual history, for to think of conversation metaphorically meant that it could be applied to the world outside the noble villa. This the humanists of the Renaissance and the courtiers of early modern Europe did more and more boldly, as genre by genre they progressively extended the scope of conversation. They did this not least because conversation provided an attractive middle way between the twin tyrannies of reason (*ratio*) and oratorical rhetoric (*oratio*). By the beginning of the Enlightenment, conversation had annexed rhetoric itself, and so had become ready to undertake a further astonishing expansion during the Enlightenment.

Here too is the story of how the thinkers of Renaissance and early modern Europe reconceived the relationship between the two halves of rhetoric, the much transformed genres of conversation and oratory. Cicero had thought conversation was meant to inform oratory – but the latter-day expansion of conversation annexed much of the traditional world of oratory and so rendered obsolete the old relationship between the two domains. The early modern conflation of conversation (*sermo*) and sociability (*conversatio*), by way of Stefano Guazzo's innovative conception of civil conversation and the natural law tradition of Hugo Grotius and Samuel von Pufendorf, made possible a new relationship between conversation and oratory. By means of the hinge of *doux commerce*, the world of oratory, now in the guise of economic interest, became a prerequisite to the world of conversation. The old complementary relationship of oratory and conversation was reconceived in historical and sociological terms.

This book further tells of how women came to speak. Doubtless they had spoken in reality, but in theory they were meant to be mute; tyranny's great monologues found their deepest analogue in the unending speech of man and the silence of women. From the Renaissance onward, this began to change. In literature and in reality, in the prescriptions and practices of women such as Moderata Fonte and Madeleine de Scudéry, the expanding bounds of conversation gave women more and more places to speak. In conversation, moreover, women were recognised as women and could speak as women. Not reason's dialectic, nor rhetoric's orations, but only the speech of conversation spoke to and with women – and so only in conversation did mankind learn to speak to one another in all their individuality and variety. The expansion of conversation to women made possible the first true universalisation of speech.

This narrative is also the first part of a yoked recasting of the history of rhetoric and of Habermasian theory. This history of the emergence and increasing universalisation and democratisation of conversation both reorganises the history of rhetoric along the broad lines of Jürgen Habermas' (1929 –) historical analysis and substitutes conversation for quasi-Kantian reason in Habermas' public sphere. This book narrates the reconception of conversation and oratory up to the beginning of the Enlightenment; its sequel will narrate the universalisation of conversation in the century from the Earl of Shaftesbury to James Madison. But let that wait; the stories of this book are complete in themselves.

Boil all that down to one paragraph. This book narrates the transformation of rhetoric between the Renaissance and the opening of the Enlightenment, especially in Renaissance Italy and seventeenth-century France. In these centuries, rhetoric shifted its emphasis from oratory to conversation, until the synecdoche of rhetoric shifted from the former to the latter. The same centuries saw a number of cognate shifts – in the interiorisation and familiarisation of friendship, in the rise of women to a central role in conversational speech, in the universalising development of sociability out of *conversatio*, and in the rise of both the Republic of Letters and the courtier/*salon* tradition as rival incarnations of conversation. Several intellectual lineages developed from this broad shift, but in the one this book traces, oratory became the predicate and dynamic fosterer of conversation via the hinge of *doux commerce*.

That is the shortest version of this book – but what is new about it?

This book in the first instance recasts the *history of rhetoric* in Renaissance and early modern Europe. The current narrative, broadly speaking, describes how the rhetoric of the ancient world was dismembered and hollowed out during the medieval centuries, to be revived by humanists from Petrarch onward. Witt describes the humanist endeavour as the classicisation of successive genres – history, letters and so on (Witt 2003: esp. 6). Rhetoric's full classicisation during the Renaissance was followed by a slow decay thereafter, as it was replaced by diverse rationalising challenges to the rhetorical word in the work of figures such as Francis Bacon, René Descartes and John Locke. Historians of rhetoric have challenged an older intellectual history that saw rhetoric disappear entirely; they, if not necessarily the larger world of historians of early modern Europe, realise the resilience of rhetorical thought, and its survival in various displaced modes. Yet in effect these historians only qualify the older narrative of rhetoric's disappearance.

This qualification rests largely upon a tacit identification, made by most modern historians, of rhetoric as a whole – of persuasive speech in all forms – with *oratory* – the persuasive speech that aimed at victory, usually in a public forum such as a legislative assembly or a law court. In so doing, modern scholars follow many influential sources among Renaissance and early modern rhetoricians, who likewise took *oratory* as synecdoche for *rhetoric*. Yet perhaps even more importantly, this synecdoche recapitulates the Renaissance and early modern *polemics against rhetoric* – the attacks against rhetoric on the grounds that because it aimed only at victory in speech it had no ability to ascertain truth in speech, hence no value, and therefore ought to be replaced by some more rational mode of discourse. To describe rhetoric as essentially oratory – to defend rhetoric as essentially oratory – is to recapitulate the old arguments of philosophy against rhetoric, and ultimately to endorse not only rhetoric's historical declension narrative but also to endorse the justification for its replacement. To describe rhetoric as oratory, no matter with what fulsome intentions, is to anticipate its obsequies.

Not all historians make this identification. Some pay attention to conversation (*sermo*) – that mode of rhetoric concerned rather with the mutual search for truth than for the agonistic desire for victory (Godo 2003). Gary Remer makes the deepest examination of the Renaissance use of *sermo* and its broader intellectual influence (Remer 1996); Virginia Cox, David Marsh and John Tinkler study Renaissance dialogues, those literary emulations of *sermo* (V. Cox 1992; Marsh 1980; Tinkler 1988a); and Judith Henderson studies the sixteenth-century debate as to whether a letter ought still to be written along ancient lines as one half of a conversation between distant friends (Henderson

1983b, 1992). At the other end of the Renaissance, Marc Fumaroli notes briefly the transition in seventeenth-century France from an age of rhetoric to an age of conversation (Fumaroli 1995: 25–45, esp. 31, 38–9). But none of these studies – excellent though they are – aims to create a coherent narrative of the emergence of Renaissance conversation, of its changing relationship with oratory, and of the broader implications that derive from the presentation of such a narrative. This book povides that narrative.

What this narrative of conversation first indicates is that we should reconceive the renaissance of rhetoric as two overlapping renaissances – one, cresting earlier, of oratory, and a second of conversation. Petrarch revived both oratory and conversation, but his humanist successors first focused upon the modes of oratory and treated conversation in a minor key. Yet conversation came to have increasing influence – partly due to the accidents of textual survival that left a disproportionate number of genre analogues of *sermo* among the ancient world's legacy to the Renaissance, and partly due to the very power of the Renaissance revival of oratory, whose tyrannising pretensions left humanists in ever more desperate search for an alternative. Conversation – a mode of discourse that sought out truth, without seeking to compel the passions or the will, and without abandoning the rhetorical framework entirely – became an increasingly attractive alternative to oratory. Indeed, the Renaissance and early modern centuries saw various writers seek to expand the scope of conversation, especially via the cognate genres of dialogue and the letter, so as to displace oratory's compulsions. The transition from Renaissance to Enlightenment saw the rise of a mode of rational discourse that challenged rhetoric entirely – but it also saw a culmination of the transition from the mode of rhetoric to the mode of conversation, whose inheritance would be at least as influential as that of the mode of purely rational discourse. The champions of oratory and of anti-rhetorical discourse both found it convenient to forget conversation and to establish their two preferred modes as mutually exclusive polarities, but the mode of conversation was a tradition at least as strong as its two quarreling siblings.

Yet this rise of conversation was not necessarily at the expense of oratory. Conversation and oratory traditionally had been conceived of as complementary modes – conversation quintessentially the private discussion of equal noblemen in their country villas, oratory the address to a mixed multitude in the forum. To expand conversation into the world of the forum could be taken as simply the suppression of oratory – and, as we shall see, was indeed taken that way in some traditions – but it also could be taken rather to call for a reformulation of the relationship between conversation and oratory. This would happen via a parallel narrative to the rise of conversation, the progressive intertwining of *sermo* (conversation) and *conversatio* (mutual behaviour, sociability).

Conversatio had long possessed affiliations with *sermo*, back to the ancient world. The Renaissance saw first a secularising, conversationalising reformulation of *conversatio* as 'civil conversation' by Stefano Guazzo, a universalisation of the concept of *conversatio* via the natural law tradition of Hugo Grotius and Samuel von Pufendorf, and finally an extended interpenetration of the two concepts, so complete that *sermo* acquired the name of 'conversation', while the nomenclature of *conversatio*, universalised, shifted toward 'sociability'. Peter Miller has written on the narrative connecting civil conversation and sociability (Miller 2008), but the significance of this narrative for the parallel reconfiguration of the relationship of conversation and oratory has not yet been explored. One effect of this interpenetration was to broaden the scope of conversation's subject matter to include the entire social realm. A further effect was to reshape the traditional complementary relationship of oratory and conversation in a new form. Prudence, the reason of rhetoric, had now come to include economic self-interest; the exercise of this economic prudence therefore become part of the realm of oratory – and sociability was now taken both to derive from and to forward this exercise of economic prudence. More precisely, the exercise of *doux commerce* was now taken to make a logical and historical sequence of economic interest, sociability, polite manners and the establishment of the material and intellectual preconditions of conversation. Conversation originally had been meant to inform oratory; now the exercise of oratory was taken as the prerequisite for conversation. This new complementary relation of conversation and oratory, built upon the hinge of civil conversation and sociability, would be the foundation for the enduring and powerful rhetorical tradition of the Enlightenment.

This book thus argues the importance of the history of conversation within the history of rhetoric. Classic *sermo* was scarcely more than an afterthought in the classical theory of rhetoric – a paragraph here, a sentence there – and the theory of the letter was scarcely more developed. The practice of conversation clearly was greater – witness the relative abundance of surviving dialogues and letters – but *sermo* remained a minor component of rhetoric as a whole. The Renaissance revival of *sermo*, however, radically magnified the importance of conversation within rhetoric. Indeed, the abstraction and metaphorisation of conversation and the slow shift of rhetoric from a default of oratory to a default of conversation by *c*.1700 made conversation the most important mode of rhetoric. Historians of rhetoric (above all Fumaroli) have written about the importance of the emergence of conversation within rhetoric, from minor part to subsuming whole, but I do not think there has been any sustained argument that this transformation was of first-order importance, both within the history of rhetoric and the larger intellectual history of Renaissance and early modern Europe. This book makes that argument.

This book further argues the importance of a broad shift in the conception of rhetoric *c*.1500 – an amoralisation of rhetoric, a shift to a pure consideration of appearances, a divorce from any essential tie between virtue and rhetoric. Eugene Garver makes this argument with reference to Niccolò Machiavelli's prudential thought (Garver 1987, esp. 88–9), but the shift was far broader. Leon Battista Alberti anticipated Machiavelli in his commendation of properly mutable behaviour toward a Prince; Baldassare Castiglione made the flexible courtier a model for European nobles; Desiderius Erasmus argued the same polypian shift with regard to letters; and Guazzo applied these lessons in changeability toward the entire realm of civil conversation. I do not seek to explain this shift – it seems a natural consequence of prolonged meditation upon the a prioris of rhetoric, but 'natural' assumes a point at issue, and this still begs the question of the shift's timing. Yet whatever the cause, the shift did occur, and it seems to have been a turning point in the history of European rhetoric – a turning point in the thought of the most influential rhetorical thinkers of the age, and not only a singular innovation on the part of Machiavelli. (The broadness of the turn, incidentally, supports the thesis that what Machiavelli did was to amoralise prudence rather than instrumentalise it, since such amoralisation was the intellectual drift of the age. But this point will be argued at greater length in this book's sequel.) A great deal of the later history of rhetoric, both in this book and in its sequel, in effect consisted of successive innovations progressively to broaden and then to universalise the scope of amorality in rhetoric – innovations whose importance were of the first order in the history of rhetoric.

Thus far this book recasts the history of rhetoric – but it also recasts broader aspects of the *intellectual history* of Renaissance and early modern Europe. The narrative of the shift of rhetoric from the oratorical to the conversational mode incorporated, articulated and forwarded several parallel shifts of cognate concepts. Ancient conversation had been defined as rational speech among equal male friends whose friendship was defined primarily around a shared virtue and only secondarily around a shared familiarity or intimacy. To begin with, the shift to conversation accompanied the intellectual shift of emphasis from reason to the passions, where conversation, mediating, became a speech of passion that sought out the rational truth. This shift brought with it a shift of friendship from freely shared rational virtue to freely shared passionate intimacy: conversation became a communication of intimacy in search of the truth, the old expressive aspect of conversation applied to conversation that sought out truth. The growing conception of conversation as possible between unequals – inherited from the innovative medieval Christian conception of conversation between God and man – most radically altered conversation by making it a discourse which women could be conceived of as capable of partaking. Oratory remained explicitly masculine in its associations; the universal discourse of reason persistently modelled itself upon implicitly male interlocutors; but conversation, precisely because it allowed for discourse involving a presumed inferior, increasingly welcomed the speech of women. The widening scope of women's discourse in the Renaissance and early modern centuries thus was above all a widening of the estimation of women's abilities to partake in conversation joined to the widening subject matter of conversation. This book does not seek to explain these cognate changes by reference to the rise of conversation; rather, it *associates* them with the rise of conversation as a coherent, complex intellectual narrative. The histories of passion, friendship, intimacy and women all find a joint link and articulation broadly in the history of rhetoric, and narrowly in the history of rhetoric's conversational mode.

The book also recasts further aspects of the *combined intellectual and social history* of Renaissance and early modern Europe around rival innovations upon conversation. The mode of conversation came to infuse both the *quattrocento* Italian court and, via the *quattrocento* Italian Academies, the *Respublica literaria*, the Republic of Letters. Castiglione gave to European court culture an enduringly conversational cast, albeit one reformed within the shadow of the power of the Prince; his seventeenth-century French successors would reformulate that court culture as *salon* culture, whose conversational structure operated in the Prince's absence – first quietly, and then with increasing self-assurance and theoretical justification. The Republic of Letters, meanwhile, formed an alternate mode of conversation, deviating toward the more rationalising rival mode of Platonic dialogue. The overlapping history of these social structures' modes of conversation – partly complementary, partly rivalrous – mattered not least as the prehistory of the alternate modes of the universal conversation of public opinion that would emerge in the Enlightenment. That public opinion, not incidentally, would be articulated via another derivation of conversation – the newspaper, the descendant of the mixedly dictaminal and conversational letter, which would oscillate in and out of conversational presumptions. The histories of court, *salon*, Republic of Letters and newspaper all intertwined with the history of conversation.

This book incorporates and recasts these related intellectual histories with a larger argument in mind – for this book is part of a larger project to fuse the history of rhetoric with Habermasian theory. Most immediately, this book's histories of rhetoric and conversation are intended to recast them parallel to the broad framework of early modern European intellectual history Habermas sketches in *The Structural Transformation of the Bourgeois Public Sphere* (Habermas 1991: 1–117) and *Theory and Practice* (Habermas 1973: 41–81). In these two books, Habermas describes the transformations of reason and its articulation in such genres as the newspaper and such social formations as the *salons* and the Republic of Letters, in terms of processes of universalisation, publicisation and democratisation that would collectively result in a critical-rational public discourse theoretically universal both in its participants and in its subject matter – the public sphere (Habermas 1991: 1–26; Raymond 1999: 111–12, 118). This book's larger historical argument is that Habermas' description of the processes (universalisation, publicisation and democratisation) operating in Renaissance and early modern Europe is the proper framework by which to understand the histories of rhetoric and conversation. This is so not least because Habermas ascribes to the public sphere and its prehistory such historical elements as the *salons* and the newspaper, which more correctly should be ascribed to conversation; Habermas' historical chronology and dynamics apply to the history of conversation because they are drawn, somewhat unawares, from that history. But I will make this argument at greater length in this book's sequel.

This book is further intended as a component of a theoretical critique and revision of Habermasian theory – but it is not itself making the direct argument, for it generally stops short of the Enlightenment and it largely consists of focused intellectual history. It should be taken, however, as narrating the emergence and describing the character of that transformed conversation which would become pervasive in the Enlightenment, and constitute one half of a *rhetorical public sphere*.[1] It further establishes the character of a *conversational rationality* which may be substituted for Habermas' conception of *communicative rationality*. I take this book's narrative to be largely self-sufficient in its purpose and its interest, but it has also been written with this larger purpose in mind, whose argument also will be detailed in this book's sequel.

This narrative is largely self-sufficient – but not entirely. The conception of a rhetorical public sphere is built around the complementary nature of oratory and conversation, but I do not here narrate the parallel transformations in Renaissance and early modern Europe of different modes of *prudence* – the reason of rhetoric in its oratorical mode desiring success rather than truth. These I have narrated in three separate articles, detailing respectively the history of amoralised prudence and *interest* (Randall 2011c), the history of economic prudence (Randall 2016b) and the history of rhetorical violence (Randall 2016a), wherein each of these emerges by the Enlightenment as components of the oratorical portion of the rhetorical public sphere. These articles, which all turn on a reading of Machiavelli as articulating prudential reasoning rather than calculative or instrumental reasoning, should be taken generally as lurking in the background of this narrative. In particular, the conception of economic interest as prudential rather than (as in Max Weber, Habermas, etc.) as calculative or instrumental lies behind the particular argument that *doux commerce* provides a hinge between oratory and conversation – for economic activity must be taken as prudential for that particular equation to be taken as valid. For the lengthier version of this argument, I direct the reader to my articles on prudence and economic prudence.

I have given some idea of the broad ambitions and implications of this book; what follows is a brief outline of the book, chapter by chapter.

The history of conversation begins with the classical formulations of the concepts analysed here. To begin with, conversation referred narrowly to actual conversations (and their literary simulations), conducted in the leisure time of noble men, and generally concerned with indefinite philosophical topics only loosely connected to the world of political affairs, which was more properly addressed by oratory. The Greeks and Romans linked together several concepts whose history we will trace throughout this narrative. These were *familiarity*, its sometimes rivalrous complement of *friendship*, the friend's doppelgänger, the *flatterer*, and *conversation*, the mode of speech inquiring after truth that articulated both familiar style and friendship. All these concepts found expression not only in conversation but also in the *letter*, the written analogue of conversation. The Romans in particular also began to emphasise during their Silver Age the concept of *conversatio*, the mutual conduct of mankind. This last concept stood at some intellectual distance from the constellation formed around familiarity, friendship and conversation, but from the beginning it possessed conceptual associations that would allow it to be linked with them more tightly in ensuing centuries (Chapter 1).

During the medieval centuries, the concepts of friendship, familiarity and *conversatio* reoriented themselves around the universalising Christian conception of community, while the *sermo* of dialogue began to concern itself with that eminently Christian subject matter, the interiority of the soul. On the other hand, the *ars dictaminis* (art of letter writing) shifted the medieval letter toward the public realm, and thus toward the traditional realm of oratory. Petrarch's rediscovery of classical conversation retained these medieval innovations. The Renaissance variant of conversation that sprang from him would partly slough the theory and practice of its medieval predecessor – but the influence of Christianity and the *ars dictaminis* would endure (Chapter 2).

Conversation, both within treatises touching on theories of conversation and in the practice of the literary genre of dialogue, underwent increasingly radical transformation thereafter at the hands of the humanists and their successors. This transformation began with the Renaissance humanists, who intensified the Petrarchan abstraction of conversation-as-metaphor from actual conversation. The changing role of Renaissance conversation was linked to the simultaneous expansion of oratory's ambitions, which inspired both the use of conversation as a refuge from oratory and, in a revolutionary riposte, the counter-claim that conversation should expand the scope of its subject matter to supplant oratory. The innovative genre of Utopian dialogue provided a climax to this last development, by transforming the old debate as to the *optimus status rei publicae* into a conversation, and thus incorporating the ends of political action within the genre of *sermo*. Finally, in seventeenth-century France, the preceding expansion of conversation culminated in a revolutionary triumph, as conversation replaced oratory as the default mode of rhetoric. These changes collectively set the stage for the centrality of conversation in the intellectual world of early modern Europe (Chapter 3).

Conversation in antiquity had been the speech of friends and familiarity – and insofar as friendship motivated conversation as a mode of inquiry, that friendship oriented conversation toward reason and virtue. The Renaissance witnessed a long shift in the conception of friendship, culminating in the thought of Michel de Montaigne, away from an alignment with reason and virtue and toward an alignment with passion and familiarity. This changing conception of friendship brought with it a corresponding change in the conception of conversation, which now also based itself upon passion and familiarity – including in its use as a mode of inquiry. In other words, the expressive aspect of *sermo*, which communicated character in an intimate manner, now became the basis of the philosophical aspect of *sermo*, the inquiry into truth. The communication of intimate, passionate friendship became a prerequisite for the search for truth. Furthermore, the development of a conception of intimate friendship and the development of a conception of friendship with and among women went hand and hand in Renaissance and early modern Europe; together, they came to associate women, as women, with conversation and the inquiry into truth. This association radically differentiated conversation from both oratory and philosophical reason, which remained the speech of wrangling and disputatious men (Chapter 4).

The humanist educational project to educate the elite of western Europe produced as one of its dizzy successes the application of conversation to the speech and behaviour of noblemen at court. This development of the ideal of the courtier took conversation from the leisurely retreat from the ancient political world to the courtly heart of the Renaissance political world. The *salons* of seventeenth-century France further transformed the conversational tradition of the court: in principle, the conversation of the *salons* began quietly to set itself to rival the world of oratory, to address itself to the same worldly subject matter. The Republic of Letters provided an alternate social matrix for *sermo*, scholarly rather than courtly – and one which migrated away from its Ciceronian roots toward the mode of Baylean critique. Where the courtly and scholarly traditions of *sermo* acted as complementary modes during the Renaissance, the increasing scope of *salonnier* conversation and the increasing abandonment of *sermo* by the Republic of Letters set them at odds with one another in the eighteenth century. Both now harboured universalising ambitions, which set these sibling modes to fierce conflict (Chapter 5).

Renaissance humanists classicised their letters so as to approximate the familiar style of *sermo* – but they also inherited the medieval tradition of *ars dictaminis*, which had shifted letters toward the public realm. Humanist letters therefore continued to depart from familiar style in practice – and in Erasmus' theory, he explicitly acknowledged that letter-writing was no longer entirely a genre of familiar communication. The Renaissance humanist letter became a mode of communication mediating between conversation and oratory, and firmly oriented toward the public world. One descendant of the humanist letter would be the newspaper – that genre that Habermas took to constitute the public sphere. The newspaper, by way of the news letter, preserved aspects of the style of familiar communication, but, as it shifted in medium toward print, transformed into a distinctly persuasive communication between anonymous correspondents and anonymous recipients. Conversation had shifted in theory to be able to address the public world; the newspaper would be the genre that embodied a familiar conversation, universal and anonymous, that discussed all the subjects of the world (Chapter 6).

Conversatio, mutual conduct, had possessed loose affiliations with *sermo* in ancient and medieval times. During the Renaissance, *conversatio* shifted far closer to *sermo* and its constellation of cognate concepts. Most notably, Guazzo elaborated an influential theory of civil conversation in his eponymous late-sixteenth-century dialogue, which reconceived *conversatio* in secular terms as the realm of society and manners intermediate between the *oikos* and the political world. This conception of civil conversation then received a universalising spin from the natural law jurisprudential tradition of Grotius and Pufendorf, transforming it into an amoral disposition toward sociability shared by all humanity. The long parallel tracks of *sermo* and *conversatio* now finally converged: *sermo* became conversation as *conversatio* became sociability. The convergence of *sermo* and *conversatio* made possible the establishment of a causal connection between the two concepts. This connection appeared via *doux commerce*, the application of sociability to the realm of economics: sociability, via the universal exercise of economic self-interest, became the conceptual and historical predicate to conversation – and, as the Enlightenment progressively yoked manners to the civic humanist tradition, the predicate in turn for both virtue and liberty. Sociability thus at last substituted for Platonic love an amoral, entirely human motivation for conversation. By this means, conversation received a coherent grounding in the selfish needs of humanity – the discourse of reason found its base in human passions (Chapter 7).

Put more briefly: the concept of conversation was born in the classical world, tightly linked to actual conversations among elite gentlemen, who conversed as friends (Chapter 1). In the Middle Ages, Christianity made the idea of friendship universal, and the shift of the primary locus of conversational style over to the *ars dictaminis* muddied the idea that a conversation was a private affair (Chapter 2). In the Renaissance, conversation became a metaphor applied to an ever widening range of activities, and in seventeenth-century France supplanted oratory as the default mode of rhetoric (Chapter 3). The Renaissance's long mutation of the idea of friendship meanwhile changed it from a relationship between members of the male elite to a relationship between any two human beings – including women. Since conversation was carried on between friends, this change in turn opened up conversation to the whole world, and notably women (Chapter 4). This new style of conversation acquired a social articulation in the *salons* of seventeenth-century France, which would be the model for the future spread of conversational culture (Chapter 5). Conversations in writing (letters) and conversations in print (newspapers) evolved in tandem in early modern Europe, and produced in the newspaper a new conversational style capable of discussing all the subjects of the world (Chapter 6). Finally, the transformation of *conversatio* into *sociability* led in turn to a new conceptual relationship between the rhetorical modes of conversation and oratory, where the exercise of oratory (especially as economic commerce) now became the historical prerequisite for the exercise of conversation (Chapter 7). These linked transformations set the stage for the vast expansion of conversation that would occur during the Enlightenment.

This outline generalises horribly – and so does the book as a whole. It is both a narrative and an interpretation of the history of conversation from classical times to *c.*1700, and each chapter could have been a monograph in itself. Inevitably, given the nature of the project, I have been more concerned to paint with a broad brush than to seek out nuance and counter-example. Among my sins, I generalise from an inevitably narrow selection of texts, largely Italian and French; I follow secondary sources for many of my local interpretations; I cite narrow and uncontextualised portions of the thought of many disparate thinkers; I do not discuss the medium (manuscript or print) in which these works first appeared, nor (usually) examine the circumstances of their composition, circulation and reception; and I reify conversation and other such abstractions as coherent entities that possess a unitary history. These choices of how to write this narrative are the inevitable consequences of writing at this length on a topic of such broad scope: I judge it tolerable for the reader to endure *European conversation did X at point Y* over the course of several hundred pages, but fear that repeated resort to *Rhetorician Z wrote about the concept of conversation in text X, with limited application to the broader, nuanced and complex histories of European conversations*, would try the patience of a saint.

Withal, I have tried to phrase my language carefully so as to minimise the effect of my generalising approach. A large number of qualifiers bestrew the narrative, and *a* or *an* substitute for *the* very regularly. Where such caution fails, I ask the reader to impute to me an editorial failure rather than a conceptual one.

Another simplification: when I cite the character of a dialogue to support the statement that 'X believed Y', I know that dialogues frequently present mutually contradictory views from their dramatis personae, none of which can be associated with absolute confidence with the author's beliefs. The reader should take 'X believed Y' to stand for 'X raised the possibility of Y, regardless of what the author actually believed'. In using this shorthand, I have tried not to conflate contradictory arguments by different characters in a dialogue. I do not think my shorthand distorts the history presented here.

I do not always write 'as Blimovich says' at the beginning of a passage that paraphrases Blimovich's interpretation of a source, but instead say (Blimovich 2016) at the passage's end. I trust I combine concision and transparency well enough. Further, I should emphasise that this book was not written to quarrel with any Blimovich. My largest argument is that this overarching narrative exists – which is not written for or against any scholar, since I don't believe any have explicitly considered the matter. My references are meant to indicate my dependence upon and gratitude to a host of scholars, to whose interpretations of the subject matter which is their expertise I have scrupulously deferred. My side of the scholarly conversation is really no more than to say 'thank you!' – as expressed by (Blimovich 2016). Any errors I have made as I rephrased their interpretations in summary paraphrase are, of course, my own.

The reader will notice a tendency to quote at length. The heart of this book concerns the changing conception of conversation and its allied concepts, and for such a project primary source quotation, not analysis, is the heart of the matter. I have preferred to err on the side of lengthy quotation. Such quotations can seem less formidable when broken up and interspersed with interpretive paraphrase – but I am not fond of interpolating my own words when I cannot improve on the original. I provide interpretation where appropriate, but not simply for the sake of breaking up a lengthy quotation.

Within this narrative, I emphasise successive intellectual moments and figures. The classic source of this rhetorical tradition, overwhelmingly, was Cicero, although Aristotle, Seneca and Quintilian, among others, also had notable roles. Petrarch resurrected both the oratorical and conversational aspects of rhetoric, and supporting roles were played in the *quattrocento* by figures such as Manuel Chrysoloras, Leonardo Bruni and Alberti. The expansion of conversation to cover all topics was pioneered in the dialogue genre, especially among figures such as Alamanno Rinuccini, Francesco Guicciardini and Thomas More. The years around 1500 saw a great shift towards amoral flexibility, among thinkers including Machiavelli, Erasmus, Castiglione and Guazzo. The mode of intimate friendship received enduring articulation from Montaigne; the shift of such friendship, and corollary conversation, to include women found notable exponents in Fonte, Scudéry and Mary Astell. The seventeenth century saw a great shift in France toward the conceiving of conversation as the default mode of rhetoric, especially important in Jean-Louis Guez de Balzac, Scudéry, René Rapin and François Fénelon. The same century also witnessed, by way of conceptions of civil conversation articulated by Guazzo and popularised by Pierre Charron, a parallel development of the ideals of sociability in the Teutonic jurisprudence of Grotius and Pufendorf. The breadth and significance of the renaissance of conversation is measured by the catalogue of notable thinkers whom it encompassed.

Yet to speak of a 'catalogue of notable thinkers' is to acknowledge the limited scope of this book, which largely narrates an intellectual history of the *concept* of conversation – the history of rhetoric, conceptions of friendship, the transformation of civil conversation into sociability and, within literary genre history, the history of the dialogue and the letter. I do not provide a history of actual conversations. Neither do I engage in a close linguistic analysis of literary evocations of conversations so as to determine (for example) what salutations reveal of actual social relationships. These approaches, to be done adequately, would require treatment in separate books with different ranges of primary sources and secondary scholarship.

This book's narrative does intersect with social history, in the history of the Republic of Letters, the court and *salon*, and the newspaper, and it intertwines with the history of women as a whole – yet these remain adjuncts to what is, in essence, a study of select books and select thinkers, a narrative of the changing attitudes and behaviour of a narrow elite. The social history of coffeehouses, schools and other locales associated with the increasingly widespread early modern culture of conversation will be discussed in this book's sequel, which explores the democratisation of conversation.

Finally, to say that this book is a history of the 'concept of conversation' requires some unpacking. This is the history of several attributes that were originally applied to, or allied with, actual conversations in the ancient world. These attributes were abstracted early on as, in essence, a conversational style that could be applied in circumstances other than actual conversation, and to literary genres such as the letter and the dialogue. I trace the evolving nature of these conversational attributes, styles and genres – as well as the broadening use of conversation as a metaphor and the social matrices which articulated these aspects of conversation. At its heart, however, the history of the concept of conversation is the history of the application of conversational style to ever wider portions of the European intellectual world.

We will now turn to the ancient origins of conversation.

Note

1. For transhistorical substitutions of rhetoric into Habermasian theory, see Farrell (1993), Hauser (1999), Rehg (1997: esp. 359) and Triadafilopoulos (1999). Donawerth anticipates my application of conversation to Habermasian theory (Donawerth 2012: 40), but only to argue that conversation developed 'a counterdiscourse of women's rhetorical theory'.

Chapter 1

The Classic Origins of Conversation

Introduction

We begin in antiquity, when the Greeks and Romans linked together several concepts whose history we will trace throughout this narrative. These were *familiarity*, its sometimes tense analogue *friendship*, the friend's doppelgänger, the *flatterer*, and *conversation*, the mode of speech inquiring after truth that articulated both familiar style and friendship. All these concepts found expression not only in conversation but also in the *letter*, the written analogue of conversation. The Romans also began to emphasise during their Silver Age the concept of *conversatio*, the mutual conduct of mankind. This last concept stood at some intellectual distance from the constellation formed around familiarity, friendship and conversation, but from the beginning it possessed conceptual associations that would allow it to be linked with them more tightly in ensuing centuries.

This portrait of classical conversation and its allied modes serves as a jumping-off point for our story. It must be a stumbling block to classicists, for I therefore render these concepts as a flattened synthesis of the long intellectual history of the classical era, to emphasise points of similarity rather than internal variation and transformation. It must likewise be foolishness to the Cambridge School as it pronounces anathema on historiographical teleology, for (indulging in blithe Whiggery) I also emphasise those aspects of this classical ensemble that would matter most in the later development of the conversational tradition – and hence focus particularly upon the thought of Cicero, the genius of conversation in the Latin West. It is a narrative conceived in sin; let us commence.

Familiarity

The concept of *familiarity* originated both etymologically and conceptually in the *oikos* (household), the *familia*. Familiarity denoted the intimate affection a man felt for what was primordially his own – his property, his family, that which belonged to him and that to which he belonged. Man, not woman: men were possessors and women the possessed. The ancients contrasted familiarity's intimacy with the friendship (*philia*) that held all things in common. They argued either that this friendship cut against the fundamental desire to love most what was one's own, or that such friendship had to be built by treating intimately that mass of strangers who constituted common humanity as if they were one's own (Aristotle 2004: 18 [1.5]; 2014: 136 [8.1], 152 [9.2], 171 [9.10]; Diogenes Laertius 1958: II, 329 [8.10]; Eden 2012: 8, 15–17).

Familiar style, the expression in words of familiarity, built upon the latter formulation. To speak intimately to strangers was to evoke in them the powerful passions associated with the intimate love of one's own. Yet the familiar mode's evocation of these passions was no casual thing: it required the speaker to express his character (*ethos*). The original meaning of *ethos* had been 'accustomed place', a definition that had distinct overtones of *oikos*, and the dual definition of character remained *what belonged to one* and *to what one belonged*. To speak familiarly was to speak with one's character; familiar style expressed this character, whose definition referred irreducibly to the intimate relations of the domestic realm (Aristotle 1986: 17 [1252b9–15], 40–1 [1261b35–1262a18]; 2004: 121–2 [3.2], 129–30 [3.7]; Eden 2012: 17–19).

To speak familiarly was also to speak appropriately – with *decorum*, with a command of *to prepon*. To act with propriety, appropriately, meant – with semantic overlap matched in the English translation – not least to act as befitted a man who owned his particular property. Such familiar style could be addressed to strangers, for public and manipulative purposes, but the ancients tended rather to use it to build intimate relationships. Cicero (106–43 BC) praised the intimate *familiaritas* possible between a few complementary characters, and distinguished it from the ordinary, utilitarian alliances of *amicitia* (friendship) (Aristotle 2004: 129–30 [3.7]; Cicero 1971: 357–61 [21–2.70–4]; 2000: 20–1 [1.55–6], 33 [1.93–4], 38–9 [1.110–13]; Eden 2012: 17–18, 27–9).

Friendship

The contrast between *familiaritas* and *amicitia* overlapped with the contrast between *amicitia perfecta* or *vera amicitia* and the more ordinary varieties of *amicitia* – between a friendship based upon selfless affection that sought no useful return and a friendship based upon utility. Such selfless affection was the domain of a select few: while ordinary *amicitia* could embrace relationships between unequals, patrons and clients, friendship *perfecta* or *vera* was usually taken to unite well-born young men of equal station. The philosophical school at the Garden of Epicurus, exceptionally, appears to have been open to women, but this rarity was immediately seized upon as an object of hostile polemic (Diogenes Laertius 1958: II, 535 [10.6–7]; Cicero 1933: 91 [1.33.93]; P. Gordon 1996: 85–8). As a rule, *amicitia vera* could only be achieved between a few, intimate male acquaintances. Yet such perfect friendship was a *philia* that both built upon and overcame the self-rootedness of familiarity, and succeeded in that unlikely endeavour of holding all possessions in common. While familiarity was defined by the relationship of separate characters distinguished by their individual possessions, perfect friendship was defined by commonality both of characters and possessions.

This common character of perfect friends was above all that of a common virtue, a common love of virtue and a common love of one another's virtue. There were exceptions: Plato (*c.*428–*c.*348 BC) in *Lysis* (*c.*380 BC) broached the idea that a fairly good man might like a friend's dissimilarity (Plato 1963: 158–9 [*Lysis*: 215d–e]). Yet *vera amicitia* generally amalgamated itself with moral purpose: to love virtue implied a desire to seek it out, and friends therefore jointly sought out the related goals of happiness, wisdom and the means to moral self-improvement. This last goal, in presaging paradox, tinged the selflessness of perfect friendship with self-interest, for it was difficult to seek to improve oneself, even morally, without some awareness of and interest in the accruing advantages.

In Aristotle (384–322 BC) and those influenced by him – in a move that was at once economically conservative and philosophically radical – the common pursuit of virtue, or its equal possession, came to substitute for the common possession of physical property as the mark of friendship. One possible corollary of this shift was that friendship could be taken as prerequisite to both virtue and wisdom. A different corollary, however, tended to make friendship a secondary appendage to virtue and wisdom. If friendship could be defined fundamentally around the affinity to one another of two men's virtues, such friendship tended (even in Aristotle's less transcendent key) toward an abstraction that rendered irrelevant the particular characters of the two friends. Ultimately, this definition even made friendship itself secondary to the self-sufficient virtue of a perfected man or to the contemplative virtue of *theoria*. Friendship's unstable alliance to virtue led with equal plausibility to both these sharply varying conceptions of friendship, as prerequisite or superfluous to virtue and wisdom. Much future discussion of friendship would build upon these alternatives posited by the ancients (Plato 1963: 145–68 [*Lysis*]; Aristotle 2013: 121–52 [7]; 2014: 136–74 [8–9]; Hutter 1978: 103–4, 111–12, 130; Hyatte 1994: 4–23; Kalimtzis 2000: 61–2, 71–2).

The portrait of friendship in Cicero's *Laelius de Amicitia* (44 BC) merits particular attention, both for its importance within the ancient world and for its future influence on the medieval West. Cicero's Romanising synthesis of many Greek writings on friendship would provide a model both for the conception of friendship and for the entire genre of the philosophical dialogue as it weathered the hard millennium between Augustine and Petrarch. Within the matrix of classic thought on friendship, Cicero emphasised that friendship joined together the agreement of unanimity (*consensio*), benevolence and love (*caritas*), that it was associated with both leisure and the search for knowledge, and that it was the basis of the political order. *Consensio* was particularly important: Cicero gave to his character Laelius the emphatic opinion that 'the true power of friendship consists – [of] the greatest possible community of interests, wishes and opinions . . . friendship is in fact nothing other than a community of views on all matters human and divine, together with goodwill and affection.' Yet Cicero's association of friendship with *consensio* was accompanied by ambiguity about *consensio*'s precise meaning, and so he bequeathed to his posterity what would become an intellectually productive debate both as to its definition and as to how it was to be achieved. Cicero's connection of friendship to the political order likewise would inspire productive debate, but only after a lapse of centuries. Friendship became apolitical during the transition from republic to empire: so Seneca (4 BC – AD 65), who otherwise followed Cicero closely in his conception of friendship. The Senecan divorce of friendship from the political order would significantly affect the later intellectual tradition. Yet Cicero's writings preserved the old link between friendship and the political realm, ready to be revived by a receptive reader (Cicero 1990: 35 [4.15], 37 [6.20]; Seneca 1917–25: I, 9–13 [3], 25–9 [6.2–7], 43–57 [9]; Hyatte 1994: 26–32, 36–8).

The flatterer

The friend came with a dark double: the flatterer, who forged a deceptive simulacrum of friendship. Plutarch (*c*.46–120 AD), in his 'How to Tell a Flatterer from a Friend', addressed the need to distinguish the true friend from his shadow. Plutarch associated friendship with sincerity and truth: 'For the character of a friend, like the "language of truth," is, as Euripides puts it, "simple," plain, and unaffected' (Plutarch 2005: 331–3). In contrast:

> The changes of the flatterer, which are like those of a cuttle fish [polyp], may be most easily detected if a man pretends that he is very changeable himself and disapproves the mode of life which he previously approved, and suddenly shows a liking for actions, conduct, or language which used to offend him. For he will see that the flatterer is nowhere constant, has no character of his own, that it is not because of his own feelings that he loves and hates, and rejoices and grieves, but that, like a mirror, he only catches the images of alien feelings, lives and movements. (Plutarch 2005: 285; cf. Cicero 1990: 69–71 [25.91–6])

The flatterer also could be distinguished from the friend because he encouraged one to wallow in the passions rather than counsel virtue and reason:

> The friend is always found on the better side as a counsel and advocate, trying, after the manner of a physician, to foster the growth of what is sound and to preserve it; but the flatterer takes his place on the side of the emotional and irrational, and this he excites and tickles and wheedles, and tries to divorce from the reasoning powers by contriving for it divers low forms of pleasurable enjoyment. (Plutarch 2005: 327–9)

The flatterer was characteristic of the tyranny, the unfree state, as the friend was characteristic of the free state – the tyrant, notoriously, had no friends and was governed by his passions (Plato 1963: 292 [*Gorgias*: 510b–d], 795–6 [*Republic*: 8.567–8]; Plutarch 2005: 283 [52D–E]; Cicero 1990: 53 [15.52]; Hutter 1978: 93–4, 166–74).

Plutarch associated the flatterer not only with tyranny, the exercise of power and the passions but also with a cognate constellation of concepts and images associated with rhetoric: *opinion, adapt, variable, polypus, chameleon, counterfeit* (Plutarch 2005: 271 [50A–B], 277 [51C], 281 [52B], 285 [52A], 287 [53D], 317 [59C]), 331 [62B]. The flatterer, in other words, could be distinguished from the friend because he applied the manipulative mode of rhetoric to a realm that was supposed to free of such craft.[1] Rhetoric's intrusion into the realm of friendship had destabilising implications. Plutarch distinguished the flatterer from the friend in that he was 'nowhere constant, has no character of his own' – his surface was not true to his interior character. Yet this stipulation shifted the measure of a friend from external virtue to inner consistence, and so made true friendship unverifiable:

a polyp might strain at virtue, but it was his métier to assume a consistence if he had it not. To pose the existence of the flatterer – to expose friendship to rhetoric – mocked the pretensions of *amicitia perfecta* with the unnerving vision that any and all perfect friends might be polyps in disguise.

Equally unsettlingly, Plutarch argued that even true friendship required rhetoric's craft in homeopathic doses. A friend, after all, should not be perpetually stern. Rather, when bringing his friend toward virtue, he ought to take account of his friend's weakness:

> The first step should be commendation cheerfully bestowed. Then later, just as steel is made compact by cooling, and takes on a temper as the result of having first been relaxed and softened by heat, so when our friends have become mollified and warmed by our commendations we should give them an application of frankness like a tempering bath. (Plutarch 2005: 389–95)

Such mollification was no very great distance from flattery, nor was forbearing to reprehend vice self-evidently to be differentiated from encouragement of the passions. The true friend's tempering virtues were the flatterer's corrupting vices, both exercises in the rhetorical mode, which the former used to make their subject good and the latter to make their subject useful. Where friendship had its own persuasive rhetoric, only a knife's edge separated the virtues of the friend from the vices of the flatterer.

Conversation

The search for truth, which partook of both familiarity and friendship, also had its own rhetoric. This mode, discussed relatively briefly in the ancient sources, was conversation (*sermo*). Cicero primarily defined conversation as a private discourse (and implicitly its literary simulation) where two or more people discussed an indefinite question – often upon an abstractly philosophical theme, but any topic, whether domestic, professional or political, could become the subject of conversational inquiry.

> [Conversation] should have its place in social gatherings, philosophical discussions, meetings with friends, and it also has a place at dinner . . . So this conversational mode, in which the disciples of Socrates are the supreme masters, must be mild, wholly undogmatic, and witty. A spokesman should not act as if entering upon his birthright by silencing others;

rather, in general conversation as in all else he should not resent others having their turn . . . Very often exchanges centre on family affairs, or politics, or cultural pursuits and scholarship; we must therefore ensure that even if the conversation begins to roam on to other topics, it should be brought back to the original theme, as long as those present consent to this – for we do not all take pleasure in discussing the same subjects all the time or in a similar way . . . Just as throughout our daily lives the golden rule is to avoid mental disturbances when excessive emotions fail to obey the reason, in the same way our conversation ought to steer clear of such feelings. We should not allow anger to obtrude, nor any grasping or world-weariness or faint-heartedness or any such attitude to surface. Above all we should demonstrate our apparent respect and affection for whose with whom we are to converse. (Cicero 2000: 45–6 [1.132, 1.134–6])

Cicero followed what he took to be the precedent of both the Academic skeptics and of Socrates (470/469–399 BC) and presented the philosophical subjects of conversation as irresoluble. No arbiter could decide such matters, no consensus was possible, and each individual was free to proffer his own probable judgement. In the circumstance, the aim of such conversation had to be the collective discovery of truth rather than the oratorical goal of individual victory in debate. The very process of deliberation pro and con (*in utramque partem*) was intended to elicit from each participant his probable judgement as to the truth of a necessarily indefinite question. The speakers were to seek truth with a becoming moderation, as it could be known with no more than probable assurance. Neither were they supposed to use either *ethos* or *pathos* to gain one another's assent. Rather they were to apply these persuasions toward the *decorum* of the conversation itself, civilly and considerately using their knowledge of one another's particular character so as to elicit free and full speech from all participants – *logos* unmingled with *ethos* or *pathos*.

Conversation's style – clear, pleasing, relaxed, mild, undogmatic and witty – forwarded this conversational decorum. So Cicero in *Orator* (46 BC) on the style of philosophers:

It is therefore easy to distinguish the eloquence which we are treating in this work from the style of the philosophers. The latter is gentle and academic; it has no equipment of words or phrases that catch the popular fancy; it is not arranged in rhythmical periods, but is loose in structure; there is no anger in it, no hatred, no ferocity, no pathos, no shrewdness; it might be called a chaste, pure and modest virgin. Consequently it is called conversation rather than oratory. (Cicero 1971: 351–3 [19.62–4])

Friendship and the desire for truth underpinned conversation, and it characteristically took place in the leisure (*otium*) of a small and elite group capable of dispassionate philosophical inquiry. This circumscription of conversation was necessary not least because the multitude was not only incapable of philosophy but also actively hostile to its practice (Remer 1996: 13–16, 26–41; and see also Lévy 1993).

On the one hand, Ciceronian conversation differed sharply from oratory: private rather than public, oriented toward indefinite rather than definite questions, oriented toward truth rather than victory, cooperative rather than contentious, refraining from rather than indulging in the persuasive use of *ethos* and *pathos*, set among a homogenous elite rather than a mixed multitude, and a speech of leisure (*otium*) rather than of business (*negotium*). On the other hand, Ciceronian conversation shared its Academic framework not only with Ciceronian disputation but also with Ciceronian oratory: just as the Ciceronian conversation elicited joint inquiry toward an unknowable truth and the more purely disputatious seeker after truth was supposed to be able to discuss both sides of every question, so also the perfect Ciceronian orator was supposed to be able to debate both sides of every question (Cicero 1989: 155 [2.3.9]; 1967: I, 109 [1.158], III, 65 [3.31.80]; K. Wilson 1985: 34–5). Ciceronian conversation's concerns also overlapped significantly with the subject matter of oratory, for conversation ultimately aimed to change the speakers' own lives and actions. Thus Cicero in *De finibus* (45 BC): 'I should have thought that to be worthy of philosophy and of ourselves, particularly when the subject of our inquiry is the Supreme Good, the argument ought to amend our lives, purposes and wills, not just correct our terminology' (Cicero 1931: 357 [4.19.52]). Conversation fundamentally shared with oratory an intent to bring about change in the world, although with less urgent and particular purpose. So the abstract consideration in conversation of what constituted a just war was meant to have some bearing, and effect, upon the oratorical consideration of a particular decision to go to war. Conversation's ultimate orientation toward worldly action presaged its future rivalry with oratory, for in the largest sense they shared the same subject matter (Remer 1996: 31, 33).

Neither was conversation entirely divorced from oratory's manipulative aims: Cicero ascribed a secondary motive to conversation, oriented toward an insinuative form of persuasion rather than toward truth.

> There are two forms of discourse, the first conversation and the second argumentation. There is no doubt at all that in pursuit of glory argumentation has the greater force, for this is the medium which we call

eloquence; on the other hand, it is hard to say to what extent friendly and affable conversation captivates men's hearts. Letters have survived composed by three men who we are told were masters of practical wisdom: the first was sent by Philip to Alexander, the second by Antipater to Cassander, and the third by Antigonus to his son Philip. Their advice in these letters is to win over the hearts of the common folk by graciously addressing them, and thus to gain their affection; and again, to soften the spirits of the soldiers by addressing them with honeyed words.

As for the argumentative type of speech made before a crowd, this is often a source of glory gained from all quarters, for there is great admiration for a person who speaks with fluency and wisdom, and his listeners believe that his understanding and intelligence transcend that of others. If indeed a speech combines sobriety with moderation, there can be no performance more admirable, the more so if these qualities are evinced in a young man. (Cicero 2000: 70 [2.48]; Kennerly 2010: 120 (note 2)

Sermo was not incapable of persuasion; rather, it could not address a large audience so effectively as oratory. Looking forward, it is thus no surprise that an increase in the size of *sermo*'s audience correlated with a shift toward persuasive aims. The *sermo*-in-writing of the Republic of Letters clearly had an eye on that same glory Cicero took to be an object of both conversation and argumentation (Goodman 1994: 17); *sermo*-in-print would have a yet wider audience, and explore even more widely the insinuative mode.

The roughly marked boundary between *sermo* and oratory was mirrored by an equally ragged border with other ancient conceptions of dialogue that aimed at truth. *Sermo* differed most from Greek dialectic, which both regarded the emotions of the participants as irrelevant and satisfied itself with syllogistic proof: 'Dialectic is the art of discourse by which we either refute or establish some proposition by means of question and answer on the part of the interlocutors' (Diogenes Laertius 1958: I, 319 [3.48]; Remer 1996: 30, 35–6). Platonic dialogue was conducted with greater awareness of emotional and social context than was dialectic – 'A dialogue is a discourse consisting of question and answer on some philosophical or political subject, with due regard to the characters of the persons introduced and the choice of diction' (Diogenes Laertius 1958: I, 319 [3.48]) – but it still fundamentally relied for its persuasive authority on the philosophical truths presented. In *sermo*, by contrast, argumentative authority derived from the known and particular character of the interlocutors – from their reputations (V. Cox 1992: 12–13; K. Wilson 1985: 23–45). Cicero put it in *Laelius de Amicitia* that, '[t]his type of dialogue, grounded in the authority of eminent men of past generations, seems somehow to carry more weight' (Cicero 1990: 29 [1.4]). Cicero himself, although he drew upon both Platonic and (now lost) Aristotelian conceptions of dialogue, explicitly contrasted his approach to Socrates, 'the source from which has sprung the undoubtedly absurd and unprofitable and reprehensible severance between the tongue and the brain' (Cicero 1967: II, 49 [3.16.61]; Remer 1996: 26 (note 91), 28–9, 32; Vickers 1988: 163-4). Cicero here was confident in his contrast; yet elsewhere he felt it necessary explicitly to affirm the competence of *sermo*, "the rhetoric of philosophers," to address philosophical matters (Cicero 1931: 99 [2.6.17]; Remer 1996: 32). *Sermo* remained close enough to Platonic dialogue and dialectic that it was vulnerable to supplantation. The status of *sermo*, Platonic dialogue, and dialectic as rival genres of speech oriented toward the collective search for truth naturally led both to anxious competition and to recurring slippages between the sibling modes.

The contrast between Platonic dialogue and *sermo* also expressed the rivalry between the Platonisers and the sceptic Academics. The Platonist conception of philosophical truth as sufficiently resoluble, hence particularly and with self-sufficient authority in the possession of the party that avowed it, logically diminished the rival authority of *ethos*. Cicero's conception of individual characters as guarantors of philosophical authority rested on Academic arguments of philosophical truth as both irresoluble and equally inaccessible to all. The word 'equally' merits further consideration: Ciceronian *sermo*'s Academic framework rendered it a more egalitarian mode of inquiry than the Platonic. In Plato's writings, by contrast, Socrates' unmatched possession of the truth was paralleled by his unmatched, formidable character. Plato delineated no other speaker sufficiently to provide rival philosophical authority, and no other characters (save, in Socrates' recollection, Diotima) were capable of engaging in equal conversation with him, of improving his character or of equal insight into the nature of truth (Plato 1963: 145–68 [*Lysis*], 553–63 [*Republic*: 201c–212a]; K. Wilson 1985: 25–9). Ciceronian *sermo* implied both Academic scepticism and an egalitarian mode of inquiry into the truth; Platonic dialogue rejected both implications.

Furthermore, the contrast between *sermo* and Platonic dialogue recapitulated the rivalry between rhetoric and philosophy. The mutual critique of these two modes was wide-ranging, but focused not least on an opposing pair of indictments. Philosophy accused rhetoric by turns of coercing or catering to popular opinion, even at the expense of inquiry into the truth, while rhetoric alleged that since philosophy depended upon a reason purified of the passions, it was incapable of motivating people to inquire into the truth (Plato 1963: 229–307 [*Gorgias*]; Abizadeh 2007; Vickers 1988: 83–213). Even Plato's own work gave some warrant to the latter accusation: however much the Socratic *elenchus* should persuade, in his dialogues that eminently rational mode of persuasion usually failed to do so (Klosko 1986). Cicero's recourse to *sermo*, 'the rhetoric of philosophers', served to vindicate rhetoric both by applying the motivating power of rhetoric to the search for truth and by providing a firm negative to the charge that all rhetoric, all concern with the passions, limited and corrupted philosophical inquiry.

Cicero was not the only Roman to favour *sermo* in this debate between rhetoric and philosophy. Seneca, although no sceptic, agreed with Cicero that philosophical communication required some rhetorical elements – some appeal to the senses as well as to the intellect. This was particularly the case where philosophical writing was intended to persuade the reader to virtues that would modify both behaviour and judgement. Style that moved the emotions was a very effective, perhaps necessary and by no means illegitimate component of such a persuasion (Seneca 1917–25: *Epist.* I, 41 [8.8], 233–5 [33.2], 329–31 [49.12], 411–15 [59.5–8], II, 139 [75.3–6], III, 29–31 [94.27–30], 233–9 [108.6–12]; Behr 2007: 97–102). Cicero and Seneca differed sharply on many subjects, but both affirmed the capacity of *sermo* to treat of philosophy and the necessity for rhetoric, in this conversational mode, to motivate the inquiry into the truth.

Letters

The letter came to be regarded as the written form of conversation – but it did not begin so. The earliest articulations of ancient rhetoric generally assumed a speaker who attempted to influence a listener. There was some consideration of the written word – Aristotle, in passing, distinguished the rhetoric appropriate for the written word from the rhetoric appropriate for the spoken word, and rhetoric operated in a world increasingly inhabited and conditioned by the written word – but rhetoric was held to be primarily a matter of structuring oral speech into persuasive form (Aristotle 2004: 142–3 [1413b–1414a]; E. Haskins 2001).

Rhetorical theory, therefore, did not at first pay much attention to written letters (Welles 1974: xlii ['Introduction']). After all, written letters were not originally supposed to be media of persuasion, but rather official messages conveying decisions and orders; as Stirewalt notes, 'the original meaning of [the Greek word] *epistolē* was an official message, an order, insistent request, decision, oral or written' (Stirewalt 1993: 5; and more generally, 4–15, 67–87). It was an expression of completed political decision, not a means by which to influence political decision-making (Welles 1974: 33–40, 60–2, 64–5, 89–100, 115–17). Yet in the fifth and fourth centuries BC, as Greek letters broadened in use from state missives to private correspondence, the *parousia* of the letter – 'the projection of the official's person, the sense of his felt presence, and the transmission of his authority' – became less peremptory (Stirewalt 1993: 5). Indeed, the letter came to be regarded as a form of conversation; the letter often still had instrumental purpose, but it was no longer the bludgeoning executor of power (Stirewalt 1993: 5–6; and see also Harris 1989: 56–7, 78, 88–9, 123, 127–8, 160–1, 208–9, 217, 229–31, 317; Van Den Hout 1949; Rosenmeyer 2001: 19–35). Seneca wrote to Lucilius that:

> You have been complaining that my letters to you are rather carelessly written. Now who talks carefully unless he also desires to talk affectedly? I prefer that my letters should be just what my conversation would be if you and I were sitting in one another's company or taking walks together, – spontaneous and easy; for my letters have nothing strained or artificial about them. (Seneca 1917–25: II, 137 [75.1])

It is this conversational characteristic of the letter that led Demetrius of Phalerum (350–280 BC) to refer to the letter as 'one side of a dialogue' and Cicero to regard it as a substitute for oral dialogue (Grube 1961: 111; Cicero 1927–9: II, 617 [12.30.1]; Malherbe 1988: 12). But once this conversational form was established in the private sphere, correspondents (by Hellenistic times at the latest) applied it to the public sphere, trying to use letters to persuade recipients to undertake particular political actions (F. Millar 1977: 227; Welles 1974: xlii–l ['Introduction']). Now, as letters joined speech as a medium of persuasion, rhetoricians began to devise rules for governing their composition.

Yet there was an imperfect sense by these rhetoricians that letters required a rhetoric distinct from oral speech. Between the third century BC and the fourth century AD, Demetrius, Cicero, Seneca, Philostratus of Lemnos (200–30), Gregory of Nazianzus (329–90) and Libanius (314–94) all considered the letter in their discussions of rhetoric, but in ways that did little to distinguish it from oral speech (Malherbe 1988: 2–3). Letters could vary quite sharply between the familiar and the formal (Cicero 1927–9: II, 261–3 [9.21.1]; Quintilian 1920–2: III, 517 [9.4.19]; Fantazzi 1989: 2) – but so, too, could oral speech. Demetrius wrote that 'letters are at times written to cities and kings; these should be somewhat more distinguished in style. One must adjust them to the personage to whom they are addressed' (Grube 1961: 113). Cicero and Seneca both called a letter nothing more than speech in the written medium (Cicero 1912–18: II, 163–5 [8.14.1]; Seneca 1917–25: 137 [75.1]; Malherbe 1988: 12).

To the extent that rhetoricians conceived letters to be a separate form, they associated them with the plain style. The plain style generally was intended for the efficient, unadorned conveyance of information, narrative and argument: as Cicero put it, 'the plain style for proof' (Cicero 1971: 357 [20.69]). It thus suited letters' purpose: Aristotle said that 'a written composition should be easy to read and therefore easy to deliver', and Demetrius wrote that 'a letter should be a brief expression of one's friendly feelings, expressing a simple topic in simple language' (Aristotle 2004: 128 [3.5.1407b]; Grube 1961: 111–13). Plain style particularly fitted private letters, which, although supposed to show awareness of the social status of both correspondent and recipient, could be more casual than letters written for public purposes (Stowers 1986: 27–31). Demetrius thought letters should be both elegant and plain – but the accent was on the plain. Significantly, he wrote about letters within his discussion of plain style (Grube 1961: 111–13).

By late antiquity, however, rhetoricians began to consider letters as an entirely separate medium that demanded a separate rhetoric of its own. The crucial figure was Julius Victor, writing in the fourth century AD, who in his *Ars rhetorica* treated letters in a separate appendix, *De epistolis*. Victor made explicit a great deal of classical rhetorical thought about the letter:

> Many directives which pertain to oral discourse also apply to letters. There are two kinds of letters: they are either official or personal. Official letters are such in virtue of their official and serious subject. Characteristic of this type are weighty statements, clarity of diction, and special effort at terse expression, as well as all the rules of oratory, with one exception, that we prune away some of its great size and let an appropriate familiar style govern the discourse ... In personal letters brevity is the norm. Do not let the display of eloquence, as Cato says, expand in all directions ... Clarity ought to radiate through the letters unless by design they are secret ... A letter written to a superior should not be droll; to an equal, not cold; to an inferior, not haughty ... The openings and conclusions of letters should conform with the degree of friendship (you share with the recipient) or with his rank, and should be written according to customary practice. (Julius Victor, *Ars Rhetorica* 27 (*De Epistolis*), cited and translated in Malherbe 1988: 63, 65)

In other words, letters resembled oral speech and hence were largely subject to the strictures of oral rhetoric, even though they constituted a genre of their own; letters could be categorised as either official or personal; plainness, brevity and clarity were the preferred qualities for letters; and letters were supposed to state the social relationship of the writer and the reader (Murphy 2001a: 195–6). These were to be the fundamental assumptions of epistolary rhetoric through the medieval centuries.

Classical letters were both public and private, both political and personal: they *could* be regarded as a mode of conversation, but they did not have to be. The later instability of the letter genre was based upon an instability already present in the ancient world. Yet it is worth emphasising the importance of the tradition wherein the letter was conceived as an unproblematic substitute for an oral conversation. Scholarly Carolingian letter-writers 'like the ancients . . . accept the conception of the letter as a kind of conversation, even though they are usually either incapable of manipulating the language to attain an informal tone or do not understand what that tone would be', and the belief that the letter was a form of spoken conversation persisted into the Renaissance (Witt 1982: 6, 10–12, 19, 27–34; 2001: 33–4). As late as 1586, the English rhetorician Angel Day wrote in *The English Secretorie* that

> *an Epistle*, which usually we term a letter, no other definition needeth thereof, then that which use and common experience hath induced unto us. A Letter therefore is that wherein is expressly conveyed in writing, the intent and meaning of one man, immediately to pass and be directed to all other, and for the certain respects thereof, is termed the messenger and familiar speech of the absent. (Day 1586: 1)

The classical world would bequeath to its medieval and Renaissance inheritors a strong, but not exclusive, association of the letter with conversation.

Conversatio

Conversatio began at a somewhat greater remove from the more tightly linked notions of friendship, familiarity, conversation and the letter. *Conversatio* appears to have been an Imperial Roman coinage of the first century AD; in Hoppenbrouwers' summary, '*Conversatio* ne figure pas dans le latin classique. Son histoire débute en même temps que notre ère et culmine dans les textes des auteurs chrétiens'

(Hoppenbrouwers 1964: 48). From the beginning *conversatio* had a remarkably wide range of meanings, including 'way of life', 'one's life as it relates to others', 'company', 'conduct', 'familiarity', 'familiar [social] intercourse', 'habitual association' and 'society' (Tacitus 1914: 40 [9.6], translated in W. Johnson 2010: 66; Furey 2003: 71, 71 (note 2); Hoppenbrouwers 1964: 47–95).[2] The range of connotation of *conversatio*, all deriving loosely from the word's literal meaning of 'with turning', involved the various aspects of people being with other people. Hence *conversatio* could be construed passively, to signify 'society', but also actively, to signify 'conduct'. *Conversatio* was both the social world and the active behaviour and interactions by which that world was constituted (Hoppenbrouwers 1964: 48–69).

This active behaviour did not generally bear the limited sense of modern 'conversation' but by late antiquity the relationship of discourse to social interaction occasionally gave *conversatio* the signification of speech. In a letter from Pope Simplicius (r.468–83) to the Emperor Zeno in 479, 'Simplicius Episcopus Zenoni Augusto', *conversatio* appears to refer to the spoken word: *ut tantas haereticorum fraudes et facinora diuinis et saecularibus legibus persequenda, quae saepius probastis esse tam noxia, de memoria et conuersatione hominum iubeatis auferri, quorum impietas nulla* (Guenther 1895: 149 [66.6]). We should note that this slippage of *conversatio* toward speech had an earlier parallel in the connotations ascribed to *sermo*. Kennerly notes that Cicero, by placing his discussion of *sermo* within his discussion of decorum in *De officiis* Book One, in turn associated *sermo* with the Stoic conception of sociability (*oikeiosis*) that framed his notion of decorum (Kennerly 2010: 124). The common embrace of sociability by *sermo* and *conversatio* set in motion their millennial mutual approach.

Conversatio likewise bore the signification of 'familiarity' in the ancient world. Roller translates Seneca's *adsidua conversatio* in his *De Beneficiis* as 'constant familiarity' (Seneca 1935: III, 422–3 [6.29.2]; Roller 2001: 115], while the *De deo Socratis* of Apuleius (*c*.124–*c*.170) provided the acid proverb, *parit enim conversatio contemptum* – 'familiarity breeds contempt'. *Conversatio* also became something practised by friends: Tacitus' (58–117) phrase was *conversatio amicorum*, while Seneca wrote that *conversari cum amicis absentibus licet*, 'you may hold converse with your friends when they are absent' (Apuleius 1866: 355; Tacitus 1914: 40–1 [9.6]; Seneca 1917–25: I, 370–1 [55.9]). *Conversatio* was not yet tightly linked to *sermo*, *familiaritas* or *amicitia*, but the threads uniting them were already thickening.

The Imperial context of *conversatio* merits further attention. Where Ciceronian *sermo* was associated with the search for truth, with potential application to the *vita activa* that remained the ideal of the late Republic, *conversatio* generally lacked political implications. *Conversatio* was the realm of Romans displaced from rule, and it suggested a correspondingly depoliticised way of life, a distance from the political world recapitulated in our modern sense of 'society'. In philosophy, *conversatio* was embedded in the search for an ideal good at some distance from any this-worldly good. In Seneca's *Natural Questions* (*c*.65), '[t]he study of nature is presented as *divinorum conversatio*', while in his *Epistles* (*c*.65) Seneca prescribed *bonorum virorum conversatio*, 'habitual association with good men' (Seneca 1917–25: III, 36–7 [94.40]; 1971: 206–7 [3.Pref.11]; Inwood 2002: 128; Stadter 2014: 236). It is true that Seneca's discussion of leisure in *De Otio* (*c*.62–4) implied a blurring of this distinction between the proper ends of *sermo* and *conversatio*. When the wise man had no proper state in which to act – a stipulation that could apply generally to the human condition or particularly to the political conditions of Imperial Rome – then his leisure would need to serve a different state.

> Let us grasp the idea that there are two commonwealths – the one, a vast and truly common state, which embraces alike gods and men, in which we look neither to this corner of earth nor to that, but measure the bounds of our citizenship by the path of the sun; the other, the one to which we have been assigned by the accident of birth . . . This greater commonwealth we are able to serve even in leisure – nay, I am inclined to think, even better in leisure. (Seneca 1932: 187–9 [4.1–2], 201 [8.1–4])

This contemplated shift in the purpose of leisure implied a corollary shift in the purpose of *sermo* toward that of *conversatio* – but that shift remained only an implication. In the ancient world, *sermo* and *conversatio* retained their different goals. This, as much as anything else, kept these words at some distance from one another.

The slighter looseness of *conversatio* also distinguished it from *sermo*. While *sermo* was associated with *consensio*, like-mindedness, *conversatio* referred rather to conduct. Like-mindedness overlapped with common conduct – the former, if not a prerequisite, facilitated the latter. Nevertheless, it was possible, and would continue to be possible, to conceive of *conversatio* flourishing in the absence of *consensio*.

Interrelations

Sermo and *conversatio* approached each other via their mutual connection with decorum and *oikeiosis*; *urbanitas* provided another hinge. *Urbanitas'* somewhat hazy definition in ancient Rome included refined and witty manners – and Ramage notes that Cicero's description of urbane manners overlapped significantly with his description of the behaviour that forwards conversation. To be 'mild, wholly undogmatic, and witty' pertained as much to urbanity as to conversation (Cicero 2000: 45–6 [1.132–6]; Ramage 1963: 399–409). Aulus Gellius' (*c*.125 – after 180) refined and agreeable banqueter, implicitly urbane, was also a pleasant conversationalist (Aulus Gellius 1927–8: II, 439 [13.11.3–5]; Burke 1993: 96). Quintilian (*c*.35–*c*.100) associated *urbanitas* with *sermo* explicitly: '*urbanitas* . . . denotes language [*sermonem*] with a smack of the city in its words, accent and idiom' – but he also associated it explicitly with oratory (Quintilian 1920–2: 446–7 [6.3.17], 499 [6.3.110]; Ramage 1963: 410–11). To the extent that conversational speech implied urbane manners, *sermo* slipped towards *conversatio*'s realm of behaviour. But this as yet was a tie of gossamer.

The loose relationship between *sermo* and *conversatio* was accompanied by significantly tighter connections between familiarity, friendship, *sermo* and the letter. *Familiaritas* and friendship both were necessary for *sermo* as a mode of inquiry. Friendship, whose alignment with virtue and reason aligned it in turn with *sermo*, provided the basic desire to join in *sermo* so as to seek the truth, while *familiaritas* provided the intimate knowledge of one's fellow conversationalists that made possible the delicate speech that motivated conversation's very continuance. Plato's *Lysis*, Cicero's *Laelius de Amicitia* and the *Toxaris* (*c*.163) of Lucian of Samosata (*c*.125 – after 180) all both discussed and represented friendship by means of dialogue, that literary evocation of *sermo*, and so both highlighted and embodied by their literary practice the interrelationship of friendship and *sermo* (Plato 1963: 145–68 [*Lysis*]; Lucian 1798: 476–536 [*Toxaris*]; Cicero 1990). Seneca used his letters as a form of *sermo* that would serve the discovery of truth, albeit more as a gentler means of pedagogy than as a process of mutual inquiry (Seneca 1917–25: I, 257 [38.1], II, 137–9 [75.1–3]). Both dialogue and epistles incorporated the rhetoric of *sermo* that united conversational style, the search for truth, friendship and familiarity.

One sort of *familiaritas*, anyway: not all *familiaritas* used *sermo* in the same manner. The philosophical *sermo* indeed employed *familiaritas* within a plain style that eschewed moving the passions, but the epistolary *sermo* instead used a style intended to communicate, to express, the intense, familiar emotions. In Seneca's *Epistles*, he conceived of letters as expressing the inner self: 'I thank you for writing to me so often; for you are revealing your real self to me in the only way you can' (Cicero 1912–18: 186–7 [9.4.1]; 2000: 45–6, 70 [1.132–6, 2.48]; Seneca 1917–25: I, 263 [40.1], II, 137–9 [75.1–5]; Eden 2012: 29–39). This expressive mode in turn highlighted the importance of spontaneity, whose apparent naturalness appeared to mark the genuine expression of the inner self. Thus Cicero in less philosophical moments wrote spontaneous letters (Cicero 1912–18: II, 53 [7.11.1], 181 [9.2a]; 2002: 65 [1.3.1]), imitated the loose order of topics in Atticus' correspondence (Cicero 1912–18: I, 415 [6.1.1]), and encouraged Atticus to yet further spontaneity, to 'write the first thing that comes into your head' (Cicero 1912–18: I, 33 [1.12.4]). Cicero likewise wrote to his brother Quintus that 'our letters must sometimes just ramble on' (Cicero 2002: 117 [2.10]; Eden 2012: 31–2). Seneca's preference for expressive letters led him to prize spontaneity even in his philosophical *Epistulae Morales*: 'I prefer that my letters should be just what my conversation would be if you and I were sitting in one another's company or taking walks together, – spontaneous and easy; for my letters have nothing strained or artificial about them' (Seneca 1917–25: II, 137 [75.1]) Yet the expressive *sermo* was not identical with the philosophical *sermo*, despite Seneca's fleeting amalgamation of the two, and the resolution of their relationship – the question of how or whether they could be durably yoked together – was to be a charged inheritance for the future.

There were further tensions in this intellectual ensemble. The letter could be public as well as private, an instrument of the state as well as a personal communication, oratorical as well as conversational. Perfect friendship's natural mode was *sermo*, but the figure of the flatterer conveyed the danger that manipulative oratory might invade the realm of conversation. As friendship was only a knife's edge away from flattery, so the conversational intentness on audience was only a knife's edge away from the manipulations of oratory, and thus the fulfilment of the philosophical accusation that rhetoric must inevitably corrupt the search for truth. The very conjugation of *familiar* and *style* contained within it the tension between truth and technique.

The same modes of speech recommended for conversation, after all, were recommended for oratory that sought to simulate the virtues of conversation. Cicero described the type of Attic orator whose plain speech was eminently conversational (Cicero 1971: 361–3 [23.75–8]). Quintilian in turn praised Cicero the orator for the 'appearance of spontaneity' and for his style that displayed 'the utmost felicity and ease', and generally Quintilian recommended that the orator should speak 'in such manner as to make it appear that they [passages of speech] are but casually strung together, and to suggest that we are thinking out and hesitating over words which we have, as a matter of fact, carefully prepared in advance' (Quintilian 1920–2: IV, 65 [10.1.111], 241 [11.2.47]). The plain, the mild, the easy, the spontaneous, the natural – these all could manifest the true expression of conversation, but they equally well could manifest the premeditated dissimulation of oratory (Cicero 1967: I, 355 [2.53.212]; Richards 2003: 51). Rome's posterity would be able to use these modes of speech for either conversation or for oratory – a useful ambiguity.

Potentialities

These concepts showed some tendency to broaden their scope. Epideictic oratory (the rhetoric of praise and blame) expressed an appropriate taste that was one's own; hence it was supposed to be expressed with elements of the familiar style (Eden 2012: 33). Epideictic rhetoric thus also came to have some affiliation with conversation: Quintilian regarded it as akin to both *contentio* and *sermo* (Quintilian 1920–2: I, 395 [3.4.10]; Remer 1996: 26 (note 91)). The proper orator was supposed to know when to incorporate a conversational style into his speech, so as to speak (Cicero prescribed), 'frankly and lucidly, with no formal train of argument or barren verbal controversy' (Cicero 1967: I, 249 [2.16.68]). Letters too could apply familiar style to persuasive political purposes. Seneca applied *familiaritas* to the very act of reading: one was supposed to read, to understand, intimately: 'When a person spends all his time in foreign travel, he ends by having many acquaintances, but no friends. And the same thing must hold true of men who seek intimate acquaintance [*familiariter*] with no single author, but visit them all in a hasty and hurried manner' (Seneca 1917–25: I, 7–9 [2.2–5], 233–41 [33], III, 277–9 [84.3–5]; Eden 2012: 39–42). Indeed, Seneca could write to Lucilius that 'Most of my converse is with books' (Seneca 1917–25: II, 37 [67.2]).

True friendship, meanwhile, had long possessed an unstable relationship with the public world. Plato, Xenophon (*c*.430–354 BC), and Aristotle shared a belief that friendship underlay the state, but Epicurus (341–270 BC) and Seneca privatised friendship and divorced it from politics. Cicero, more ambivalently, did not rely upon true friendship to underpin the political order of the republic, but rather upon concord, which harmonised unlike members of the polity; he also recognised that ordinary *amicitia*, and its doppelgänger *factio*, threatened to destroy the republic's order.[3] Among all these philosophical schools, the ability of perfect friendship to function in the political world was thematically problematic. Consider the contrast Aristotle made in *Nicomachean Ethics* between true friendship and the more ordinary friendship that, among other things, underpinned the *polis*:

> To be a friend to many people, however, in a way that accords with complete friendship, is not possible, just as it is not possible to be in love with many people at the same time. For erotic love is like an excess and something of that sort naturally comes about in relation to a single person. And it is not easy for many people to please the same person intensely at the same time, nor, presumably, for them to be good. But he must actually acquire experience of them and become intimate with them, which is very difficult. If, however, the friendship exists because of pleasure or because of utility, it is possible for many people to please someone, since there are many of the requisite sorts and the services involved take little time. (Aristotle 2014: 143 [8.6])

This contrast generated a question whose implications were remarkably ambitious: could that perfect friendship shared among an intimate few be generalised by some means to the *polis* or the republic? The answer to this question lay in the realms of familiarity, friendship and conversation, each of which possessed their own expansive dynamic, whose effects had already begun to transform these linked conceptions.

Conclusion

The expansion of familiarity, *sermo* and the letter into the realm of oratory, and the posed query as to the potential of friendship to encompass the *res publica*, jointly set the stage for the future development of this conceptual constellation. It is too Whiggish to say that these shifts within antiquity in the characterisation of these concepts already posed a question that the Enlightenment would answer: could *sermo*, the discourse of intimacy, friendship and equality, be applied (not least via the letter) to the political world of dissimilar strangers? Piously we may affirm that the later development of these concepts was contingent and no latency in antiquity should be deemed a teleological inevitability. Nevertheless, it is notable that the thinkers of the Enlightenment drew upon aspects of the conversational constellation already present in the ancient world. The later development of that constellation, through all its transformations, would remain in good measure a meditation upon the thought of Greece and Rome.

Notes

1. For the history of classical rhetoric, see Kennedy (1999: 1–182), Vickers (1988: 1–147).
2. The definition 'society' anticipates: 'society', 'sociability' and cognate words emerged in the late seventeenth century to denote the range of meanings covered by *conversatio*, as it narrowed to refer exclusively to the spoken word (see below). The totality of the replacement may be measured by the need for modern definitions of *conversatio* to use 'society' and its cognates (e.g. Hoppenbrouwers 1964: 64).
3. Plato (1963: 795–6 [*Republic*: 8.567–8], 1287–8 [*Laws*: 3.693b–e, 3.694b]); Aristotle (1986: 122 [1295b23–6]; 2013: 139–44 [1241a–1243a]; 2014: 163–4 [9.7]); Diogenes Laertius (1958: II, 645 [10.119]); Xenophon (1979: 139–41 [2.6.24–7]; Cicero (1998: 58 [2.69]); Cassidy (1999: 45–54); Hutter (1978: 91–174); Kalimtzis (2000: 51–86); McEvoy (1999).

Chapter 2

The Medieval Reformulations of Conversation

Introduction

The Renaissance humanists, as we shall see, attempted to restore classical rhetoric in general and classical conversation in particular; in so doing they both discounted and frequently tried to eliminate the transformations of rhetoric during the intervening medieval centuries. Yet the humanist recuperation of classical rhetoric did not restore conversation and its cognates unchanged. On the one hand, the concepts of friendship, familiarity and *conversatio* had reoriented themselves around the universalising Christian conception of community during rhetoric's long medieval sojourn, while the *sermo* of dialogue had begun to concern itself with that eminently Christian subject matter, the interiority of the soul. On the other hand, the *ars dictaminis* (art of letter writing) had shifted the medieval letter toward the public realm, and thus toward the traditional realm of oratory. Petrarch's vaunted rediscovery of classical conversation retained these medieval innovations. The Renaissance variant of conversation that sprang from him would partly slough the theory and practice of its medieval predecessor – but the influence of Christianity and the *ars dictaminis* would endure.

This chapter narrates medieval developments very briefly. This concision is partly because there are smaller amounts of primary source evidence and historiography on medieval conversation and its cognates than for their Renaissance successors, save for the extensive literature on the *ars dictaminis*. This brevity is also due to my limited knowledge of medieval theoretical vocabularies, especially those of Christian theology; I am hesitant to venture too deeply into these waters. The sketch here should be taken more as a placeholder than as a sufficient narrative; I would be grateful if a properly equipped scholar of medieval rhetoric would write the fuller narrative that I cannot.

Friendship and familiarity

The ancient conception of friendship persisted into medieval times, but refracted through the prism of Christian thought. To begin with, God himself became the model for what a friend should be: Saint Ambrose (337–97) wrote that, 'He has given us the pattern of friendship we should follow: we are to do whatever our friend wishes, open up to our friend every last secret we have in our heart, and not be unaware of his innermost thoughts either. We must show him our heart, and he must open his heart to us' (Ambrose 2001: 435 [3.136]). Christian thought also began to change the medieval conception of the character of friendship. Saint Augustine (354–430) asked, 'What else is friendship? It has received its name from nothing else but from love and is faithful nowhere else but in Christ, in whom alone it can also be everlasting and blessed' (Augustine 1998: 116 [1.1]). Accordingly Augustine's *Rule* (*c*.400) preserved friendship (within the Christian community) as a joint seach for (revealed) truth, and as (Christian) opinions and (Christian) spirit held in common (Augustine 1996; McEvoy 1999: 20). Saint Anselm (1033/4–1109) applied an often ecstatic imagery of friendship to the monastic structure and heavenly goals of his religious life (Southern 1990: 138–65; McEvoy 1999: 12–13). More generally, Christian Ciceronians reinterpreted the *consensio* underpinning friendship as Christian faith and sacramental practice. So Aelred of Rievaulx (1110–67) in *Spiritual Friendship* (1164–7): 'close to perfection is that level of friendship that consists in the love and knowledge of God, when one who is the friend of another becomes the friend of God, according to the verse of our Savior in the Gospel: "*I shall no longer call you servants but friends*"' (Aelred 2010: 73–4 [2.14]; McEvoy 1999: 19–22).

The Christian *contemptus mundi* also became prerequisite for and oriented toward true friendship: Abba Joseph, by John Cassian's (*c*.360–435) report in 'On Friendship' (*c*.420), said that 'The first foundation of true friendship, then, consists in contempt for worldly wealth and disdain for all things we possess. For it is unrighteous and blasphemous indeed if, after having renounced the vanity of the world and of everything in it, we should prefer the paltry household articles that remain to the most precious love of a brother' (Cassian 1997:

560 [16.6.1]; McEvoy 1999: 19–20). To divest oneself of worldly possessions was to possess nothing which could not be shared, and thus to instantiate in photonegative the ancient precept that friends held all things in common.

Friendship in all these aspects infiltrated the different corporate structures of Christendom, which were held to institutionalise and to be constituted by friendship. Among these Christian structures were the universities, those high medieval incorporations dedicated to instruction and inquiry, which also were intended to institutionalise a spirit of friendship (McEvoy 1999: 19–23). Indeed, *amicitia* was so omnipresent in medieval Christendom that its language decayed into mere formula. In letters, the invocation of *amicitia* became a hollow remembrance that such epistles were supposed to be a conversation between absent friends (Hyatte 1994: 40).

These reformulations Christianised friendship, but did not fundamentally change its nature. Yet medieval Christians also universalised the concept of friendship in ways that would change it greatly from what it had been in the ancient world. The ancients generally had taken *vera amicitia* as an intimacy necessarily restricted to a few, thematically contrasted to the broader political and social relations of mankind. Seneca had had more universalising notions packed into his conception of the friendship shared by wise men – and St Paulinus of Nola (354–431) recapitulated the Senecan dynamic as he articulated Christian *caritas* as a friendship given by God, unaffected by distance, and rooted in shared faith (Seneca 1917–25: III, 257–9 [109.4–12]; Lienhard 1990: 284–9; McEvoy 1999: 12–13). Ambrose's conceptions of *misericordia* (compassion) and *benevolentia* (goodwill) in *De officiis ministrorum* (386) likewise stretched and universalised the ancient conception of friendship: *benevolentia* was 'the source from which friendship springs', 'bringing people together and uniting them in friendship', and it suffused the varied relationships of man until 'it has filled the whole world'. Love and friendship now were to be extended without regard to the merit of their object and equality of virtue was made the goal of this benevolent friendship instead of its prerequisite (Ambrose 2001: 215–19 [1.167–72]; Cassidy 1999: 55–60). By the twelfth century, the Christian conception of friendship was embedded in the universalising definitions of early scholastic thought as part of the very fabric of human nature. So Aelred of Rievaulx wrote in *Spiritual Friendship* that 'nature itself first impressed on human minds the feeling of friendship, which experience then developed and the authority of law finally sanctioned' (Aelred 2010: 65 [1.51], 67 [1.58]; Southern 1995: 28–9).

Medieval Christians now also conceived of friendship as something that could exist between unequals – as something that could make equals of the unequal. They modelled this possibility of inequality in friendship not least on the inherently unequal friendship between God and man: Ambrose wrote in *De officiis* that 'God himself makes us his friends, though we are really the very lowliest of his servants' (Ambrose 2001: 435 [3.136]; Mews and Chiavaroli 2009: 98). Aelred of Rievaulx in turn wrote in *Spiritual Friendship* that 'thanks to the influence of friendship, *the greater and the less become equal*' (Aelred 2010: 110 [3.90]). Building upon that model, Dante Alighieri wrote to Can Grande of Verona:

> Nor do I think I shall incur the imputation of presumption in assuming the name of friend, as some perchance might object, since those of unequal rank are united by the sacred bond of friendship no less than equals. For if one chooseth to glance at pleasant and profitable friendships, very frequently it will be evident to him that persons of preëminence have been united with their inferiors; and if his glance is turned to true friendship – friendship for its own sake – will it not be acknowledged that many a time men obscure in fortune but distinguished in virtue have been the friends of illustrious and most great princes? And why not? Since even the friendship of God and man is in no way hindered by disparity? (Dante 2013: 188 [11.2])

This conception of friendship as something that could exist between unequals would in time infiltrate the idea of conversation, and make of it too something that could be conducted between unequals, so as to make of them equals. The heavenly friendship of the medieval Christians would infuse the consciously egalitarian discourse of their secularising *salonnier* successors.

Familiarity also found itself altered within the Christian conception of friendship. In medieval Christian theology, the Trinity came to be conceived of as intimate friends who shared all things in common. The intimate friendship among the members of the Trinity thus became part of the *imitatio dei* to which all good Christians were supposed to aspire. The incarnate person of Christ also became a means by which to facilitate the universalisation of Christian friendship. Any Christian could share an intimate friendship and love with Christ, who was God and Virtue personified, and Christ as intermediary therefore made it possible for all mankind to share that intimate friendship and love with one another. Aelred of Rievaulx put it that 'a friend clinging to a friend in the spirit of Christ becomes *one heart and one soul* with him. Thus mounting the steps of love to the friendship of Christ, a friend becomes one with him in the one kiss of the spirit' (Aelred 2010: 75 [2.21]; McEvoy 1999: 33–6; Southern 1995: 28–30). All good Christians were supposed to imitate God's intimate friendship, Christ made it possible for mankind to partake of intimate friendship with one another, and universal intimacy thus became at once a possibility, a duty and a heavenly joy.

Medieval Christianity thus had preserved, universalised and rendered possible between unequals those ancient conceptions of friendship and familiarity. Within this new matrix, the conception of personal friendship began to re-emerge in the twelfth century from its long post-classical recession. Where Ambrose had identified friendship with the universality of goodwill, Aelred of Rievaulx in *Spiritual Friendship* once more began to distinguish friendship from such undiscriminating virtue: 'Through the perfection of charity we have perfect love for many who are a burden and a bore to us. Although we consult their interests honestly, without pretense or hypocrisy, but truthfully and voluntarily, still we do not invite them into the intimacies of friendship' (Aelred 2010: 75 [2.19]). This twelfth-century revival was the beginning of a long efflourescence that would provide the foundation for the Renaissance humanist cult of friendship (Mews and Chiavaroli 2009: 839). That cult would reclassicise the conception of personal friendship – but always within the medieval Christian framework, where God made possible the friendship and familiarity of all to all.

Conversation and dialogue

Sermo seems to have gone into recession during the medieval centuries as a mode of joint discovery of the truth. Of actual such conversations, little record remains. So far as their literary simulation is concerned, Augustine's dialogues transformed the genre by shifting it from free inquiry *in utramque partem* to the transmission of revealed authority. Medieval dialogues retained this Augustinian spirit and the scholastics further transformed medieval dialogues into fig leaves for the monologies of dialectic. But if the Augustinian dialogue lost the sense of a joint inquiry into truth, it gained a new dimension, of dialogue internalised as an individual's examination of his conscience. This medieval innovation acquired conscience for the ensuing tradition – secularised, the inner self – as both participant and subject of *sermo* (Marsh 1980: 3–4; Novikoff 2013).

The *ars dictaminis:* the medieval art of letter writing

As the medieval centuries progressed, the distinction between spoken rhetoric and written rhetoric survived, and became wider as the self-conscious tradition of epistolary rhetoric gathered strength (Witt 1982: 9–10, 26–7). There is scattered evidence between the fifth and eleventh centuries for the survival of late Classical epistolary theory, particularly in collections of letters such as the seventh-century *Formulae Marculfi*, which followed dictaminal forms (pertaining to the *ars dictaminis*) although they did not explicitly acknowledge them (Lanham 1975: 90–3; Murphy 2001a: 200). From the eleventh century, when Alberico of Montecassino (*c.*1030–*c.*1105) wrote the *Flores rhetorici* (also known as the *Dictaminum radii*), there is certain evidence of manuals on the art of letter writing – the *ars dictaminis.*[1] These dictaminal manuals, and dictaminal theory, spread rapidly through Italy and western Europe in the twelfth and thirteenth centuries (Fantazzi 1989: 3–5). By the thirteenth century a mass of letter-writing manuals provided models for letters, derived from the parts of a speech prescribed in Ciceronian spoken rhetoric (Murphy 2001b: xv–xvii ['Introduction']). These letters, written with the aid of the *ars dictaminis*, were used first and foremost in the medieval Italian city-states by their rulers and subordinate officials for diplomatic and administrative purposes (Camargo 1991: 17–18; Constable 1992; Grafton 1991: 10–11). With the ever-increasing size of medieval bureaucratic apparatuses came an ever-increasing flow of letters. Letters had become subject to rhetoric in antiquity only when they moved from the realm of the state into the realm of private correspondence, but in the dictaminal era epistolary rhetoric, whether used for public or private purposes, modelled itself primarily on letters concerning state business.

As the primary use of letters shifted from private to public, the purpose and the contexts of the epistolary plain style also shifted. For workaday official letters, the brief, clear, to-the-point and unadorned *stilus humilis* – the plain style reborn – was most useful and appropriate (Witt 2001: 44). When (repeating the evolution of the letter in ancient Greece) the style of the official letter began once again to spill over into that of the familiar, the *stilus humilis* also provided a suitably plain style, albeit no longer so pleasantly personal as in the ancient world. Indeed, the *stilus humilis* was attractive, in part, because it could provide double service in official and in familiar letters – and its dual nature neatly reflected the similarly dual nature of medieval Italian officials, who retained much of their personal identity while working for the state (Witt 1982: 6). In the service of clarity, bureaucratic convenience and familiar letter writing, the *stilus humilus* was the standard accompaniment of the *ars dictaminis* through the centuries.

Yet the public purposes which provided the central justification and model for the *ars dictaminis* meant that the *stilus humilis* varied significantly from the plain style of antiquity, when the letter had been associated with familiar subjects and recipients. As the primary subject matter of letters shifted to public affairs, the *stilus humilis* likewise shifted to incorporate an elevated diction suitable for reading aloud in a public setting (Patt 1978: 134). The rhythmic prose style called the *cursus*, with roots stretching back to the letters of Cicero and the Church Fathers (Denholm-Young 1969: 43), was formulated in the late twelfth century, adopted by the Roman chancery in 1178 or 1179 and disseminated throughout western Europe in the following generations; it survived as a significant influence upon epistolary rhetoric until the early fifteenth century (Witt 2003: 137, 509–14). Predicated upon oral delivery, with the aim of persuading within that medium, the *cursus* associated the *stilus humilis* with artistically oratorical methods of aural persuasion (Witt 2003: 137). In its elevated, aural diction, early dictaminal rhetoric associated the plain style of the *stilus humilis* with extra-logical forms of persuasive argument.

Furthermore, dictaminal rhetoric emphasised those parts of a letter that specified what would have been apparent in face-to-face settings, the identity of the correspondent and the recipient and their expected social relationship. The *ars dictaminis*, drawing upon the model of a classical oration, generally divided a letter into five parts – salutation (*salutatio*), introduction (*exordium*), narrative (*narratio*), petition (*petitio*) and conclusion (*conclusio*) – and dictaminal rhetoric focused upon the salutation (unique to dictaminal rhetoric) and the conclusion, which were concerned with particularising these social identities and relationships. Substantial proportions of dictaminal treatises and model-letter manuals consisted of the enumeration of the social categories of recipients and the combinations of possible salutations from all prospective correspondents to all types of recipient. Almost half of the *Rationes dictandi* (Bologna, 1135) was devoted to the salutation alone, and the anonymous author stated that 'very often the largest part of securing the goodwill is in the course of the salutation itself' (Murphy 2001b: 17; Shepard 1999: 10). Thus, although the narrative would provide the bulk of the logical argument in the dictaminal letter, it received relatively little attention in the dictaminal manuals; in Hugh of Bologna's similarly titled *Rationes Dictandi* (Bologna, *c.*1119–24), '[persuasive] effectiveness depends on the general nature of the problem at hand, and not on the specific contingencies' (Shepard 1999: 8; Witt 2003: 172). In other words, early dictaminal rhetoric's theoretical emphasis on the salutation and conclusion, and its de-emphasis of the narrative, resulted in a corresponding stress on persuasion by the statement of social status on the part of known correspondents and recipients rather than by logical argument.

We may sum up these various developments – the shift to a public mode, the use of aural technique for persuasive purposes, the emphasis on social standing of both correspondent and recipient, the de-emphasis on reason and, most tellingly, the adoption of the five parts of an oration into the structure of a letter – as the shift of the letter from the mode of *sermo* to the mode of *oratio*. The dictaminal letter retained the formulas of friendship, but it largely served the purposes of power and persuasion. Traces persisted of the letter's roots in friendly and familiar private conversation, and these traces would allow the humanists to reclassicise the letter, to reorient it back toward *sermo*. Yet when they did so, they would do so within the public, oratorical tradition and potentialities established by the *ars dictaminis*.

Finally, we should note an unintendeded consequence of the development of the letter as a mode of communication during the recession of the spoken conversation. The letter was supposed to be a conversation in writing – but the prominence of the *ars dictaminis* meant that most 'conversations' in medieval Europe were actually being conducted in writing. The ancient assumptions of the primacy of orality were slowly being undermined by the practice of medieval letter-writers. The ease with which the conversations of Renaissance humanists would slip into writing and then into print was another inheritance of the medieval centuries.

Conversatio

The otherworldly orientation of *conversatio* made it particularly amenable to Christianisation in late antiquity. *Conversatio* became a conduct, a way of life, oriented toward the good of God; so in the late fourth century Evagrius of Antioch translated the Greek *askesis* ('the ascetic way of life') as *conversatio* (Benedict 1981: esp. 268–9 [58],

294–5 [73]; Conwell 1997: 493 (note 4)). By a happy slippage, *conversatio* also came to acquire a more active connotation by conflation with the related *conversio*, the moment of conversion, or adoption of a reformed (Christian) life. When Saint Benedict (*c*.480–543/547) referred in his Rule to *conversatio morum* (the monastic way of life) – a choice of words that would immensely increase the medieval world's familiarity with the concept of *conversatio* – it would be (mis)read in following centuries to encompass the moment of conversion to a monastic life as much as that monastic life itself. The durative sense of *conversatio* thus acquired something of the dynamic overtones of *conversio*, the turn-with of men becoming a turn-toward God. *Conversatio*, as it emerged from late antiquity, bore as a primary signifier a (Christian) conduct or way of life, embedded within and oriented toward a (Christian) community, overlappingly virtuous, godly and monastic, and oriented toward an active pursuit of a perfected life (Conwell 1997: 214–15, 493 (notes 6, 8, 10)).

The Christian intellectual framework also added a new political overtone to *conversatio*. Evagrius of Antioch, an anonymous translator into Latin of Athanasius' *Life of Antony*, and, most influentially, Saint Jerome (347–420) in the Vulgate – *nostra autem conversatio in caelis est* (*Philippians* 3: 20) – all translated the Greek *politeia* and *politeuma* as *conversatio* (Conwell 1997: 493 (note 4)). *Politeia* and *politeuma* indeed both bore the sense of 'conduct' or 'way of life', but with a more political context – the conduct befitting a member of a *polis* (Collins 2008: 53–6). The translations of these words as *conversatio* served to depoliticise the Latin Christian texts and thus are significant markers of the translators' hermeneutics. On the other hand, at the very least for any reader who sought out the original Greek of the New Testament, and perhaps for any reader sensitive to nuance, they also served to shade *conversatio* with a tinge of the political ends of *politeia* and *politeuma*. This effect should not be overstated: *conversatio* usually rendered other Greek words, notably *anastrophe*, which shared with *conversatio* an etymological derivation from *turning* and which lacked the political charge of *politeia* and *politeuma* (Bhaldraithe 1984). Yet neither was this minor incident of translation trivial: henceforward 'we are citizens of heaven' would linger behind 'our conversation is in heaven' as a palimpsest available for innovation.

In the later medieval centuries, *conversatio* largely would retain the meanings it had acquired by the time of Augustine and Benedict (Quondam 2007: 21–9). Skating forward a millennium, the high- and late-medieval Italian *conversazione* preserved *conversatio*'s denotation of 'custom', 'way of life' and 'familiarity'. In that vernacular, *sacra conversazione* became the term of art for one's life as it related to God, for converse as communion (Furey 2003: 71, 71 (note 2); Goffen 1979: 199–201). The social resonances of *conversatio*, in telling register of the societal form of the day, gave it the meaning of 'hierarchy' in the early medieval centuries. By Dante Alighieri's (*c.*1265–1321) time, it also was used as a rough synonym for 'civility' and both Saint Thomas Aquinas (1225–74) and Dante used the compound phrase *conversatio civilis* to indicate 'the common life in society' (Robiglio 2006: 125–9).

Yet the sociative meaning of *conversatio* continued to imply verbal communication; both Aquinas and Dante also used the term to refer to the spoken word (Robiglio 2006: 125–9). Petrarch (Francesco Petrarca, 1304–74), in a letter rehearsing the ancient conception of the letter as a conversation between distant friends, referred to *conversatio* instead of to *sermo*. In another letter, Petrarch associated the *familiaritas* of reading with *conversatio*: 'nobelium ingeniorum familiaritas et clarorum virorum conversatio' (Petrarca 1997: 83 [2.6], 162 [4.2]; 2005: I, 89 [2.6], I, 182 [4.2]). In these usages, Petrarch registered *conversatio*'s continuing association with *familiaritas*, friendship and *sermo*. But this use of *conversatio* to denote speech, if perhaps a shade more frequent in the *trecento* than in the ancient world, remained a minor register.

Petrarch

Petrarch's role in the history of *conversatio* was minor; in that of *sermo*, it was enormous. In this narrative, he played a triple role. Petrarch amplified and greatly forwarded the impulse to restore classical *sermo*, he grafted medieval conceptions of *sermo* into the humanist tradition that would follow him, and he added to *sermo* distinctive innovations of his own. These last, in particular, indeed would alter the arc of conversation's history.

While Geri d'Arezzo (*c.*1270–1339) had pioneered the classicising of the private letter in the early fourteenth century, it was Petrarch's discovery in 1345 of Cicero's letters (those of *Epistulae ad Atticum*) that led him to amplify Geri's efforts into a self-conscious and influential programme:

I shall offer my friends not only my deliberations, but the thoughts and movements of my mind, which are called spontaneous; nor will I write merely summaries and conclusions, but the particulars of their beginnings and their progress; to the friends whom I meet I shall relate early in the morning whatever occurred to me during the night. If upon sitting at table I change my mind, upon arising I shall tell my friends, and I shall take pleasure in seeing my opinions struggle until the better wins. This will more easily occur if my loyal friends are allowed to participate in my deliberations from the very beginning. As I was saying this and similar things in defense of my daily routine, I happened by chance to come upon Cicero's letters, a magnificent book replete with great variety and with this kind of friendly discourse. In it I read a similar defense and was delighted that, whether because of similar reasoning – which I would like to believe but dare not hope for – or simply because of similar subject matter, I had expressed what that great man had long ago stated without my knowing until that moment. (Petrarca 2005: III, 58 [18.8]; Eden 2012: 49–72; Randall 2008b: 12)

Petrarch's rediscovery of the familiar letter thus firmly re-associated the letter genre with *sermo* and its 'plain, domestic and friendly style' (Petrarca 2005: I, 6–7 [1.1]; Eden 2012: 29–33; Remer 1996: 29). Perhaps as importantly, Petrarch made the return to ancient *sermo* a return to Ciceronian *sermo*. Roman theorists of rhetoric such as Quintilian and Julius Victor had also written about conversation, but it was Cicero's formulation – the Cicerolatry of the age given new direction by Petrarch's happy discovery – that would have most influence in the Renaissance (Marsh 1980: 8; Remer 1996: 26 (note 91), 28).

Petrarch's re-association of *sermo* with the letter was matched by his revitalisation of the dialogue as a literary genre, which returned it from its Augustinian peregrination as a medium of revealed truth to the Ciceronian mode of joint inquiry. Petrarch inspired generations of his humanist successors in turn to compose Ciceronian dialogues and make of 'the genre of interior dialogue . . . a mode of [ethical] inquiry' (Marsh 1980: 3, 13, 16–23; Remer 1996: 86; Struever 1985: 85; 1992: 24; Tateo 1989). To this dual revival of Ciceronian *sermo*, Petrarch added a revival of Seneca's conception of friendship as a rational affection in pursuit of a philosophical goal (Seneca 1917–25: I, 315 [48.2–3], II, 227–9 [81.12–14]; Miller 2000: 51–3). Petrarch's revival of both ancient *sermo* and friendship flourished most in his own practice: Petrarch's own familiar letters constituted that community of discursive friends necessary, in dynamic relation with meditative solitude, for the lived practice of a mode of free inquiry (Seneca 1917–25: I, 35 [7.8]; Petrarca 1978: 162–5 [1.5.4]; 2005: II, 254–7 [15.3]; Struever 1992: 4–21). Petrarch's revival of ancient conversation was more than matched by his resurrection of conversationalists in the ancient mode.

Yet Petrarch did not merely revive the Roman dead: the phrase 'genre of interior dialogue' above alerts us that Petrarch's revival made no *tabula rasa* of the medieval centuries. 'Interior dialogue', after all, was Augustinian dialogue. So, for a notable example, Petrarch's revival of Ciceronian dialogue in his *Secretum* (1347–53) both restored the ancient dialogic mode of free inquiry and retained the Augustinian characteristics of a focus on the internal examination of conscience and an abstraction from historical particularity (Petrarca 2003).

Petrarch signifed the return to free inquiry in the very choice of the participants of the dialogue. The *Secretum* began with a conversation between Franciscus (Petrarch) and Truth, but it shifted swiftly into a dialogue between Franciscus and Augustinus (the saint himself) in the silent presence of Truth.

> I realized that this could be none other than Truth herself . . . Eager to see her, I looked up, but my human vision could not bear her ethereal light. Again, I lowered my eyes to the earth. She took note of this. After a short silence, she again spoke, and asking me many questions, she led me into a long conversation with her. From this conversation I know I gained doubly: I won a little knowledge, and also the very act of talking with her gave me some measure of confidence. I found myself slowly becoming able to look at the face whose splendor had at first so scared me . . . I am very grateful to you for many things and especially for these three days of conversation, because you have cleared my blurred vision and you have dispelled the dense cloud of error that swirled around me. And what great thanks I owe to Truth, who, not troubled by our extensive talk, has stayed with us until the end. (Petrarca 2003: 46, 147)

Truth was still to be sought together in dialogue, but Truth's silence was the sign of Truth receding from the known, shared and revealed. Neither did Augustinus speak in the *Secretum* as a transmitter of revealed truth, but rather as an equal participant with Franciscus in the mutual search for truth.

Yet Petrarch applied this classicising mode to medieval subject matter: as had Augustine, Franciscus sought truth so as to heal his soul's discontents. This combination of ancient mode with medieval subject matter led Petrarch to an innovative conception. The truths that would heal him most effectively had to come from a fellow human being, able to give good counsel precisely because he was possessed of the same passions and discontents: 'Furthermore', Truth said to Augustine:

> unless your present happiness has made you forget your former sorrow, you remember that when you were shut in the prison of the body, you suffered similar things. And so, as you are a most worthy physician for diseases from which you yourself suffered, I ask you, even though I know that of all things silent meditation is for you the most agreeable, please break your silence and try somehow to bring calm to this man who is so deeply distressed. (Petrarca 2003: 47)

Such counsel, moreover, would be persuasive as well as good, because Franciscus would listen to his fellow human being more carefully than he would to any incorporeal abstraction of Truth, precisely because he knew him to share his passions and discontents – and his delights, for Petrarch enjoyed the pleasure of conversation (Petrarca 2003: 47) as much as Augustine had enjoyed the pleasure of confession. God's truth was not directly challenged thereby, but, *contra* Augustine, Petrarch substituted conversation for revelation as the remedy for his troubled soul. Petrarch's synthesis of ancient and medieval was to make the soul a subject for conversation – to devote conversation's exercise of reason to the study of the passions – and to make the soul's salvation, the proper ordering of its passions, an end for conversation (Marsh 1980: 4, 16–22).

Petrarch revived, Petrarch grafted, but Petrarch also innovated. To begin with, Petrarch took up the Senecan reinscription of writer and reader as intimate friends, and broadened it to include reading across time. Intimate reading now was meant to create *familiaritas*, a familiar conversation, with writers of the past: 'When I read his letters', Petrarch wrote of Cicero, 'I feel as offended as I feel enticed. Indeed, beside myself, in a fit of anger I wrote to him as if he were a friend living in my time with an intimacy that I consider proper because of my deep and immediate acquaintance with his thought.' This intimate reading and understanding was meant to be as expressive of one's individual self as one's writing; what Eden calls 'a *hermeneutics of intimacy*'. Petrarch offered all of himself – indeed, demanded that he be read comprehensively:

> I wish my reader, whoever he may be, to consider me alone, and not his daughter's marriage, not a night with his lady friend, not the wiles of his enemy, not his security or his home, not his land or his money. Even as he reads me, I want him to be with me; if he is pressed by affairs, let

him defer his reading. When he decides to read what I write, he must lay aside the burden of his affairs and the anxieties of his home life in order to direct his attention to what is before his eyes.

Such reading was also, among other things, a *historical* reading – an understanding across time that therefore was aware of time, that sought to understand the character of a writer's historical 'home'. As Petrarch had made of the soul, so now he made of historical understanding, a subject and an end of conversation (Petrarca 2005: I, 12 [1.1], II, 191 [13.5]; Eden 2012: 63–8; and cf. Hyatte 1994: 196–201).

But not of literal conversation – and this too should be emphasised as a Petrarchan legacy. Petrarch revived *sermo*, but he also began the Renaissance dislocation of the concept from the literal to the metaphorical, which would be prerequisite for the later, increasingly elastic applications of *sermo*. To conceive of reading Cicero as an exercise in *sermo* was perhaps the most dramatic example of this shift to the metaphorical, but more influential was Petrarch's shift in emphasis from the spoken to the written, from *sermo* as actual conversation (and its literary simulation) to *sermo* as an epistolary exercise. To speak of this shift in emphasis does not – cannot – allow fully for the effect of Petrarch's actual, necessarily unrecorded conversation; but neither should we deny Petrarch's focus on his own (familiar and private) letters – so carefully written, so carefully edited, collected and published (Enenkel 2003: 96–104). To some extent, the shift of emphasis toward letters registered the influence of the *ars dictaminis*, noted above. The monastic inheritance also mattered in this transformation. Monks had devoted their leisure to copying – *writing* – holy texts, and Petrarch's quite monastic devotion to the written word acted as a conduit of influence that would make of humanists, in effect, a scholarly species of *gyrovagus* (wandering) monks who would devote their leisure to *writing letters* devoted to the common good and the search for truth (Fumaroli 1988: 141–3). Petrarch made thematic the articulation of *sermo* in writing.

But to use *sermo* as a metaphor, to shift its primary mode from speech to writing, opened *sermo* to new dangers as well as to new opportunities. *Sermo*'s mode of friendship was meant to entail both unmanipulative spontaneity and actual familiar knowledge – and Petrarch certainly both practised and explicitly emphasised the spontaneous element of his correspondence (Petrarca 2005: I, 31 [1.5], 415 [8.7], III, 56, 58 [18.8]; Eden 2012: 54–5). Yet Petrarch's letters were highly polished evocations of spontaneity, meant to evoke a familiar, intimate style (Eden 2012: 58–9). Petrarch's exercises in spontaneity avowed their debt to Ciceronian *sermo*, and made the tie to *sermo* all the tighter by Petrarch's own influential epistolary practice – but their very polish also shifted such *sermo* toward oratory's realm of manipulation and dissimulation.

Furthermore, since Petrarch wrote not only to unknown contemporary addressees but also (continuing the conversation formed by reading the letters of the ancients) to the unknowable readers of the future (Petrarca 1992: 672–9 [18.1 ('To Posterity')]; 2005: I, 15–21 [1.2]) – and in both cases with a consciousness that he was engaged in a mode of public address – the familiarity he invoked was also entirely fictional. Petrarch's artful and impersonal evocation of artless familiarity *could* make a friend of the reader, and thus create in him the condition of lived practice that made possible the mode of shared inquiry – but the success of the gambit depended upon the choice of the readers to respond in a friendly fashion, to commit themselves to the subject of inquiry. Nor did the Petrarchan correspondent necessarily desire true *amicitia*: it was all too easy for artfulness to decay into a manipulation and empty courtesy that hollowed out the friendliness that made possible this mode of inquiry. Petrarch's infiltration of the familiar address into letters concerning the realms of epideictic and public affairs heightened the possibility that an oratorical subject matter would contaminate *sermo* with oratory's unfriendly, manipulative mode (Petrarca 2005: II, 49–54 [10.1], III, 305–7 [23.21]; Struever 1992: 9–29). Similarly, although Petrarch's address to socially diverse correspondents allowed him to emphasise his flexible attention to their individually diverse characters (Petrarca 2005: I, 9 [1.1]; Tinkler 1991: 72), it entailed a further drift from the realm of *sermo*, used between a socially homogenous elite, to the realm of oratory, used toward a socially diverse audience. Petrarch had disentangled *sermo* from dictamin and dialectic, but only to cast it out once more on a long turn toward oratory.

Conclusion

Christianity pulled *sermo* and *conversatio* toward God, outward toward the universal friendship of mankind and inward toward each man's soul. The *ars dictaminis* pulled letters in the opposite direction, toward the world and the myriad of necessary sins that make up public life. The consequence of these discordant shifts was to stretch the bounds of *sermo* and *conversatio*, to universalise them and to dislocate them from their classical framework. Petrarch's resuscitation of classicising *sermo* preserved many of its medieval stretchmarks – and dislocated conversation further still, making it fundamentally a metaphor rather than a descriptive category. This would be the inheritance of the medieval and Petrarchan transformations of *sermo* and *conversatio* – universalising impulses toward God, the soul and the world, and an unmoored conceptual malleability. A wild ride was about to commence.

Note

1. For the dictaminal tradition, see Camargo (1991), C. Haskins (1929), Murphy (2001a: 194–268), Patt (1978), Witt (2001).

Chapter 3

The Renaissance of Conversation

Introduction

The previous chapters unite the narratives of several linked concepts – friendship, familiarity, conversation and *conversatio*, and the literary genres of the dialogue and the letter. The history of these concepts and their derivatives became far more complex in the Renaissance, such that they must be traced in parallel narratives. I begin in this chapter with a study of the transformation from roughly 1400 to 1700 of the conception of conversation itself, both within treatises touching on theories of conversation and in the practice of the literary genre of dialogue, that literary emulation of *sermo* whose changing form registered conversation's transformations. This transformation began with the Renaissance humanists, who intensified the Petrarchan abstraction of conversation-as-metaphor from actual (and literary) conversation. The changing role of Renaissance conversation was linked to the simultaneous expansion of oratory's ambitions, which inspired both the use of conversation as a refuge from oratory and, in a revolutionary riposte, the counter-claim that conversation should expand the scope of its subject matter to supplant oratory. The new genre of Utopian dialogue provided a climax to this last development by innovating upon the old examples of Plato's and Cicero's *Republics* and thereby transforming the debate as to the *optimus status rei publicae* into a conversation that incorporated the ends of political action within the genre of *sermo*. Finally, in seventeenth-century France, the preceding expansion of conversation culminated in a revolutionary triumph, as conversation replaced oratory as the default mode of rhetoric.

This narrative provides the theoretical core of the transformation of conversation in Renaissance and early modern Europe – an examination of conceptions of conversation itself, rather than of the applications of conversation to other spheres of European culture. Yet this transformation of conversation was only one of a number of simultaneous and intertwining metamorphoses concerning conceptions of friendship, women, the court, letters and *conversatio*, among others. These several metamorphoses will be presented in discrete, parallel narratives for the purpose of analytical clarity, but they should be regarded as integrally linked in their development.

Humanist expansion

Petrarch's influence set the mould for humanist consideration of conversation – but his example was reinforced a generation after his death by the émigré Byzantine Manuel Chrysoloras (1355–1415), who largely resided in Italy from 1397 to his death in 1415 (Kristeller 1972: 73–4, 76; C. Smith 1992: 133–97).[1] Chrysoloras practised and promulgated in Italy a Byzantine tradition of conversation, not least for the purposes of education.[2] Chrysoloras' theory and practice of conversation appears to have provided a direct influence on his student Leonardo Bruni (*c.*1370–1444), whose dialogues *Ad Petrum Paulum Histrum* (1401–6) explicitly acknowledge his debt to Chrysoloras. In Bruni's dialogues, the character Niccolò says, 'And that Chrysoloras, from whom they learned Greek, once when I was present (which, as you know, I often was) particularly exhorted his pupils to talk over some topic among themselves.' *Quattrocento* humanist conversational practice would appear to owe some debt to the Byzantium that formed Chrysoloras, even if their fundamental desire to converse was not Byzantine in origin (Bruni 1987: 66 [Bk. I]; C. Smith 1992: 144–8).

Petrarch and Chrysoloras both steered the *quattrocento* humanists toward a close engagement with *sermo* – and so did the accidents of literary survival. Ancient rhetorical theory had focused on the branches of oratory, especially on judicial rhetoric; *sermo* had received only brief and scattered discussion. The Renaissance humanists, by contrast, inherited from the ancients a corpus largely composed of dialogues, histories, letters and other representatives of those overlapping categories of *sermo*, deliberative rhetoric and demonstrative rhetoric. Where so much of their textual inheritance consisted of examples of *sermo* and allied genres, it was only natural that the humanists would focus much of their intellectual effort upon these modes. *Contentio* (contentious oratory) receded in the humanist horizon, while the uncontentious genres of demonstrative oratory, deliberative rhetoric in its aspect of advice and opinion, and *sermo* (potentially encompassing in its informal mode any genre of rhetoric) came to the fore (Tinkler 1987: 280–6).

The marginal position of the humanists' studies in relation to their professional lives reinforced the shift toward *sermo*. The genres of oratory, judicial and deliberative, were the genres of *negotium*, while *sermo* was the genre of *otium*. The humanists' studies were either a leisured avocation or the calling card of the marginally employed among them, perforce at leisure; therefore they justified their inquiry into and engagement with the classical past as a leisured exercise of *sermo* meant in the present to inform and contribute to the *vita activa* of their professional lives (Tinkler 1987: 286–93, 302; 1988a: 209–14). As the character of Salutati put it in Bruni's *Dialogues*:

> I see that you are dull and have insufficient regard for your own advantage: you neglect to make a habit of practicing disputation . . . What sharpens the intellect, rendering it more clever and versatile, better than disputation, since in a brief space of time one must apply one's self to the topic and thence reflect, discourse, make inferences and conclusions? So that it is easy to understand how a mind stimulated by this practice becomes swifter at discussing other things. (Bruni 1987: 64 [Bk. I])

Sermo also relied on character (*ethos*) – and the authority of character, created by self-expression, also mattered most to the institutionally marginal humanists, who had little or no institutional authority upon which to draw. By contrast, the scholastics, who did have the institutional authority of the universities, relied, not least in their dialogues, 'on the impersonal validity of method' in preference to subjectivity (Tinkler 1987: 296–9; 1988a: 202–3). The shift toward *ethos* in turn created as a further corollary an increasing emphasis among Renaissance humanists upon familiar style as the means by which to express their selves. So Desiderius Erasmus (1466–1536): 'As each individual has his own appearance, his own voice, his own character and disposition, so each has his own style of writing. And the quality of mind is manifest in speech even more than the likeness of the body is reflected in a mirror" (Erasmus 1992: 76–9; Eden 2012: 87–8). Familiar style was necessary, in other words, to convey the authority of their newly salient characters. The humanists' embrace of *sermo* entailed a particular emphasis upon *familiaritas*.

These several influences impelled the *quattrocento* humanists toward a deepening engagement with the classical mode of *sermo* – and in particular toward a further abstraction of *sermo* from its association with actual and literary conversation toward a generalisable model of discourse and intellectual inquiry. Petrarch had taken his engagement with Cicero as a conversation across time; the *quattrocento* humanists not only followed Petrarch in framing their engagement with the classical world as a conversation between themselves and the ancients but also began to assimilate conversation with both historical inquiry in particular and with the discovery of knowledge – understanding – in general. In so doing, they began generally to conceive of the Ciceronian dialectic between conversation and activity in the world as a dialectic between communication with the ancients and their communication with their fellow citizens. So Niccolò Machiavelli (1469–1527) wrote to Francesco Vettori (1474–1539) in 1513 of his conversations with the ancients: 'I am not ashamed to speak with them and to ask them the reason of their actions; and they, out of their humanity, answer me.' Such conversations had present-day application: 'I have noted those things that profited me in their conversation and composed a little book, *De principatibus* where I go as deeply as I can into thoughts on this subject' (cited and translated in Najemy 1993: 234–5). Likewise, the character of Bernardo del Nero in Francesco Guicciardini's (1483–1540) *Dialogue on the Government of Florence* (1527) says that:

> [Y]ou have the advantage of being well read. Thanks to this, you are able to learn from the dead what happened in many past eras, whereas I can only converse with the living and see nothing other than the events of my own time . . . For having read so many histories of various nations in ancient and modern times, I am certain you have also thought about them and gained a familiarity with them, so that it won't be difficult for you to judge what the future will be . . . But someone with a sharp eye, who knows how to compare and contrast one event with another and consider what the substantial differences are and which matter less, easily recognises it and with calculations and measurements of past events knows how to calculate and measure quite a lot of the future. (Guicciardini 1994: 9, 16 [I])

This dialectic may be phrased in terms of genre and tense: the *quattrocento* humanists strengthened the application of the demonstrative (epideictic) genre of history to the deliberative genre of counsel, applying the study of the past to consideration of the best action in the future. At the same time, the *quattrocento* humanists created a new dialectic for *sermo*: if Petrarch and Bruni substantially had liberated *sermo* from its old yoke to Augustinian revelation, the Platonising generation of Marsilio Ficino (1433–99) created a new tie to Platonic idealisation. The *quattrocento* humanists made the relationship between Ciceronian and Platonic conceptions of knowledge thematic to their conception of philosophical inquiry. As Pocock notes – although without emphasising as I do the genre specificity of *conversation* – conversation became the means to acquire sure knowledge of philosophical universals, the historical concern with the past became linked with moral philosophy's concern for the present and the future (Pocock 2003: 61–5).

> Truth itself became less a system of propositions than a system of relationships to which the inquiring spirit became party by its inquiry. In consequence, participation in the humanist conversation, in one or other of its forms, became in itself the mode of relation to the universal, and the universal could be known and experienced by perpetual engagement in the conversation with particulars. The question was what form the conversation should take, what manner of conversation most fully realized the universal.

Baldassare Castiglione's (1478–1529) *The Book of the Courtier* (1528), as we shall see below, exemplified this melding of humanist conversation with Platonic universals. For now we shall note more generally that conversation's double dialectic with sure knowledge on the one hand and the *vita activa* on the other rendered it the suture by which sure knowledge could inform oratory and political action, and by which deliberative counsel was assimilated to the goals of moral philosophy (Pocock 2003: 61–5; Tinkler 1987: 294, 304; 1988c: 458–9).

The sixteenth-century humanists further broadened the application of conversation. Erasmus applied the conventions of *sermo* to his conception of the divine Word and to his notion of tolerance, and his influence generally amplified the role of conversation in Renaissance thought and practice (McConica 1969: 90–1; Remer 1996: 43–230, esp. 90–6). The Italian theologian Jacob Acontius (*c.*1520–*c.*1566), broadening the social class that could participate in conversation, applied *sermo* (in Remer's summary) to 'the method that churches, though large and diverse, should use to investigate doctrinal matters' (Acontius 1651: 94 [3]; 1940: 132 [6]; Remer 1996: 123). *Sermo*, as tolerance and theological discussion and in the practice of churches, became an ever more influential model throughout the century. These examples all register the practical and particular expansions of conversation – but, to repeat, they are even more important as examples showing that the *quattrocento* humanist cast of mind that took conversation as a metaphor capable of indefinite extension and application had inspired the humanists of the sixteenth century to begin actually to apply that metaphor to different aspects of communicative practice.

The genre of dialogue: conversation's struggle with oratory

Second only in importance to the metaphorisation of conversation was its first great expansion to cover the range of political topics – in other words, into the realm of oratory. This expansion occurred most dramatically in the rapidly multiplying genre of humanist dialogues (Vallée 2004: ix–x) – an incident that requires that we also establish that these dialogues should indeed be taken as examples of *sermo*, so as properly to substantiate this aspect of the argument. So as to avoid repetition, this section combines an account of the humanist genre of the dialogue, a discussion of the relationship of conversation to the political world of oratory, and an account of how the subject matter of humanist dialogues expanded to cover a remarkable amount of the political world.

In the first place, the characters in *quattrocento* dialogues explicitly stated that they were engaging in *sermo*, not in an agonistic genre. In Poggio Bracciolini's (1380–1459) 'On Avarice' (1428–9), Bartolomeo da Montepulciano said that 'none of you should expect any polished speech or wise opinions from me, for after dinner no learned or dignified discourse or well-ordered oration should be required', while Andrea of Constantinople explained that 'I didn't come here invited to an academic disputation' (Bracciolini 1978a: 248–9). In Bracciolini's 'On Nobility' (1440), Niccolò noted that, 'the debate is hardly suited to this time and place' (Bracciolini 1978b: 125). Looking ahead to the *cinquecento*, we may note that Guicciardini's *Dialogue on the Government of Florence* continued this stipulation of genre. When Bernardo del Nero demurred from discussion, 'since we are bound to get upset by arguing and disagreeing about matters of such importance, however amicably we do it, and instead talk of pleasant things,' Piero Guicciardini reassured him that the company can 'continue our earlier conversation. Far from being upsetting, it is bound to be extremely enjoyable, as a discussion – I won't say between friends, rather between father and sons, for this is how we regard our relationship' (Guicciardini 1994: 8 [I]).

Furthermore, the *quattrocento* dialogues recapitulated in their settings the old association of *sermo* with leisure in the villa or garden, *otium* in counterpoint to the *negotium* in the city. Bracciolini set his 'On Avarice' in the 'little country house' of Bartolomeo da Montepulciano, where, '[a]s often happened, the guests this time sat around discussing various topics' (Bracciolini 1978a: 243). Bracciolini's 'On Nobility' likewise was set in his own country house: 'For one day, when I had retired to the country from the city for a change of air, there joined me at my invitation, Niccolò Niccoli and Lorenzo de' Medici, my closest and most learned friends. I had lured them to my villa mainly to show them some sculptures I had brought there.' The dialogue itself began '[w]hen they were in the garden' (Bracciolini 1978b: 122). The Florentine humanist Alamanno Rinuccini (1426–99) in 'Liberty' (1479) spoke extensively of the country villa and garden setting of his conversation – although here (as we shall note again below) it was thematic that his leisure was enforced, exile from the tyrannical city of Medicean Florence (Rinuccini 1978: 193–4, 198–9, 211). Looking forward to the *cinquecento*, Thomas More (1478–1535) likewise situated the dialogue of the *Utopia* (1516) in a garden: 'After making a few stock remarks, as people generally do when first introduced, we adjourned to the garden of my hotel, where we sat down on a bench covered with a layer of turf, and began to talk more freely' (More 2003: 17).

Dialogues thus explicitly described and located themselves as evocations of *sermo*. Their character also emulated quite successfully the character of ancient *sermo*. Early on, Bruni's *Dialogi* initiated the *quattrocento*'s move beyond Petrarch toward a more exact imitation of ancient (Ciceronian) dialogue. The *Dialogi* itself exemplified, and its characters prescribed, free and leisurely discussion among friends who joined affection for one another's character, joy in common studies and a taste for conversation both as '[t]he practice of our studies' and (since *sermo* partly remained an artificial, agonistic exercise for its humanist practitioners) for 'love of glory for triumph in disputation' (Bruni 1987: 64, 66, 71 [Bk. I], 84 [Bk. II]; Marsh 1980: 4–5). The *Dialogi*, and its *quattrocento* successors, thus completed the return from internal contemplation to external discussion begun by Petrarch. In so doing, they thematised the combination of competitive rivalry and mutual interest that moved the passions both to sustain inquiry into morals and ethics and to move the soul to believe (Marsh 1980: 12–13).[3]

To sustain inquiry: in pursuit of this goal, Bruni and his *quattrocento* successors both classicised and followed Petrarch's treatment of Augustinus in his *Secretum*. So Salutati in Bruni's *Dialogi*, an authority to parallel Augustinus, also encouraged and sustained conversation rather than pronouncing a final truth. Poggio in Bracciolini's 'On Nobility' struck a characteristic note of philosophical diffidence: 'It would be pleasant to know the answer and well worthwhile . . . I am not surprised, myself, that the nations agree so little, when even philosophers argue enough to leave me in doubt as to the right opinion' (Bracciolini 1978b: 125). So likewise Rinuccini in 'Liberty': 'Since you two started the argument, I think you should finish it. I shall, like an honorable judge, keep watching to see which of you comes closer to the truth, and I may on occasion give my own opinion' (Rinuccini 1978: 197–8).

The humanist authors preferred a moderate tone that encouraged the continued joint inquiry into truth over a decay into contentiousness that would end both the dialogue and the inquiry. They also declined to indicate whether the last opinion given in a dialogue should be taken as their preferred opinion. Embracing the reader within the conversation of free inquiry, the dialogues, so often adjourned rather than resolved, remained open-ended, leaving the readers to continue inquiry into the subject themselves. Bracciolini, again, expressed this concisely: 'Which of us is right, let others judge, who have more talent. All are free to judge for themselves' (Bracciolini 1978b: 147). The friendliness that was meant to unite both the characters within the dialogue and the author and reader of the dialogue contributed to this open-endedness. Humanists were reluctant to commit the unfriendly act of judging among friends, or the equally unfriendly arrogation to themselves of a judgement they thought more properly belonged to their readers. Such actions pertained rather to those inflexible dogmatists the humanists disparaged – those mustachio-twirling scholastics, often in Stoic drag, always good for a hiss from the humanist claque (Marsh 1980: 11, 21; Tinkler 1988a: 205–6).

Thus far the *quattrocento* humanists returned in their dialogues to the modes of their ancient predecessors. In certain respects, however, they went beyond ancient practice. Sometimes they assigned a given belief to a character whose historical original did not share it. Such carnivalesque role-reversal – and Tinkler notes that 'Bruni's *Dialogi* and [Lorenzo] Valla's [(c.1407–57)] *De voluptate* [(1431)] take place explicitly on *festi dies*' – suspended the normal social hierarchy and thus provided a further encouraging context for the practice of free speech (Bruni 1987: 63 [Bk. 1]; Valla 1977: 53 [1.1]; Marsh 1980: 14–15; Tinkler 1988a: 211–12). The humanists also stretched beyond the traditional Ciceronian use of dialogue. In Marsh's summary:

> The dialogues of Bruni, Poggio, and Valla exhibit a variety in the presentation of arguments which is inconceivable in Cicero's balanced discourses *in utramque partem* or in the rigorous syllogisms of Scholastic *sic-et-non* disputations. [Leon Battista] Alberti and [Giovanni] Pontano employ the dialogue in a more discursive exposition, insisting that their interlocutors enjoy a freedom of organization.

Their loosened forms of discussion, presaging Erasmus' rejection of the rigidities of Ciceronianism, were as free as their mode of inquiry (Marsh 1980: 13–14). The *quattrocento* intensification of the mode of *sermo* thus began to dissolve *sermo*'s own genre conventions.

As they began to dissolve *sermo*'s genre conventions, so the *quattrocento* humanists began to dissolve its genre boundaries. Now they applied conversation and dialogues to a broadening range of topics – which rapidly came to include subject matters traditionally assigned to oratory. To explain properly this peculiar and complex expansion of *sermo* into the realm of oratory, we must first recollect that the rise of *sermo* within that progressive extension genre by genre of reclassised rhetoric that constituted Renaissance humanism (Witt 2003; and see Bouwsma 1990; Gray 1963; Kristeller 1961: 92–119; Seigel 1968) proceeded in tandem with a parallel rise in oratory, *oratio*. As noted above, the humanists' conception of oratory was peculiarly violent. This peculiarity proceeded not least from the increased Renaissance estimate of the power of the passions and of the will, both for good and for ill; as Coluccio Salutati (1331–1406) put it in *De nobilitate legum et medicinae* (1399–1400, published 1542), the will's 'force . . . is so great and its hegemony over the other powers of the soul so large that even though the instruments of the senses receive the images of sensible things, the effect of such reception scarcely proceeds further without the commands of the will' (Salutati 1947: 184 [23], translated in Trinkaus 1970: 67; Bouwsma 1990: 79). If the passion and the will were so strong, then rhetoric, which could address and constrain them, must be itself more desirable and more necessary. Rhetoric must also be brutally strong, for what but such brutal strength could control the passion and the will? So, while ancient writers often had conceived of rhetoric as violent in nature, and described it with military imagery, the humanists assimilated the conception of forceful rhetoric with the notion of lordship itself. The orator's seizure of an audience's passions to compel their assent blended with the prince's seizure of his subjects' wills to compel their obedience (e.g. Du Vair 2000: 246). Such rhetoric became 'the very *paradigm of rule*' (Abizadeh 2001: 558; Dawson 2007: 83; Kennedy 1994: 39; Rebhorn 1995: 23–31, 34–56, 83–94). Only such fearsomely powerful rhetoric, armed cap-a-pie, could suffice to joust with passion and with will.

At the same time, this equation of an audience's passions with subjects' wills led to a significant analogy and a corollary nightmare vision. The traditional division within the soul of reason and passion, where reason was supposed to control the passions, now was reinscribed, with new emphasis, onto the body politic. The elites were that state's reason and the populace its passions and its will; a rebel orator, therefore, challenging the rightful rule of the lordly orator, could seize control of the populace's passionate wills and lead them on a path of sedition, anarchy, civil disorder and rebellion. The French political philosopher Jean Bodin (1530–96) stated in *Six Books of the Commonwealth* (1576) that:

> Besides these causes of unrest there is another which proceeds from the freedom which is allowed to orators, who play upon the emotions and fan the desires of the people as they choose. There is nothing which has greater influence over men's souls than the art of eloquent speech . . . He [the orator] can excite the most cowardly to overcome the bravest, he makes the proudest cast aside their arms, turns cruelty into gentleness, barbarity into humanity, revolutionizes a commonwealth, and plays upon the people at will. (Bodin 1967: 143 [4.7])

The only antidote to such destabilising rhetoric was the proper exercise of the sovereign's rhetoric. Bodin also stated in *Six Books of the Commonwealth* that:

> There is no better means of appeasing discontent, and persuading subjects to obedience than to employ a good preacher, for he will find a way to soften and turn the hearts of the most obstinate rebels. This is especially true in a popular state where an ignorant people is master, and cannot be restrained except by orators. (Bodin 1967: 144 [4.7]; Rebhorn 1995: 127–32)

Yet the prince was all too frequently – *sotto voce*, almost always – a subject of his own passions. As Bracciolini put it in 'On Avarice':

> [W]hen one is in a position of power it is very difficult (and, indeed, beyond the abilities of most rulers) always to follow reason and be moderate. The tasks of ruling disturb the mind, inflame the intellect, upset reason, and

incite various desires, so that it is no great wonder that when rulers are seized by anger or lust they feel that they should do whatever pleases them. (Bracciolini 1978a: 270)

So likewise Guicciardini in *Dialogue on the Government of Florence*: 'There's no denying that the Medici regime was of this type – as are almost all one-man governments today, which mostly don't represent the will or the natural inclination of the subjects but are based on the appetite of whoever is in control' (Guicciardini 1994: 11 [I]). Oratory's solution to the disordered passions of the rebellious multitude was a rhetoric so compulsively powerful as to capture the will of any subject – and this rhetoric was as likely as not to be itself the creature of the disordered passions of the tyrant.

With increasing strength as the Renaissance progressed, rhetoric – as oratory usually was called – assumed a double image of despotism and anarchy, the unbridled domination of the single will or the unbridled wills of the multitude. Actual rhetors discoursed fantasies of their power over rulers, usually tactfully referred to as tyrants (Peacham 1593: sig. A.B. iii[r-v]; Rebhorn 1995: 106–10). Yet Renaissance rhetors could not entirely disguise, even from themselves, their actual powerlessness vis-à-vis the sovereign rhetoric of their lords (Rebhorn 1995: 118–22). Abizadeh notes that military imagery in classical Roman discussions of rhetoric contributed to the early modern distrust of rhetoric; that distrust more precisely derived from the Renaissance's even more coercive conception of rhetoric (Abizadeh 2007: 447).

This image of a fearfully coercive rhetoric gathered strength through the Renaissance, partly in tandem with the rising strength of the princely governments of Renaissance Europe – whose strength rose particularly in Italy and France, where most of the texts I will now discuss were written. At the beginning of the *quattrocento*, however, the humanists appeared to be more troubled by popular opinion than with its twin, tyrannous power. (Although they may already have been writing self-protective and concealing Aesopian language, with a wary eye to the power of the world's passions – see below.) Humanist dialogues notably registered this concern. To begin with, while such dialogues frequently appealed to judgements derived from the cognate authorities of experience, public consensus and general practice, the people's opinion and judgement – rough cognates for their passions and their wills – simultaneously remained highly problematic (Marsh 1980: 13, 21). In Bruni's *Dialogi*, this issue crystallised around popular approval of the *trecento* poets, which was taken, in successive alternation, as grounds both for condemnation and for praise (Bruni 1987: 72–5, 79 [Bk. I]; Marsh 1980: 36). Indeed, the character Salutati articulated ambivalence about popular judgement: if on the one hand he relied upon the 'universal agreement' praising the worth of the *trecento* poets, elsewhere he stated that, '[t]hroughout my life nothing was more pleasing to me, and I sought nothing so much as getting together with learned men whenever possible and explaining to them what I was deliberating upon and undecided about, and asking for their judgment' (Bruni 1987: 65, 75 [Bk. I]).

The distaste for popular judgement registered in discussions of poetry also manifested itself in Bracciolini's 'On Nobility', in which he condemned the mutability of popular opinion. Bracciolini also contrasted popular judgement and reason, the latter of which he denoted as the means by which to discover truth. But Bracciolini had shifted the subject matter of this condemnation from the apolitical realms of poetic reputation to that of the definition of nobility. He wrote in 'On Nobility':

> 'If you deny that such renown comes from the things we just mentioned, you run against the general opinion and universal sentiment of men[,' said Lorenzo.] . . . 'If you respect our own customs, then, and our traditional ideas, and if you consider the general opinion authoritative (for in such matters, it has the most authority), you will have to accept my description of nobility.'
>
> 'Who do you think should decide this issue?' Niccolò asked, 'the wise or the masses? If you choose to be guided by the beliefs and habits of people in general, however, you will find that there is no basis at all for nobility, for these popular beliefs and customs differ widely and contradict each other. No fixed standard can be derived from them, as far as I can see . . . If nobility is really something, standing, as it must, on a definite rational basis, it ought to be one and the same thing for all people. The masses, however, when they call someone noble are thinking of everything but virtue and reason, and the significance of the term fluctuates to suit the beliefs and habits of different classes – beliefs and habits that are contradictory . . . I am forced to doubt, on this account, that the common everyday word, 'nobility', is more than an empty name.
>
> 'If it means anything at all, it must originate in either vice or virtue. But it is foolish to think that nobility arises from vice. And if it arises from virtue, it must be always one and the same, not vary with local custom. Nobility must be a fixed reality. But among us nobility is not much like this, it varies and goes from this extreme to that, seemingly without any firm basis.' (Bracciolini 1978b: 124–5; Marsh 1980: 53–4)

This mid-*quattrocento* discussion registered several changes. In the first place, to discuss the definition of nobility was to discuss a topic necessarily possessed of political charge – to begin to infringe upon the realm of oratory. In the second place, Bracciolini both defined nobility as it was as a creature of the vagaries of popular opinion and local custom, and defined nobility as it should be as properly defined by the beliefs of the wise, which would possess stability, universality, rationality and virtue. In this contrast of opinion and reason, and in this stipulation of the need for the reason of the wise to define a concept with no fixed meaning, this discussion of nobility provided a first rehearsal of the later arguments that public opinion (communicative rationality, etc.) should provide norms in general. Bracciolini did not explicitly constitute the opinions of the wise in terms of conversation – but to place this argument within a dialogue implicitly subjected the definition of nobility to the conversation of his readers, whose dialogic judgement could then provide the desired rational and virtuous definition of nobility. 'On Nobility' not only condemned popular opinion but also hinted that *sermo* itself might provide a solution to such opinion's insufficiencies (Rigolot 2004: 4).

The dialogues discussed so far did not directly address political subject matter, although Bracciolini's 'On Nobility' registered a shift in that direction. Rather, they all registered an unease with popular opinion, while 'On Nobility' only implicitly presented the mode of *sermo* as a potential rival to such opinion. Such muted unease, however, may have signalled deeper critiques. In contrast to Cicero, who wrote clearly and openly in the dwindling but real liberty of the late Republic, Cicero's *quattrocento* imitators wrote in markedly unfree Italian states and had to be wary of offending either the powerful or the masses. In Bracciolini's *On Avarice*, for example, Cencio cuts short his condemnation of avarice among present-day priests with the note that 'on these matters I think it is better to remain silent than to say only a few words' (Bracciolini 1978a: 273–4). The *quattrocento* humanists wrote dialogues in a mode of ambiguity and irony, aware that there might be dangerous eavesdroppers listening to their conversations. The free inquiry of dialogue had to come to orthodox, inoffensive conclusions. Even the professed desire in dialogues to speak so as to spark discussion – 'My only reason for attacking yesterday', said Niccolò in Bruni's *Dialogi*, 'was to stimulate Coluccio to praise them' (Bruni 1987: 78 [Bk. II]) – while genuine, also allowed an easy means by which to recant an argument and disclaim any essential tie between it and one's true beliefs

(Marsh 1980: 9–15, 28, 52–4; Tinkler 1988a: 211–12). To disparage popular opinion in reference to poetry, or to discuss the need for the wise to define the nature of nobility, might well disguise a more subversive point.

All such arguments of protectively self-concealing and coded Aesopian language must be to some extent speculative – yet by the later *quattrocento* and the beginning of the sixteenth century, humanists were beginning to address political subject matter directly in their dialogues: among these would be Rinuccini's 'Liberty' (1479), Giucciardini's *Dialogue on the Government of Florence* (1527) and Thomas Starkey's (*c.*1495–1538) *A Dialogue between Pole and Lupset* (1529–32). These dialogues, as we shall see, articulated increasingly severe critiques of the dangers of tyranny. At the same time, however, they registered by their willingness to discuss political matters at all an increasing boldness, an increasing willingness to oppose *sermo* (instantiated in the dialogues themselves) against such tyrannies – an increasing willingness to shift from Aesopian condemnations of the passions of popular opinion to open condemnations of the disordered passions of tyrants. The practical reality of some sufficient sphere of liberty, and perhaps a growing one, made it possible for such unprecedentedly frank dialogues to be written at all. The threat of tyranny, of coercive oratory, provoked an increasingly self-conscious turn toward dialogue as a means of critique and as a refuge. Conversation, after all, was by definition a mode of rhetoric that did not seek to compel the will – a mode where *logos* spoke uncompelled by *ethos* or *pathos* – and hence, aside from its positive allurements, a welcome alternative to oratory.

So these dialogues now explicitly contrasted the realm of *sermo* and the threatening political world beyond. In the first instance, this contrast was defensive – a description of the realm of *sermo* as a rare haven. For Rinuccini in 'Liberty', the country villa and the garden were an escape from a city explicitly given as unfree: 'Would you agree now that one is happier living in the fresh air, among wide fields, amidst the gratuitous bounties of nature? Or would you still prefer to be walled in on all sides by the city, to live as if in prison, and hardly to breathe freely?' (Rinuccini 1978: 193, 211). The enforced leisure of exile allowed for conversation that could only be productive in *negotium* if and when the city again became free: 'I am always learning something and becoming potentially more useful, should the state ever require my services' (Rinuccini 1978: 217). Guicciardini in *Dialogue on the Government of Florence* posited the same situation for such conversations as Rinuccini: exile from a tyrannical city, enforced leisure and discussion in hopes that it might someday be applied to the *negotium* of a free city. So he wrote that

> it is not at all reprehensible either to think or to write about the government of our city; and much less so because of the present situation. For although the city may seem to have lost its freedom . . . a one-man regime could at any moment revert to its former liberty . . . If it did change back, this meditation and discussion of mine might not be totally useless. (Guicciardini 1994: 2 [Preface])

The frame of the dialogue reinforced this situation of enforced leisure in exile, for Guicciardini set it in 1494, when his grandfather Piero, '[h]aving been excluded from public affairs . . . was living tranquilly in his villa nearby (Guicciardini 1994: 3 [Preface]). Conversation, leisure, the garden – these now also were endangered botholes, refuges from the political world.

Yet for all their defensiveness, these dialogues dared to concern themselves with government, and to discuss it with remarkable freedom. Rinuccini's 'Liberty' provided an extensive and detailed critique of the tyrannical aspects of Medicean Florence – although the characters in the dialogue had to be kept pseudonymous, 'lest, if some of the talk that took place among us seems to attack a certain person, these men might have reason to complain that I published the freely spoken words of a friendly conversation' (Rinuccini 1978: 194). Where Rinuccini discussed Medicean Florence in particular, Guicciardini declared the discussion of government, both practical and theoretical, generally a proper subject of dialogue:

> How splendid and honourable it is to meditate on government and public administration, on which our well-being, our health and our life depend – as do all notable deeds that are performed in this earthly life below! Quite apart from the useful and relevant material they provide for many aspects of our daily lives, the subject-matter is extremely worthy and worthwhile in itself. So that even if there were no hope at all of the things we think about or design ever happening, anyone who devotes time and mental energy to contemplate them certainly deserves to be praised – unless we believe that Plato, when he thought and wrote about the republic, did so in the hope that his imaginary government would be adopted and put into practice by the Athenians. (Guicciardini 1994: 1 [Preface])

Guicciardini further specified that this discussion of government should include the full range of judicial, demonstrative (epideictic) and deliberative topics: 'I think that in a government of a city like ours there are three main topics to be considered: how to administer justice fairly, how best to distribute the honorary political offices and the salaried public offices, and how to conduct foreign affairs, that is, concerning the defence and expansion of our dominion' (Guicciardini 1994: 24 [I]). Guicciardini's dialogue, in other words, encompassed the subject matter of all three modes of oratorical rhetoric.

Guicciardini's dialogue also engaged in a prolonged and innovative transposition of the object of the wary use of persuasion and reason, from the prince to the people. The people were the subject of pleasing flattery: 'Those who enjoy leading positions in the city do not primarily seek liberty as their objective as much as the increase of power and making themselves as superior and outstanding as possible. As long as possible, they strive to conceal their ambition with this pleasing title of liberty' (Guicciardini 1994: 36 [I]). In a popular regime, the dialoguing gentlemen would have to accommodate themselves to the wishes of the people: 'consider that it will be a lesser evil – not only for the city but also for yourselves – to temporise and accommodate yourselves as best you can to the present times' (Guicciardini 1994: 81 [I]). They also would have to use persuasion on the irrational people:

> Then it would be difficult to draw the people with you, since one always has to use persuasion with them, and yet the majority are incapable of understanding reason and do not recognize things from afar. Nor are we planning to legislate for a city ready to receive the ordinances that were provided; instead it has to be led to what is good for it by means of persuasion . . . we must look for a government that we are reasonably confident could be introduced by persuasion. (Guicciardini 1994: 89, 96–7 [II])

Yet the passions of the people, while still considered the subjects of rhetoric, were also considered as amenable to stability: 'A good government will also stabilise the feelings of the subject population' (Guicciardini 1994: 165 [II]). Looking backward, Guicciardini's consideration of the passions of the people in a political context connected these political dialogues with the earlier, Aesopian dialogues that discussed popular opinion in a literary frame of reference. Looking forward, the full implications of this transposition would not flower until eighteenth-century England – but already in Guicciardini that passionate sovereign who was subject to the flatteries and persuasions of reason began his abstracting shift from prince to people.

Finally, dialogue extended itself within the realm of oratory to consider the old question of the best republic – *optimus status rei publicae*. Plato's and Cicero's respective *Republics* had addressed this subject in antiquity in dialogue form (Plato 1963: 575–844 [*Republic*]; Cicero 1998), but the scholastics and early humanists had made it a subject of disputation and debate rather than of conversation. More's *Utopia*, of course, provided the foundation for making this topic once more a subject of dialogue: 'I must start by recording the conversation which led up to the first mention of that republic' (More 2003: 19; Chordas 2004: 27–34). This bald statement was only the beginning of the dialogic structure of More's work. The book *Utopia* was a nest of conversations within conversations, the island Utopia was a site of 'constant dialogue' and Utopia was an imperfect *exemplum* that, in addition to providing a sort of experimental model by which to test abstract theories of the best state, was meant to involve the reader to further active contemplation both of how much Utopia in particular approximated the best state and what in general should be the nature of the best state (More 2003: 63–4; Logan 1983: 44–5, 62–5, 142–3, 231–43; Surtz 1964: xxvi). The nature of the best state became an uncertain question, where the ambiguities of dialogue deliberately left the question unresolved and open to the reader.[4]

At the same time, More also implicitly tied conversation to the related question of how to get from the very imperfect present of Europe to the best state. This topic might be stated as one of the efficacy of counsel: in Hythloday's challenging query, 'if I said things like that [recommendations to improve the world as it is] to people who were quite determined to take the opposite view, do you think they'd listen to me?' (More 2003: 41; Logan 1983: 111–30). Yet this was also a question of rhetoric: if persuasion could work at all, what mode of persuasion – what mode of rhetoric – could bring people to create the best state? Relevant here is Tinkler's analysis of *Utopia*, which takes More's interweaving of deliberative and demonstrative rhetoric both to thematise the gap between practical reality and the praiseworthy ideal and to seek how to bring them into alignment (Tinkler 1988b). We should also recollect Pocock's contention that it was precisely the humanist conception of conversation that was intended to bridge the gap between the practical and theoretical knowledge. Put Pocock and Tinkler together – that is, take More's use of conversation in *Utopia* as Pocockian humanist conversation applied to Tinklerian rhetorical ends – and the corollary would be that for More *conversation was the means by which to achieve the best state.* To engage readers in a dialogue about the best state, to allure them to think actively upon the subject, was itself the surest means of persuasion by which to achieve the state in reality. In effect, the very fact that More wrote *Utopia* as a dialogue subtly argued that conversation provided both the means of determining the nature of the best state and the means of achieving it. As Guicciardini had made the nature of government a topic of dialogue, so More had made the ends of government likewise dialogue's subject.

The literary genre of the dialogue thus registered as early as Guicciardini and More an ambition to apply conversation to the entirety of the political world. The continued flourishing of the dialogue thereafter must therefore be something of an anticlimax. We may note briefly that other notable examples of sixteenth-century dialogues included Erasmus' *Colloquies* (1518–33) (which discussed virtually every topic of inquiry in sixteenth-century Europe), Castiglione's *Courtier* (1528), Stefano Guazzo's (1530–93) *Civil Conversation* (1574) and Justus Lipsius' (1547–1606) *Constantia* (1584). We may also note that sixteenth-century dialogues, dethroning Cicero, increasingly assimilated the techniques and philosophical assumptions of the Platonic, Xenophontic and Lucianic dialogues. The dialogue spread from Italy to flourish in the nations beyond the Alps, hundreds of dialogues were published in each of at least four major vernaculars (Italian, Spanish, French, English) and large numbers were written in Latin, Portuguese, German, Polish and Czech. The dialogue would provide an influential model for emerging genres of early modern Europe such as the essay and the novel, and large numbers of dialogues would continue to be published (at least in England) into the eighteenth century.[5]

Yet by the end of the sixteenth century – perhaps precisely because the dialogue now addressed itself to the realm of oratory and thus began to be infiltrated by the imperatives of the search for victory – the genre began to decay as a genre devoted to mutual inquiry toward an uncertain truth. In Torquato Tasso's (1544–95) *Discourse on the Art of Dialogue* (1585), dialogue reverts to an artful exercise in dialectic and Socratic dialogue (Tasso 1982: 27–31; V. Cox 1992: 94–5, 194–5 (note 59)). *Cinquecento* Italy saw a progressive restriction of the dialogue as a mode of inquiry, constrained on the one hand by the restraints of political and religious authority and on the other by the strengthening belief that philosophy and science needed to be argued in monologic form. Decorum now became a partner in restricting inquiry rather than forwarding it, and dialogue became an increasingly hollow literary convention (V. Cox 1992: esp. 61–113; Leushuis 2004: 1302; Carron 1991: 102). Most sixteenth- and seventeenth-century

English dialogues were likewise essentially exercises in catechism and polemic in dialogic guise (J. Warner 2004; Puterbaugh 2004). After about 1600, the dialogue's genre characteristics and associations generally survived in the genres to which it had given birth rather than in the senescent husks that copied its form rather than its spirit (Burke 1989: 6). Significantly, some portion of this shift had to do with a sense that these new genres – above all the novel – modelled conversation more successfully than their dialogic forebears (Mee 2011: 4; Prince 1996: 244; Valenza 2009: 46). What remained of the dialogue genre largely disappeared from the scene during the eighteenth century (Dykstal 2001: 198 (note 5)).

This afterlife was somewhat beside the point. What mattered about the dialogue, for this narrative, was that in the late *quattrocento* and early sixteenth century the humanists formulated within its genre the conception of conversation as a refuge from the coercive claims of oratory, the ambition for conversation to discuss both the nature and the ends of government, and the revolutionary idea that the practice of conversation itself might provide a means toward achieving the best state. In all this, conversation provided a limited mode of rebellion against oratory – it was, after all, also a mode of rhetoric. To the rhetoric-besotted humanists, this presumably provided part of its attraction: conversation was a halfway house, a mode of rhetoric without its usual vices. So, within the genre of dialogue, the humanists articulated the general abstraction of conversation into a radical thrust to subsume the political world.

Conversation triumphant

Even as conversation grew in importance, the *quattrocento* humanists had continued to take speech as fundamentally persuasive in character, concerned with victory. This conception began to shift in the later Renaissance, as speech came to be seen as oriented toward the ideal of truth. This shift recuperated those aspects of the ancient tradition, most influentially articulated by Cicero and Quintilian, that had emphasised both rhetoric's ability to convey truth and its dependence upon truth for its power. So Quintilian: 'Therefore I would have the orator, while careful in his choice of words, be even more concerned about his subject matter. For, as a rule, the best words are essentially suggested by the subject matter and are discovered by their own intrinsic light' (Quintilian 1920–2: III, 189 [VIII.20–1]). Yet the ancient tradition had remained fundamentally ambivalent about whether speech aimed toward truth or victory: Quintilian's *intrinsic light* was matched by Cicero's judgement that 'all speaking is oratory' (Cicero 1971: 353 [19.64]). The earlier humanists also had emphasised speech's aim toward victory. Now, however, an increasing number of humanists emphasised speech's fundamental tie to truth.

As early as the late fifteenth century, the Dutch humanist Rudolph Agricola (1443–85) wrote in his *De inventione dialectica libri tres* (1479; first printed 1515) that, 'if speech is a sign of the things which are contained in the mind of him who speaks, then it follows that its proper task is to show and bestow these contents of speech' (1538 edition, cited and translated in Dawson 2007: 69). The English rhetorician Henry Peacham the Elder (1546–1634) likewise had stated in the *Garden of Eloquence* (1577) that 'the Lord God hath ioyned to the mind of man speech, which he hath made the instrument of our vnderstanding, & key of conceptions, whereby we open the secreates of our hartes, & declare our thoughts to other' (Peacham 1577: Aii^r; Dawson 2007: 66–9). English clergyman Richard Allestree (1621/2–81) wrote in his *The Whole Duty of Man* (1684) that 'speech is given us as the instrument of intercourse and society one with another, the means of discovering the mind which otherwise lies hid and concealed, so that were it not for this, our conversations would be but the same as of beasts' (Allestree 1684: 272).

This broad shift in the perceived ends of language (although by no means universal – see Mandeville 1988: 289–93 [342–8]) naturally entailed a shift in the preferred means of language, toward those best suited to achieve the ends of truth and mutual understanding. As a means to convey the inward truth of the mind, the ancient precepts of lucidity and perspicuity (taught variously by Aristotle, Cicero, the author of *ad Herennium* and Quintilian) now received new emphasis. '[P]layne wordes' were commended by, among others, Richard Sherry (*fl.*1550) in *A Treatise of Schemes and Tropes* (1550), Richard Brathwait (1588–1673) in *The English Gentleman* (1630), John Bulwer (1606–56) in *Chironomia: or, The Art of Manuall Rhetoricke* (1644), Clement Ellis (1633–1700) in *Gentile Sinner* (1660), Obadiah Walker (1616–99) in *Instructions concerning the Art of Oratory* (1659) and Richard Allestree in *Government of the Tongue* (1667) (Dawson 2007: 70; Prostko 1989: 44). Furthermore, to shift the perceived ideal of speech implied a corollary shift in the mode of rhetoric best suited to attain its ends – from oratory, the speech aimed at victory, to conversation, the speech aimed at truth.

The rise of conversation correlated with the continued rise of monarchical power in much of Renaissance Europe, and upon the consequent monopolisation of oratorical speech by the sovereign. These shifts were particularly pronounced in sixteenth- and seventeenth-century France, to which we will now turn. As in the ancient shift from republic to empire, deliberative counsel went into deep decline, to be replaced by an emphasis upon the epideictic.[6] In 1582, the French humanist Marc Antoine Muret (1526–85) stated in his *Oratio XVI* that:

> Of the three genres defined by Aristotle, only the epideictic, which was formerly little esteemed, remains in use. It remains, however, so that they who are in a position to write letters well, that is to say eloquently, with prudence, and taking into account things, persons, and circumstances may easily reach the intimacy of Princes, be entrusted with the most important affairs, and grow from honor to honor. (Muret 1834: 406, translated in Fumaroli 1983: 258)

The counselling orator, deliberative and persuasive, was out of fashion, and his place was taken by the courtier, whose epideictic praise of the sovereign became the means by which subterrraneanly to provide counsel. This shift of counsel from the deliberative to the epideictic also led to a shift of counsel into letters and conversations, not least because their increased emphasis on *delectare* had allied them with the epideictic. Cicero's letters thus become the model for a constrained eloquence modulated to a pleasing note. So Jacques Amyot (1513–93) drafted for Henri III (1551–89; r.1574–89) a *Projet d'éloquence royale* (unprinted until the nineteenth century), focused upon the conversations between the king and his courtiers, whose preferred style was, *en français*, Pietro Bembo's (1470–1547) delighting Ciceronianism. Indeed, during this period the delightful sound of such pleasing style – the music of Ciceronianism – became an increasingly important rival to the rhetorical mode that favoured the plain sense of the words (Amyot 1992; Fumaroli 1983: 258–61). Conversation's ascendancy owed as much to its delightful surface as to its truthful aims.

With this background in mind, we may turn to Pierre Charron's (1541–1603) consideration of eloquence in *Of Wisdome* (1601). This influential work, which (among other effects) did so much to popularise Michel de Montaigne's (1533–92) thought, presented a vision of rhetoric that set the stage for the seventeenth-century expansion of conversation. Charron, a champion of both the plain and the delightful – although perhaps more the former than the latter – believed that rhetoric should be Attic and conversational rather than ornately Asiatic: sober, true, 'natural, modest, and chaste: not accompanied with vehemencie and contention, whereby it may seeme to proceed from passion', serious and profitable, not offensive, gentle and pleasing, constant, strong and generous. Charron also was profoundly aware of the tyrannous abuses to which oratory lent itself: 'it hath not lesse force and violence then the commands of tyrants environed with their gards and halberds; It doth not onely lead the hearer, but intengleth him, it raigneth over the people, and establisheth a violent empire over our soules.' Yet to this fear of the power of oratory, Charron added a belief that eloquence was necessary to defend virtue against vice, since passionate men were not always disposed to virtue and truth (Charron n.d. [after 1612]: 584–8 [III.43]). Charron's analysis of rhetoric pointed toward a conversationalised rhetoric, perhaps not least to constrain the tyrannical abuses attendant upon oratory – but it also recognised that oratory had a powerful role in the preservation of virtue and that any replacement of oratory would need to substitute for this beneficial function. This ambivalent analysis would set the stage for much of the next century's development of French theories of rhetoric.

The quotation from Charron indicates how conversation had already permeated French thought by the beginning of the seventeenth century. Within this generally conversational *milieu*, the claim for conversation made particularly swift and influential strides in the circle associated with Jean-Louis Guez de Balzac (1597–1654) – Guez de Balzac's letters and essays were themselves notably influential examples of derivative genres of *sermo*, as well as making the theoretical case for conversation. Yet these claims were made with scarcely an acknowledgement of how radical they were. So Jacques de La Motte Aigron's preface to Jean-Louis Guez de Balzac's *Lettres* of 1624 registered in understated tones the rising claims of letters to the status and subject matter of oratory:

> Yet are there reasons, whereby wee may vnderstand the merit of Letters to bee of no lesse regard then that of Orations . . . But as concerning the Subiects, they are common to both kinds of writings, and it is an errour to imagine, there are some so particular to the one, that the other cannot touch vpon the same without iniurie thereunto . . . wee are therefore to confesse Oratoricall Treatises to haue no other subiect then Letters. (La Motte Aigron 1634: A2ᵛ, A3ᵛ; Carr 1990: 8)

Guez de Balzac's own influential 'De la Conversation des romains' (1644) further deprecated oratory and political speech and championed instead the freedom and authenticity of private conversation, which he now argued had been the quintessential speech mode of the Romans:

> And if some of them [the ancients] have said that they reign'd all the time they Oration'd, so soveraign was the power they exercised over mens mindes; we may speak even of those which in their conversation restored the liberty which they had taken away in their Orations, That they set at large and at ease the minds of those they opprest and tormented; and that they drew them from that admiration which had agitated them with violence, to make them sensible of a sweeter transport, and ravish them with less force. (Guez de Balzac 1652: 73–4)

This interpretation did not go unchallenged: Antoine Gombauld, Chevalier de Méré (1607–84), thought Guez de Balzac's history faulty, and accurately enough cited *De oratore* as evidence for the relatively slight interest the Romans paid to private conversation as compared to public rhetoric. He made his points with admirable courtesy in a letter to Guez de Balzac himself:

> J'admire principalement tant de choses nouvelles que vous dites des anciens Romains; & puis que vous m'ordonnez de vous en parler sincerement, je voy que les portraits que vous faites des conversations des bon mots & de l'urbanité de vos Romains sont plus agreables que les originaux ... car en verité leurs bons mots à les bien examiner n'estoient pas fort bons; on en dit de meilleurs en France. (Méré 1682: 267–8 [56])

Guez de Balzac acknowledged that the record of ancient private conversations was scarce, preserved essentially in a few dialogues and letters – but nevertheless he gave great weight to those few survivals (Guez de Balzac 1652: 96–7). His Rome was a Rome of conversation – and *salonnier* as well, devoted to the cultivation of pleasing manners and polite society (Guez de Balzac 1652: 65–74, 94–100; D. Gordon 1994: 112–15). We shall see below the affiliations of conversation with the *salons*; but we may note here that Guez de Balzac dedicated 'De la Conversation des romains' to that great *salonnière*, Catherine de Vivonne, Marquise de Rambouillet (1588–1665) (Guez de Balzac 1652: 41). The vision of a conversational Rome rose directly from the conversational social circles of France.

Indeed, Fumaroli identifies Vincent Voiture's (1597–1648) *Oeuvres* (1650), Paul Pellisson's (1624–93) prefatory 'Discours' to Jean François Sarasin's (1614–54) *Oeuvres* (1656) and Guez de Balzac's *Les Entretiens* (1657) as emblems of the inflexion in the long transition from the age of eloquence to the age of conversation, from the reign of *oratio* to the reign of *sermo* (Voiture 1650; Pellisson 1656; Guez de Balzac 1657; Fumaroli 1995, esp. 32, 38–9; and see Strosetzki 1984). Voiture and Guez de Balzac exemplified the new conversational mode; Pellisson provided admiring pointers to its use. Notably, Pellisson's praise of Sarasin's dialogues, by way of prescription on how to write in that enduring genre, also delineated the nature of the artful conversation that was coming to ascendancy in France:

> En dernier lieu, il faut posseder l'art du Dialogue, pour faire que cette conversation qu'on represente, quoy que plus sçavante & plus soustenuë que les conversations ordinaires, soit pourtant vne conuersation. C'est à dire vn entretien libre, familier, & naturel, semé par tout des ieux, de la gayeté, & de la ciuilité des honnestes gens, qu'on y distingue le caractere particulier de chacun de ceux qui parlent, qu'on les y connoisse, qu'on les y ayme. (Pellisson 1656: 13–14)

We may add to this, following Donawerth, the contribution of Madeleine de Scudéry's (1607–1701) *Les Femmes Illustres or the Heroick Harangues of the Illustrious Women* (1642), which likewise remodelled discourse upon the casual pleasantries of conversation – and linked this to a specifically female imagery and mode of speech, whose aesthetic excellence in the revelation of private sentiment was now also characteristically female, the artful artlessness of female self-adornment now the model for the artful artfulness of rhetoric.

> The delicacie of art consists in making believe there is none at all. You carrie flyes on your faces, which by your dressing are put there, to make the whiteness of your Complexion shine the clearer: Yet they are placed so orderlie, that it might be said they are living, and that they fly at hasard. You make curles and rings of your hair, but with such subtile negligence and agreeable cairlessness, that it might be judged rather the wind, than your hands had been helping to nature. Just so heir I have endeavoured to make my Heroines Eloquent. (Scudéry 1681, esp. sig. A2[r–v]; Donawerth 1997; Morlet-Chantalat 1994: 345–86)

Here, at the crux of this narrative, we should emphasise that the substitution of conversation for oratory was intimately linked with the substitution of a female model of speech for a male model of speech. We will return to this link but for now we will simply note that by the middle of the seventeenth century, in the thought of Guez de Balzac, Voiture and Scudéry, conversation, epochally, had substituted itself for oratory as the synecdoche of rhetoric.

This bald statement by Guez de Balzac and his fellow-travellers was accompanied by many descriptions of rhetoric, of oratory, with attributes associated with conversation. So Nicolas Faret's (*c.*1596–1646) *L'honnête homme* (1630) described an oratory marked by the artful artlessness of *sprezzatura*: 'Orators haue no greater Art, then to couer it in their Orations, the which being once knowne they lose their credit, and are not able by their eloquence to perswade even the most simple and ridiculous' (Faret 1632: 55–6). The Jesuit René Rapin (1621–87) put it in his *Reflections Upon the Use of the Eloquence of These Times* (1672):

> That Eloquence in general which takes too much care to range it's words, and to deck it's exterior parts, scarce ever succeed's well. Men ordinarily distrust what ever appeares artificial and unnatural . . . When the artifice of Eloquence is too apparent, all the effects it produces are against it self. (Rapin 1672: 37–8)

Archbishop François Fénelon (1651–1715) in his *Dialogues on Oratory* (written 1679, published 1718) emphasised the Longinian note that the most effective rhetoric concealed its own artistry, and the most effective rhetors succeeded in self-effacement (Fénelon 1722: 98–9; Bullard 2012: 267; Howell 1975: 123–40). Fénelon likewise praised Cicero as a model of artfully artless oratory:

> When he endevour'd to support and revive expiring Liberty, and to animate the Commonwealth against Antony his Enemy; you do not *see* him use Points of Wit and quaint Antitheses: He's *then* truly eloquent. Every thing seems artless, as it ought to be when one is vehement. With a negligent Air he delivers the most natural and affecting Sentiments; and says everything that can move and animate the Passions. (Fénelon 1722: 72)

Cicero, retrospectively, was imputed a Castiglionean mien.

Artlessness was equated with the 'natural' – and the conversationality of rhetoric became explicit by way of the prescription to speak naturally. So Fénelon followed up his praise of Cicero with a further prescription of naturalness in oratory:

Every Look and Motion shou'd in an easy natural manner represent the Speaker's Sentiments, and the Nature of the Things he says; but so as to avoid all Mean and Theatrical Gestures . . . The more artless and *natural* such a convincing perswasive Eloquence is, it must be the more powerful. (Fénelon 1722: 88–9, 141)

His dialogue's Speaker B then brought up the lurking conclusion: 'But, Sir, you seem to think that one who speaks in publick ought to use no other Action than what is proper for ordinary Conversation' (Fénelon 1722: 90). Speaker A demurred, but distinguished oratory from conversation very little:

> You mistake me, Sir: I think the Sight of a great Assembly, and the Importance of the Subject an Orator treats of, ought to animate him far more than if he were talking familiarly with his Friends. But both in private, and in public, he ought always to act naturally. He shou'd use some Action when his Words are moving: but when his Expressions are quite calm and simple, there is no occasion to move the Body; except it be in the gentlest manner. (Fénelon 1722: 90)

The Oratorian Bernard Lamy (1640–1715) in his *The Art of Speaking* (1675) likewise made explicit the equation between the natural and the conversational: 'Natural Discourse is that which is us'd in Conversation to express our selves, to instruct and signifie the motions of our Will, and the thoughts of our Mind.' To this Lamy added his own proviso: 'that Art may be call'd in sometimes to our assistance: matters of natural Discourse are not always so austere, but they may admit of some little Divertisement' (Lamy 1676: second pagination, 146 [3.3.1]). Rapin likewise indicated that the artlessness of eloquence did need to be artful:

> But because that Eloquence which is purely naturall never attains at perfection without the succours of art: she being commonly destitute of this help, by reasons of the false principles which men take up, or by the little diligence of her professours; she cannot rise so high, as to deserve the generall admiration of men, by those wonderfull effects which she would produce in hearts if she were accomplish. (Rapin 1672: 45)

But generally, eloquence was to be natural and therefore had to be conversational.

In Rapin's *Reflections Upon the Use of the Eloquence of These Times* (1672), the desire to be natural shifted toward the late-rhetorical notion of *the imitation of nature*: 'The greatest & most soveraign art of Eloquence consists in exactly following of nature as its true model & first original' (Rapin 1672: 32). But ultimately, the imitation of nature was also the imitation of conversation: Fénelon wrote that

> the whole Art of good Orators consists in observing what Nature does when unconstrain'd. You ought not to imitate those Haranguers who chuse always to declaim; but will never talk to their Hearers. On the contrary, you shou'd address yourself to an Audience in such a modest, respectful, engaging manner, that each of them shall think you are speaking to him in particular. And this is the Use and Advantage of natural, familiar, insinuating Tones of Voice. (Fénelon 1722: 98)

Oratory that imitated nature fundamentally was to be modelled on conversation.

Scattered other attributes also registered the conversationalisation of oratory. Fénelon variously recommended simplicity of speech, unmemorised speeches whose small errors would indicate naturalness and negligence, a conversational tone as a background so as to give greater power to those surprising and moving moments when one resorted to lofty eloquence, and perspicuity by way of carefully selecting the number and kind of details to present (Fénelon 1722: 93, 104–7, 129–31). Rapin addressed eloquence to the inner man, not the outer: 'Now this [true Eloquence] cannot be put in practise without a perfect knowledge of the heart of man, wherein lies the chief Art of an Orator' (Rapin 1672: 43). Rapin further described eloquence with the significant word *insinuate*, and followed up with recommendations as to style that came as corollaries to the need to insinuate:

> True Eloquence never dazel's, nor surprises, because by little and little it insinuates it self into the mind. Those reasons which are most capable of touching us are ordinarily (as *Aristotle* tell's us) the most common ones, and that language which is most natural, and to which men are inclin'd by the desire alone which they have to make themselves understood, is certainly the best and most proper. (Rapin 1672: 39–40)

Lamy's *The Art of Speaking* registered the interpenetration of oratory and conversation by applying the use of rhetorical figures to both: 'We may demand the Judgment of our Auditors, and interrogate them, to fix and retain their Minds in more serious attention, and make our reflexions upon what they have said. Thus has Conversation its

Figures, as well as Speeches, and Declamations' (Lamy 1676: first pagination, 147–8 [2.4.4]). In all these descriptions of the details of the nature of rhetoric, Fénelon, Rapin and Lamy together provided a remarkably conversational portrait.

Although Guez de Balzac and his peers had significantly conversationalised rhetoric by blandly assuming the point at issue, their later seventeenth-century followers were aware that the nature of their rhetoric had changed. Lamy spoke of the old identification of rhetoric with oratory as something now in the past:

> Those who have writ hitherto of the *Art of Speaking*, seem to have intended their Rules only for Orators. Their precepts relate only to the Style of an Orator; and those who study that Art, do look upon the copiousness and richness of Expression so much admired in the Discourses of great Orators, as the chief and only Fruit of their Studies. (Lamy 1676: third pagination, 41 [4.3.2])

Yet Lamy also took conversation to have persuasive purpose:

> As much as we may, and the matter of which we treat will permit, we must give our discourse this latitude and liberty of Conversation. Doubtless when a person in conversation speaks easily and pleasantly, it goes far towards towards [*sic*] the putting us into the same humour; the pleasure we take in his discourse, renders every thing easy that he says. (Lamy 1676: third pagination, 70 [4.4.2])

Rhetoric had become conversationalised, but conversation likewise had acquired persuasive goals. Rapin's extended comparison in 'A comparison between Demosthenes and Cicero, for eloquence' of the two ancient orators' modes of rhetoric likewise implicitly rein-scribed the new conversational rhetoric as, indeed, a form of rhetoric (Rapin 1716: I, 99–103). In their different ways, Lamy and Rapin both recognised that the conversationalised rhetoric was new – and that conversation had in the process to some extent adopted the ends of oratory. The transformation of eloquence occurred not entirely unbeknownst to those engaged in its great transformation.

This shift toward conversation also affected the tradition of René Descartes (1596–1650), which is often described as a total rejection of rhetoric. So even the Jansenists Antoine Arnauld (1612–94) and Pierre Nicole's (1625–95) Port-Royal *Logique* (1662), that great Cartesian rebellion against the rhetorical mode of inquiry, allowed some role for 'manières favorables', if only as 'a means of easing the communication of truth once it has been found *by another method*: 'It is fitting that those who wish to persuade others of some truth they have recognized apply themselves to clothing it with the favorable manners that will win approval and to avoid the shocking ones that are only capable of driving people away' (Arnauld and Nicole 1662: 298, translated in Carr 1990: 72; H. Davidson 1965: 50, 79–82, 100). Nicole later greatly emphasised in 'Of the means to conserve Peace amongst Men' the importance of eschewing a dogmatic tone:

> It is also a very great fault to speak in a decisive tone, as if what we advanc'd could not in reason be question'd. For those we speak to in this manner, are either offended because they are made to understand that they question what is out of dispute; or else it seems, that we have a mind to take from them the liberty of examining and judging by their own proper light, and this they look on as an unjust domination. (Nicole 1677: I, 214)

Nicole, not incidentally, noted that a dogmatic tone was a characteristic flaw of the learned (Nicole 1677: I, 218). In these varied aspects, the Cartesian revolution overlapped with the conversational one. This overlap was not total – no amount of juggling can entirely reconcile the thought of Descartes and Guez de Balzac, friends though they were. Yet we should keep in mind that the conversational transformation was a complement as well as a rival to that of Descartes, that the arguments of reason themselves were couched in a conversational style.

Conversational rhetoric thus was both self-aware of its past and influential upon its great Cartesian rival. Yet for all this self-consciousness and strength, it did not entirely supplant oratory. As late as the reign of Louis XV, Charles Rollin (1661–1741) wrote in *Traité des études* (1726–31) that conversation was insufficient to persuade most people:

> Some people are averse to all ornaments of discourse, and think no eloquence natural but that whose plain style resembles the language of conversation; these look upon everything as superfluous that is added to mere necessity; and think it a dishonour to truth to give her a foreign dress, which they fancy she does not want, and can serve no other end than to disfigure her. If we were to speak before philosophers only, or people free from all passion and prejudice, this notion might perhaps appear reasonable. But it is far otherwise; and if the orator did not find

the art of winning his auditors by the pleasure he gives them, and by leading them by a gentle kind of violence, justice and truth would often be borne down by the attempts of the wicked. (Rollin 1734: II, 77–8)

Even the *violence* of oratory was now supposed to be *douce* – but Rollin, as much as Charron a century earlier, was aware of the limitations of conversation and the irreducible virtues of oratory. The triumph of conversation, as most such triumphs, was decisive without being annihilatory. Oratory survived, albeit in a minor key.

Conclusion

Renaissance humanist thought witnessed a series of innovations in the conception and application of conversation. The great innovation was to make conversation a metaphor rather than a description of actual and literary conversations: this allowed a series of abstractions to render conversation the synechdoche for all conversational modes of inquiry. So conversation, abstracted and rendered metaphorical, came to be regarded as the medium that united the contingent actions of the world with the Platonic norms toward which such actions might lead. Meanwhile the dialogue, conversation's literary emulation, registered the perception of the strengthening power of the realm of oratory – of passion, of will – both by increasing defensiveness and by a willingness to apply conversation both to the present and the (Utopian) future of the political world. These two Renaissance transformations were capped by a shift in seventeenth-century France, wherein conversation supplanted oratory as rhetoric's default mode.

These changes collectively set the stage for the centrality of conversation in the intellectual world of early modern Europe. To make conversation abstract, a metaphor, was the basic prerequisite for making it applicable to a long catalogue of European intellectual endeavours and social contexts: some part of that catalogue will appear in the chapters below and more of it in this book's sequel. To make rhetoric a form of conversation was likewise the prerequisite to shifting all the forms of intellectual activity previously conceived of as rhetorical to the conversational mode. To apply conversation to the political world, to take conversation as the instrument by which to meld contingent action and ideal norm, to incorporate within conversation the Utopian ends of politics and the means by which to arrive at that Utopia – all this was to lay the theoretical foundations for all later attempts to wrest the political realm from oratory, to be delivered to conversation. These conceptions of conversation – these dialogues and treatises – rehearsed the entire conceptual revolution that was to follow.

Notes

1. For Byzantium's influence on the Italian Renaissance, and especially the influence of Byzantine rhetoric, see Kristeller (1972) and Monfasani (1983). For rhetoric in Byzantium, see Jeffreys (2003) and Valiavitcharska (2013).
2. For conversation and dialogue in the Byzantine tradition, see Cunningham (2003).
3. For Renaissance dialogue, see Burke (1989) and Godard (2001).
4. For the ambiguities of dialogue as it applies to utopia, see Bevington (1961), Logan (1983: 122–3) and Surtz (1964: xxv–xxix).
5. Erasmus (1965), More (2003: 41–2), V. Cox (1992: 9–33), Dykstal (2001: 5), Hart (1990), Heitsch and Vallée (2004: ix–x), Kinney (1989: 128), Leushuis (2004: 1295), Marsh (1980: 5–6, 8), Prince (1996), Richards (2003: 25, 29), Rigolot (2004: 5–7, 13–16), Skinner (1987: 131–2), K. Wilson (1985: 75–107), Winn (1993), Yeo (2009: 13).
6. For the greater survival of deliberative counsel in England's 'mixed monarchy', see Elyot (1533: sigs. 7^{r-v}), Colclough (2005: 62–76), Guy (1993: 13–22; 1995), Lehmberg (1961), McLaren (2004: 161–97). For the parallel exercise of civic oratory in the Dutch Republic's Golden Age, see Weststeijn (2012: esp. 69–140). Yet just as a strong English tradition of dialogue developed in the Tudor mixed monarchy (Deakins 1980; Puterbaugh 2004; Warner 2004), so the Dutch Republic's tradition of civic oratory coexisted with a tradition of dialogue: Harline (1987: 52–6), Weststeijn (2012: 318–20, 323, 343). The stronger oratorical tradition in England and the Dutch Republic may have stunted the development of conversation in those two countries.

Chapter 4

Intimate Friendship

Introduction

Conversation in antiquity had been the speech of friends and familiarity – and insofar as friendship motivated conversation as a mode of inquiry, that friendship oriented conversation toward reason and virtue. The Renaissance witnessed a long shift in the conception of friendship, culminating in the thought of Montaigne, away from an alignment with reason and virtue and toward an alignment with passion and familiarity. This changing conception of friendship brought with it a corresponding change in the conception of conversation, which now also based itself upon passion and familiarity – including in its use as a mode of inquiry. In other words, the expressive aspects of *sermo*, which communicated character in an intimate manner, now became the basis of the philosophical aspect of *sermo*, the inquiry into truth. The communication of intimate, passionate friendship was now the prerequisite for the search for truth.

Among the consequences of the transformation of friendship into the mode of passion and intimacy, perhaps the most important was that it opened up the conception of friendship from a relationship between men only. Reason and virtue were taken to be masculine attributes, as therefore was friendship, and women had been taken to be incapable of conversation, the mode of speech conducted between friends that communicated such reason and virtue. Yet women were certainly considered capable of passion and intimacy – indeed, such modes were if anything taken as characteristically feminine. To recast the conception of friendship upon such passion and intimacy therefore was to broaden friendship to include relations between men and women, or even, eventually, between women and women. To think of women as capable of friendship in turn implied that they were capable of conversation, inquiry into truth – and even of reason, to the extent that conversation mediated the passions and reason. Conversation, the speech of friends, by this chain of conceptual correlation became a mode of speech that embraced women and their speech – uniquely, for both oratory and philosophical reason remained masculine modes, rejecting women or rendering them invisible. The conception of mixed-sex conversation, in turn, provided a model for actual mixed-sex social settings. The development of a conception of intimate friendship led by a high road to the emergence of women into the world of conversation, both in theory and in practice, and thus into the previously masculine world of public speech.

Familiar friendship

The Renaissance detachment of the concept of friendship from its old attachment to virtue and the public world, and its reattachment around familiarity and the private world, should probably be attributed generally to the growing sense in the Renaissance (noted above) of the power of the passions and the will, of oratory, of the political world. These, in sum, vitiated belief in the power of reason and virtue – and as *vera amicitia* based itself upon reason and virtue, so the traditional conception of friendship also began to weaken. The conception of friendship had to rebuild itself around the passions and the will – and, as it would turn out, upon a new emphasis on familiarity, and on innovations upon the concepts of sincerity and interiority. In its new mode, such friendships would be associated with the private world, away from the pressing corruption of the public world, of power and oratory. The conversational communities that continued to be formed around friendship and familiarity would be formed around these concepts in this new, privatising mode.

The *quattrocento* and early sixteenth century still largely preserved a classicising conception of friendship. So the Renaissance humanists generally continued to practise and extol the classicising cult of friendship throughout the sixteenth century (Burke 1999). Emblematic of traditional friendship's importance was Erasmus' choice of 'Between friends all is common' as the first of his adages in the *Adagia* (1500–36). Erasmus' intimate knowledge of Greek and Roman authors displayed in the *Adagia* likewise preserved the humanist conception of friendly conversation with the ancients (Vallée 2004: 44). Baldassare Castiglione's *Courtier* continued another aspect of humanist friendship, the friendship of author and reader: as Rigolot puts it, '[e]nlightened readers are invited to join the open-ended discussion as new, full-fledged members of an honourable and joyful *amorevole compagnia*' (Rigolot 2004: 10). Thomas More's *Utopia* incorporated friendship as the basis for discovering Utopia, both in the paratext that cited the (often epistolary) friendship of Erasmus, More and the entire humanist community as necessary for the production of the text, and, within the dialogue's text itself, through the friendship of the characters of Thomas More, Peter Giles and Raphael Hythloday. The character Giles' friendship is particularly noteworthy: Giles 'shows so much genuine kindness, loyalty, and affection [towards his friends], that he must be almost unique in his all-round capacity for friendship' – and it is that friendship that allows More to learn about Utopia in the first place.

> 'Do you see that man over there?' he [Giles] asked, indicating the one he had been talking to. 'I was just bringing him along to visit you.'
> 'If he's a friend of yours,' I said, 'I'll be very glad to see him.' (More 2003: 16; Vallée 2004: 44–5, 49–55)

More, as had Castiglione, also continued the humanist tradition by inviting the reader of *Utopia* to become a friend too, to read with *amicitia* – and so enter into and continue the discussion of what made a utopia, the nature of the *optimus status reipublicae* (Vallée 2004: 55–6).

Yet even as early as the middle of the *quattrocento*, Leon Battista Alberti (1401–72) began to bend friendship toward its ancient double of flattery. In 'Dell'amicizia' (1440), the fourth part of his *I Libri della Famiglia* (1434–44), Alberti's Piero, with much reference to the courtier's arts of winning the favour of princes, talked of *amicizia* as political and useful, as a means by which the individual who represented his family to the state gained favours for his family, as something (along with familiarity) that one must set out very deliberately to acquire: (Alberti 1971: 263–6 [Bk. 4]). Virtue was no longer prerequisite for such friendship: Piero deemed a relationship with the plainly wicked Pope John XXIII to be *amicizia* (Alberti 1971: 271–3 [Bk. 4]).

This emphasis on the practical coin of friendship echoed Cicero's ordinary *amicitia*, itself scarcely more than *factio* seen from the inside. Yet Alberti (via his character Adovardo) went on to identify this sort of friendship with *amicizia vera*, for such practicalities were the necessary means to create true friendship:

> [N]o one is born heir to friendship as he may be to property, and unless we acquire our own friends we shall not have as many as is convenient. Since in this world mortals cannot both create and perfect something

at the same time, I should like them to show me how to bring a new friendship to a condition which they consider good, honest, and perfect in every respect . . . who could ever hope to gain any but harmful and bothersome friends, or even mere acquaintances, relying only on his simplicity and virtue when, as you know, men are so different in character and opinions, when desires are so uncertain, customs so perverse, beliefs so ambiguous, mysterious, and varied, when there are so many deceitful, faithless, perfidious, reckless, and rapacious men, and when everything is so unstable? . . . For these things I should want a practical man who would teach me how to gain and use friendship rather than show me how to describe and almost draw it. I should want philosophers, therefore, to teach me how to acquire friendship, strengthen it, undo it, regain it, and preserve it forever. (Alberti 1971: 275–6 [Bk. 4])

In any case, the friendship of old was not possible in the modern court: as Alberti's contemporary and employer Enea Silvio Piccolomini (Pope Pius II, 1405–64, r.1458–64) put it in his *De curialium miseriis* (comp. 1444, ed. 1472), 'If truly you wish to persevere at the court, you must be ready at the command of the king, to go to war, to go through thieves, to go to sea . . . No freedom of words or of action will remain for you' (Piccolomini 1928: 34–5 [12], translated in Langer 1994: 199 (note 25)). Politics, oratory, placed on friendship the deforming stamps of prudence, decorum and protean flexibility: Alberti prescribed the behaviour of Alcibiades (*c.*450–404 BC): 'We shall do what they say Alcibiades knew well, that is, imitate the chameleon' (Alberti 1971: 320 [Bk. 4]; Langer 1994: 202–3, 203 (note 33)). A recently rediscovered letter of (Pseudo-)Quintus Cicero's *Commentariolum Petitionis* provided the keynote to Alberti's redefinition of *vera amicizia*: 'For it is vile when flattery is used to corrupt a man, but less execrable when used to conciliate friendship, and indispensable for a candidate, whose facial expression and conversation must be modified and adapted to the humour and the inclination of all whom he meets' (Cicero 2002: 433); Langer 1994: 205 (note 37). Even if genuine virtue and friendship were the most effective means in the long run to gain reputation, they were more things of the past than of the present. Simulation and deception were now the means to good opinion. In Alberti's conflation of true friendship with mere *amicitia* and the means of flattery, we may see, in effect, an early analogue of Machiavellian thought, whereby amoral means were yoked to produce virtuous ends (Alberti 1971: 274–95 [Bk. 4]; Hyatte 1994: 174–6, 180–3; Langer 1994: 196–207).

This early shift, however, was a harbinger of the future more than a characterisation of its times: it would take another century for

Alberti's problematisation of *vera amicizia*, the steady disalignment of friendship and virtue, to bear fruit. The end of the sixteenth century, however, saw a sudden recrudescence of such Albertian doubts. The late Renaissance perception of the growing power of interest (the realm of power, the realm of oratory) as a mode of thought and as a malign infuence upon the practice of friendship in the public world finally disintegrated the traditional conception of friendship among an influential cross-section of Renaissance humanists. So Cardinal Jacques Davy du Perron (1556–1618) wrote in the dedicatory epistle of his translation of *Laelius de Amicitia* of the 'Perversion of our time, in which friendships are smothered as soon as they are born; in which the shadow of interest, the idol of vain honor divide even those friendships that are based on blood and nature' (Du Perron 1618: 7, cited and translated in Langer 1994: 156, 156 (note 24); Langer 1994: 156–7).

Stefano Guazzo's *Civil Conversation* (1574) provided a notable corollary to this lament. Where Cicero had based friendship upon shared virtue, prescribed ending friendship with the insufficiently virtuous and contrasted the honest speech of friends with the speech of flatterers, Guazzo, by contrast, advised rather patience with the flaws of friends, who were likely to fall short of perfect virtue, although they were capable of being wooed to it. He likewise prescribed a gentle speech suited to their frailty that Cicero would have found smacked all too much of flattery.

> When you perceive your self to prevaile nothing by reasoning with your friende, and that there is doubt of some disorder, you ought rather to bowe then to breake, feeding his humour, if it bee not in such a case as silence may breede greater offence . . . But forsomuch as at this day we can not finde either friendes or parentes, which are in all pointes agreeable to our disposition and nature, wee must frame our selves too beare with the imperfections of others, and according to the saying, we must love a freend with his imperfection. (Guazzo 1967: I, 78–83, 93, 104 [Bk. 1]; 1993: I, 55–8 [1 C68d–1 Ac9d], 64 [1 A83], 72 [1 A110b]; Olmsted 2005: 163–4)[1]

Furthermore, although Guazzo echoed Plutarch on the nature of flatterers, those mutable counterfeits of friends, he was less confident than 'some famous writers' that a flatterer could be distinguished from a friend: 'yet is it in my opinion verie harde (that I may not say impossible) to attaine to that knowledge, as well for that the worlde is full of these tame beastes [flatterers], as also for that it is harde to discerne the evill which resembleth the good' (Guazzo 1967: I, 82–3

[Bk. 1]; 1993: I, 57 [a A69b–c]). In this he suggested a corollary to Alberti's conflation of the true friend with the flatterer: that it was difficult to the point of impossibility to discern a friend from a flatterer. Another man's virtue could not be known certainly, and so any friendship that pretended to a base in virtue could well be a relationship of the flatterer and his gull.

Guazzo's scepticism of the ability to know a friend's character found a radical complement in the work of Michel de Montaigne. Montaigne took interest to motivate the ordinary processes of the world, and therefore concluded in 'Of friendship' that perfect friendship should not be motivated by interest in any sense of the word: 'For in general, all associations that are forged and nourished by pleasure or profit, by public or private needs, are the less beautiful and noble, and the less friendships, in so far as they mix into friendship another cause and object and reward than friendship itself.' Perfect friendship, in consequence, had to be utterly private, disinterested from any social or political end. Indeed, the solipsistic aspects of Montaigne's *Essays* (1570–92) reflected the requirements of disinterest: Montaigne's friendly act of writing could avoid the temptation to decay into persuasive rhetoric only if it was devoted entirely toward no end, no subject, outside himself. Friendship, moreover, could not be motivated – interested, constrained – by either reason or virtue, but had to be an arbitrary choice: 'If you press me to tell why I loved him, I feel that this cannot be expressed, except by answering: Because it was he, because it was I' (Montaigne 2003: 165, 169; Langer 1994: 157–76; 1990: 182–90). Although Montaigne's line of critique did not entirely coincide with Guazzo's, it is noteworthy that only in the arbitary choice proffered by Montaigne, only in such disinterested privacy, could true friendship avoid the danger Guazzo sketched, the polished flatterer's perfect deceptions.

Antoine Hotman's (c.1525–96) *Deux paradoxes de l'amitié et de l'avarice* (c.1598), whose praise of avarice and interest (disclaimed by the prudent author as mere hypothesis) entailed blame of friendship, gave theoretical structure to Montaigne's apothegm. Friendship was exclusive, particular and constrained by passion, a corruption of judgement radically disjunct from the universal, liberating and rational love of God, society and the public good:

> Nothing distracts us from the duty we owe to the public as much as friendship, and there is no better way of containing oneself in a sociable mood, than by chasing from us this passion of friendship, which emprisons and ties us brutally to certain particular affections, and makes us lose all reason, and forget the duty we owe to the public.

The person, too, was radically disjunct from the virtues he possessed: 'he who loves another because of the virtue he knows is in the person does not love the person but the virtue that he likes.' For Hotman, therefore, friendship was a cognitively empty and irrationally unjustifiable affection for a person distinct from any attributes he possessed (Langer 1994: 69–87; Hotman 1616: 114, 128–9, translated in Langer 1994: 74 (note 25), 84 (note 43)).

Montaigne and Hotman did not invent these conceptions *ex nihilo*, but rather shared in a common movement of the time. Across the English Channel, Thomas Churchyard (*c*.1520–1604) presaged these linked conceptions of Montaigne and Hotman in *A Sparke of Frendship and Warme Goodwill* (1588):

> It seemeth and may bee well aduouched, that friendship of it selfe is so secrete a mysterie (shrined in an honest hart) that few can describe it, and tel from whence comes the priuie and inward affection, that sodainly breedes in breast, and is conuayed to the hart, with such a content and gladnesse, that the whole powers of man leapes in the bowelles of the bodie for ioye at that instant. (Churchyard 1588: fol. B4v)

Yet the main nexus of influence in the seventeenth century would be in France, from Montaigne and Hotman. Looking forward, we may see the operation of their framework in Faret's *L'honnête homme* (1630), where in the desire for friendship 'the motion of the heart is the true Iudge, and the soueraigne Arbitrator' (Faret 1632: 143). Madeleine de Scudéry in the ninth volume of her *Clélie* (1661) likewise conceived of friendship as an inner inclination of the heart motivated neither by interest nor by the merit of virtue: 'For finally friendship and gratitude are two different things; so I am persuaded that one must be grateful to all those from whom one receives favors, and friendship only for those who touch our heart, whether by their merit, by their friendship, or by our inclination' (Langer 1994: 176–7; Scudéry 1661: 362, translated in Langer 1994: 177 (note 74)). Hotman's paradoxes and Montaigne's apothegms inspired both Faret and Scudéry, among many others, to the same conclusion: friendship was mere tautology.

This conclusion did not end the concept of friendship, but rather shifted it decisively toward familiarity, toward intimacy. This was not an unprecedented innovation: friendship, as we have seen, had been associated back to ancient times both with particular familiarity and with universalising virtue, despite the tensions between these different values. The late Renaissance shift described above thus deepened an old association of friendship with familiarity. Yet now friendship had cast off its association with universal virtue. Friendship thus came to be defined not so much as the association of two men sharing a common virtue as the familiar association of two selves known to one another in mutual intimacy. 'Because it was he, because it was I' – this was a description of friendship based on familiarity alone, not rationalised by shared virtue.

Familiarity, however, was not enough to sustain friendship. The flatterer, casting his deceptive shadow here too, could simulate an alluring character to woo intimacy just as much as he could simulate virtue. There also had to be some proof that the familiar self presented was in harmony with the familiar self as it actually was. Hence, therefore, *sincerity* rose to the fore, as the means by which to guarantee the truth of familiar speech, 'to connect speech with feeling'. We may put it that the sixteenth century saw the rise of a dual conception: a prudent Albertian self, decorous, public and rational, and a sincere Montaignean self, honest, private and passionate. This dichotomy should not be overstated: Montaigne himself, aware of the attractions of both the prudent and the sincere self, ultimately articulated the idea that one must know – prudently! – when it was appropriate to display the sincere self and when to display the prudent one. He wrote in 'Of Husbanding Your Will' that:

> We must live in the world and make the most of it such as we find it. But the judgment of an emperor should be above his imperial power, and see and consider it as an extraneous accident; and he should know how to find pleasure in himself apart, and to reveal himself like any Jack or Peter, at least to himself. (Montaigne 2003: 941; Martin 1997: 1326–38)

Yet, such ironies acknowledged, the dichotomy was real and ever more influential; friendship had to choose between the Albertian and the Montaignean modes. In the waning of the Renaissance, it shifted decisively toward that of Montaigne.

This shift to an arbitrary, irrational mode of friendship also possessed distinct political implications. The contemporaneous sobriquet of 'sovereign' – 'frenship the moost sovereyn blys' in John Lydgate (*c.*1370–*c.*1451), 'sovereign and masterful friendship' in Montaigne – adhered to such arbitrary friendship, both because it was effective and because it was freely – sovereignly – given. As Charron put it, perfect friendship – sharing all, universal in scope, was '[v]ery free, and built upon the pure choice and libertie of the will, without any other obligation, occasion, or strange cause. There is nothing more free and voluntary than affection.' This free and mutal gift was an innovation upon the old Ciceronian *consensio* of friendship, with *consensio* now rendered as consent, signifying both an agreement of the hearts and friends' mutual consent to one another's authority. In the latter sense, friendship acquired significant charge against monarchical authority, for the sovereign freedom to choose one's friends could not be appropriated by the monarch. Indeed, the ability to have friends was an attribute of sovereign equals in which the monarch could not share. A king might seek friends, but his power tended to deform friendship and instead create, deliberately or unavoidably, flatterers, parasites and favourites (Lydgate 1897: 6 [16.109]; Montaigne 2003: 171; Charron n.d. [after 1612]: 460 [III.7]; Langer 1990: 182–90; Shannon 2002: 6–8, 30–46, 125–55). The mutual consent of friendship could flourish precisely because it confined itself to the private sphere and defined itself unpolitically. Yet it provided an implicit challenge to monarchical sovereignty, for friendship was formed by the free consent of sovereign individuals.

At the same time, such sovereign friendship provided a challenge to the emerging conception of sovereign reason, to whose authority people were increasingly being called to bind themselves – without arguing the point at length, I will allude on the one hand to Thomas Hobbes (1588–1679) and on the other hand to the discourse of the Republic of Letters. Friendship in this arbitrary mode was voluntary as compelling reason was not. The familiar relationship of private friends, whose intimate knowledge of one another formed the basis for their mutual consent, was an inverse both of the political realm of oratory and of the emerging realm of pure reason – for both, no matter their mutual quarrels, relied upon compulsion. The voluntary nature of friendship – and friendship now in a mode of privacy, familiarity and intimacy – would in time underpin an alternate mode by which to challenge both these compulsive forms of communication and politics.

An immediate consequence of this shift toward intimate friendship was an intensification of interest in the familiar style. Erasmus and Montaigne, for notable and influential examples, continued their humanist predecessors' understanding of reading as an exercise in intimate understanding; in so doing they further emphasised the importance of style as the *sine qua non* by which to convey, in familiar communication, the intimate expression of the individual self. Erasmus wrote in *Ciceronianus* (1528) that 'The very thing which the reader enjoys is getting to know the writer's feelings, character, disposition, and type of mind from the way he writes, just as he would by living on familiar terms with him for several years.' So also Montaigne in 'Of vanity':

> Besides this profit that I derive from writing about myself, I hope for this other advantage, that if my humors happen to please and suit some worthy man before I die, he will try to meet me. I give him a big advantage in ground covered; for all that long acquaintance and familarity could have gained for him in several years, he can see in three days in this record, and more surely and exactly.

Montaigne's example would be particularly influential, because he transferred the dialogue's genre characteristics of familiarity and friendship – the genre characteristics of conversation – to the essay, and therefore to all its descendants among the prose genres (Erasmus 1986: 440; 1992: 24; Montaigne 2003: 911; Eden 2012: 87–9, 101–12). More precisely, we should say that Montaigne gave to the essay and its genre inheritors a variation of the dialogue's genre characteristics transformed so as to communicate properly his new conception of intimate, private friendship, which radically had recast the the ancient ties of familiarity and friendship. Montaigne thus acted as an inflexion point in the history of European conversation and literature. He wrote his new conception of friendship in conversational style, all later expressions of Montaignean friendship likewise would inherit the style of *sermo*, and the extraordinary permeation throughout Europe of Montaigne's conception of intimate friendship increasingly made *sermo* the default mode of communication.

Friendship with women

The ancients, we may recollect, had excluded women both from friendship and from conversation, not least because women were considered incapable of masculine levels of either reason or virtue – incapable of the equality with men that was also a prerequisite to be included in conversation with them. The Renaissance witnessed an increased estimation of female capacity to reason by male humanists – from whose point of view this narrative unavoidably proceeds – which by itself made it possible to conceive of women as partaking in some fashion in friendship and (as a corollary of friendship) conversation. The shift from the friendship of reason and virtue to the friendship of familiarity and intimacy reinforced the shift to include women in friendship and conversation, since women were deemed insufficient in the former qualities, while the latter were considered entirely reconcilable with femininity. The changed conception of friendship played a crucial role in the inclusion of women both in friendship and in conversation's friendly speech.

The near-exclusion of women from friendship began to crack far before the Renaissance – but only slightly. As far back as the eighth century, male and female religious sometimes referred to one another as friends; this friendship presumably was inflected by Christian notions of *amicitia* (Classen and Sandidge 2010: 81–2 [Classen]). More broadly, the Christian notion of *amicitia* as extending between unequals presumably made it easier for men and women to conceive of one another as friends, in Christ. Switching to a different cultural milieu, medieval courtly romances often described men and women as friends, in *amicitia* – but, as this was usually a prelude to a passionate relationship, this was not precisely classical friendship. In medieval and early modern Europe, men legally or financially responsible for unrelated women sometimes were called their *friends*; and women could on occasion use the word *friend* as a claim to patronage and support (Classen and Sandidge 2010: 92–105 [Sandidge]). But women were not conceived of as true friends with men, and this evidence is generally of scattered exceptions to a rule that did not speak of women as friends at all.

For this last point, it is also worth emphasising that there is little evidence either of language referring to women as friends with other women. This is not to say that close emotional attachments between women did not exist or that women lacked the relationship that we would now call friendship. The point, rather, is that the explicit textual evidence that such relationships were conceived of as friendship is relatively scanty, not least because the literary tradition found it so difficult to conceive of friendship between women. Friendly relationships – and the evidence is often thickest among religious women, who combined literacy with non-familial communities – were often expressed in familial terms, as the relationship of a mother to a daughter or a sister to a sister. So Abbess Hildegard of Bingen (1098–1179) wrote in the middle of the twelfth century of 'my daughter Richardis [of Stade], whom I call both daughter and mother, because I cherished her with divine love, as indeed the Living Light had instructed me to do in a very vivid vision' (Hildegard 1994: 51 [13r]; Classen and Sandidge 2010: 83 [Classen]). At other times the relationship was articulated as that of a counsellor or a confidante. It was not until late medieval times that a close relation between unrelated women was articulated in terms of friendship with any frequency. In Christine de Pizan's (1364–*c*.1430) *Le Livre du duc des vrais amans* (1403–5), the Lady repeatedly called the Dame de la Tour her *friend*; this invocation of female friendship appears to have been something of an innovation (De Pisan 1908: 100–2; Classen and Sandidge 2010: 81–91 [Classen]).

As women could not be conceived of as friends, so they could not be conceived of as taking part in conversation – where conversation was defined as a species of rational discourse. This is not to say that women were thought incapable of speech – the trope of excessive, unruly speech in women is very old – but that neither they nor their speech was considered reasonable. The tie of insufficient female friendship to insufficient female conversation is especially evident in English, where the traditional name for female friends was *gossips* – the irrational inverse of conversation the metonym for the irrational inverse of female friendship. The 'appearance' of female friendship was more precisely the transposition of female friendship from the realm of gossip to the realm of conversation, from the realm of irrationality and vice to that of reason and virtue (Parsons 2009: 92–118).

So women, still generally conceived of in the overwhelmingly male intellectual culture at the dawn of the Renaissance as inferior, irrational and incapable of true friendship or conversation, were effectively silent and excluded at the beginning of the humanist tradition. Yet as early as the late fourteenth century, an Italian woman essayed a linked experiment in letter-writing and friendship (expressed in terms of familiarity). James and Kent narrate that:

> As it happens, we do know something of the epistolary education of Margherita Datini [(1360–1423)], the wife of Iris Origo's 'Merchant of Prato,' Francesco Datini [(c.1335–1410)], in the late fourteenth century. As an act of friendship extended to his friend's wife, the notary Lapo Mazzei taught Margherita, then in her mid 30s, to read and tutored her in the art of composing a letter. To demonstrate her new mastery of the letter of recommendation – an essential vehicle for winning and keeping friends in Renaissance Europe – Margherita wrote to her teacher using the conventional masculine forms, which, however, she adapted to the purposes of her own gender. This was a very daring thing to do in a society where the rules of decorum made it almost impossible for a woman to write a friendly letter to someone other than her husband or a relative, even if the manuals had supplied the vocabulary with which to do so. 'This familiarity is pleasing to me,' Margherita assured her friend, '(and) you should treat me as if I were your younger sister since

I love you as an elder brother. I don't believe there exists a person to whom I am more attached and, I can tell you, you are never out of my thoughts.' (James and Kent 2009: 124)[2]

That Datini wrote friendly letters at all, and that their existence was conspicuously rare and noteworthy, tells us something of both the possibilities and limitations for women's communications late in the *trecento*. So too does the fact that Datini was not a prodigy of learning, as Laura Cereta (1469–99) would be a century later, but rather an ordinary woman who learned a skill then extraordinary for her sex. Datini's example was not (apparently) typical or influential, but it does still tell us something of the world in which the irruption of women into the humanist world would emerge.

This irruption of women appeared first within the dialogue genre by way of a consideration of the relation between husband and wife. The textual discussion of domestic and familial subject matter was not entirely innovative: works such as Xenophon's dialogue *Oeconomicus* and Plutarch's essay *Precepts of Marriage* had provided literary precedents. These ancient models had stretched to include consideration of the education of women, and even to allow for the participation of female characters in discussions about the management of the household, as that was taken to be women's proper sphere of action (Plutarch 1999; Xenophon 1994: 105–211, esp. 119–21, 139–63; Smarr 2005: 3–4). On the other hand, although in the ancient world the relation between husband and wife had been taken to be one kind of *philia*, that relationship generally had not been taken to be *vera amicitia*. It was indicative of the disjunction between the two categories that the Epicureans had argued that the wise man should not marry or have children: 'The Epicureans do not suffer the wise man to fall in love . . . Nor, again, will the wise man marry and rear a family: so Epicurus says in the *Problems* and in the *De natura*' (Diogenes Laertius 1958: II, 645 [10.118–19]; Hutter 1978: 109, 117). Now, however, the *quattrocento* humanists would begin to combine these two strands of the ancient inheritance and apply the conception of friendship and dialogue to the *domus*, to the *familia* and to women.

The amalgamation of women to the status of friends in dialogue was hesitant to begin with: in the early *quattrocento* dialogues, women did not actually participate. This silence partly imitated the general absence of female participants in classic dialogues, and partly registered the presumption that *quattrocento* women lacked the rhetorical education necessary to take part in the conversations simulated by these dialogues. Yet women became the subjects of dialogues: the topic of Francesco Barbaro's (1390–1454) *De re uxoria* (1416) was the proper training of wives by their husbands. Moreover, Barbaro's dialogue briefly addressed itself directly to a female reader – which, in a generation that identified readers with friends, implicitly gave to those silent female readers an attribute of a friend. In Barbaro's influential work, wives were supposed to possess distinctly feminine virtues – silence, humility and modesty and housewifely diligence and frugality. On the other hand, they were also supposed to possess self-control (i.e. temperance) over all of their bodily motions and prudence, that quintessentially rhetorical virtue. Their modesty (Knox 2000) was to be displayed in public, in support of the family's reputation, and women were to practise their virtuous habits by means of the introspections of silent, internal dialogue. The wife's modesty was meant to sustain the relationship of charity – akin to *amicitia* – between husband and wife. Throughout, Barbaro ascribed to women characteristics of friendship and dialogue:

> Now we come to conjugal love, whose extraordinary force and unmatched dignity (as we learn from illustrious authors) seem to constitute a model of perfect friendship . . . So I would wish wives, in sum, to live with their husbands as though their souls were somehow intermingled – so that, as Pythogoras describes friendship, the two become one. (Barbaro 2015: 99–100 [2.2]; Frick 2004: 196–203)

In the next generation, wives began to be described with even greater emphasis as not only friends but also true friends. In the 'De re uxoria' dialogue of Leon Battista Alberti's *I libri della famiglia* (1434–44), concerned as was Barbaro's *De re uxoria* with the proper training of wives, Alberti's eponymous character adapted the description of true friendship – the union of utility, pleasure and virtue – to describe marriage, despite the inequalities of the marriage relation, as well as to praise the intimacy between husband and wife.

> Conjugal love may be judged to be very great, for if love arises from pleasure, marriage offers many pleasures and delights. If love becomes stronger through companionship, then there is no one with whom we are more familiar than with our wives. If it becomes a strong bond through confiding our wishes and desires, then there is no one in whom it is possible to confide with greater ease than our wives who are our constant companions. If friendship goes hand in hand with honesty,

then no relationship can be more sacred than that of marriage. You may add that strong bonds of pleasure and utility are formed to strengthen and preserve our love. Children are born, and it would take too long to describe how they form a common and firm bond to give two souls identity of thought and desires, that is, the union which is called perfect friendship. (Alberti 1971: 104–5 [Bk. 2])

The character Leon Battista was a bachelor lacking authority on the subject, so (as was characteristic of humanist dialogue) this cannot be taken definitely as the author Alberti's opinion. In the 'Dell'amicizia' dialogue of *I libri della famiglia* (1441–4), *per exemplum*, the Albertis' buffoonish client Buto argued that a husband could not be true friends with his wife: 'Perhaps those learned men of yours who wrote those beautiful things about friendship did not care to have women as friends, or perhaps they thought everyone knew you cannot have true friendship with a woman.' The Alberti elders implicitly agreed with him by neither disagreeing with him nor providing contrary examples (Alberti 1971: 257–8 [Bk. 4]; Hyatte 1994: 172, 179; 1999: 257–8). Nevertheless, tentatively, Alberti was expanding the conception of *vera amicitia* to include women. This expansion both raised women's status to something closer to equality with the men with whom they could be friends and stretched true friendship to include the unequal relationship of husband and wife, of man and woman.

Furthermore, Barbaro's *De re uxoria* and Alberti's *Libri della famiglia* pioneered the Renaissance association of dialogue with *ragionamento domestico*, a discussion of the household and its economy, and of the proper domesticating treatment of wives. This association applied ancient learning and philosophy not only to the present day but also to a realm of life distinct from that of either philosophy or politics (Marsh 1980: 79–81). Indeed, the informal subject matter of domestic affairs, in contrast with philosophy, which requires rigorous logic, allowed for the free, even improvisational organisation and development of the dialogue (Alberti 1845: 58 [II], translated in Marsh 1980: 90; Marsh 1980: 90–1). To make women the subject of dialogue, therefore, stretched the subject matter of conversation beyond the traditional political subjects of oratory, to the new realm of economy, of society, that mediated between the traditional subject matters of the public and the private realms. Habermas identified Thomas More's *Utopia* as the origin of discussion of this subject matter (Habermas 1973: 50–9), but it is Barbaro and Alberti, and the discussion of women, that is (should no predecessors be found) the *fons et origo*.

Women now also began to appear as actual participants in the humanist world. Literary *exempla* provided models for living practice: the tradition of exemplary learned women, subject to imitation, slowly created conceptual space for the actual practice of female learning and eloquence: Laura Cereta's 'Defense of the Liberal Instruction of Women', written in 1488 to the possibly pseudonymus Bibulus Sempronius, cites a formidable list of learned women from fabulous antiquity to the present day (King and Rabil 1983: 82–3). Such precedents buttressed Italian humanist women in the *quattrocento* such as Cereta, Cassandra Fedele (1465–1558) and Isota Nogarola (1418–66) as they began to circulate and publish letters – in which, as had Datini, they rehearsed as formal exercises female *amicitia* outside of marriage. Some such letters were to other women: so Cereta wrote to Santa Pelegrina of the friendship she desired between them as essentially a form of *vera amicitia*: 'I am so concerned about you that nothing is more precious to me than my being loved in return by you, who are the most beloved of friends' (Cereta 1997: 137–8). Yet the letter was perhaps more important as a means to allow women to converse with men outside their family. Since the conventions of modesty inhibited participation in actual dialogues with men, these letters, conversations in writing, conducted in domestic isolation from one's interlocutors, provided a reputable substitute – a commerce of thought without insinuating implication (Gill 2009, esp. 1119, 1121–3; Robin 2000; Smarr 2005: 117, 130–1, 138, 152–3). By 1500, these pioneers had begun to make female friendship, consciously so denominated, a reality outside of marriage as well.

The *quattrocento* adaptation that allowed marriage to be conceived of as an example of perfect friendship continued into the sixteenth century. In his *De institutione feminae christianae* (1524; trans. *Education of a Christian Woman* 1531), Juan Luis Vives (1493–1540) also described marriage as a form of friendship: 'If husband and wife love each other mutually, they will want and not want the same things, which in the last analysis is staunch friendship' (Vives 2000: 212 [2.51], 284 [2.149]). Meanwhile, both Nicolas Denisot's [?] (1515–59) novel *L'amant resuscité de la mort d'amour* (1555) and Montaigne's 'Of friendship' articulated a conception of friendship that united men and women – if, in Montaigne's case, as we shall see below, a hypothetical one (Montaigne 2003: 167; Furey 2013: 30; Hyatte 1999: 258–9). In England the *Homilie of Marriage* defined marriage first (1563) as a 'perpetuall friendly felowshyp' and, in later revision (1623), as 'a perpetual friendship'. Furey notes that '[t]he standard marriage sermon in Elizabethan England enjoined husbands and wives to live together lawfully in "perpetuall friendship"' (Furey 2013: 29; Luxon 2005: 35). Even Moderata Fonte (pseudonym of Modesta Pozzo, 1555–92) in *The Worth of Women* (1592; posthumously published 1600), somewhat dubious (as we shall see below) in general about the male sex and its capacity for friendship, identified friendship with marriage: 'For it is friendship that keeps the world alive: friendship seals the marriages that preserve the individual in the species' (Fonte 1997: 128).

Erasmus innovated more strikingly in his conception of marital friendship. In his matrimonial writings in general, and particularly in his *Praise of Marriage* (1518), Erasmus further deepened the notion of marriage as a form of *amicitia*:

> For what is sweeter than living with a woman with whom you are most intimately joined not merely by the bonds of affection but by physical union as well? If we derive much spiritual delight from the kindness of other close relatives and acquaintants, how much more pleasant to have someone with whom to share the secret feelings of the heart, with whom you may talk as if with yourself, to whose loyalty you can safely entrust yourself, who regards your fortune as her own! What happiness there is in the union of husband and wife, than which none greater nor more lasting exists in all of nature! For while we are linked with our other friends by benvolence of mind, with a wife we are joined by the greatest affection, physical union, the bond of the sacrament, and the common sharing of all fortunes. (Erasmus 1996, esp. 69, 72; Furey 2013: 30)

Erasmus also gave the *amicitia* of marriage a theological underpinning by conceiving of the sacrament of marriage as a sign of that bond (Leushuis 2004). Moreover, the spiritual and physical intimacy of marriage began to affect Erasmus' general conception of friendship; for a notable example, the friendship of writer and reader (Leuishuis argues) became more intimate for Erasmus in imitation of the friendship of marriage (Leushuis 2004: 1291). Finally, in a pregnant association of the realm of marriage with the realm of politics, Erasmus stated in the *Institution of Christian Matrimony* (1526) that 'marriage is rather like a kingdom, but must be far from any semblance of tyranny. Nothing is accomplished here by force; all is done by persuasion and good will' (Erasmus 1974: 343; Leushuis 2004: 1302–3). The friendship of men and women, in other words, was no longer merely modelling itself on the friendship of men. By the time of Erasmus, the friendship of men and women was itself becoming a model for thought in other realms – to reshape them around a model of humanity in which women emphatically were both present and (more nearly) equal.

Sixteenth-century dialogues registered yet further female advancement. Women were no longer merely the silent subjects of dialogues on wives: now they participated as characters in dialogues, were the subjects of dialogue (and not just in their character as wives) and, perhaps most daringly of all, themselves wrote and published dialogues. This was particularly noticeable in Italy; the cultural lag between Italy and the outlying regions of Europe meant, for a notable example, that the Portuguese and Polish versions of the *Courtier* deleted the female characters, since in those countries they were not yet seen as plausible participants in conversation. In Italy, however, female characters frequently did participate in dialogues, pioneeringly in Pietro Bembo's *Gli Asolani* (1505) and Castiglione's *Courtier* (on which more below), and later also in works such as Giuseppe Betussi's (*c*.1512–73) *Raverta* (1544) and *Leonora* (1557), Sperone Speroni's (1500–88) *On Love* (1542) and the fourth book of Guazzo's *Civil Conversation* (1574). Some Italian dialogues were entirely populated by women: Pietro Aretino's (1492–1556) *Ragionamenti* (1534), his dialogue among courtesans, and also Alessandro Piccolimini's (1508–79) *Rafaella* (1539), Lodovico Dolce's (1508–68) *Education of Women* (1545) and Bartolomeo Gottifredi's (*c*.1500–*c*.1570) *Mirror of Love* (1547). Women were also the subjects of dialogue – especially those dialogues with female characters. This subject matter, if not simply that of wifehood, did remain generally confined to more-or-less sex-typed topics, such as love, marital love, beauty, the status of women, women's education, spiritual counsel and the role of women in the family. Finally, women themselves began to write and publish dialogues: Tullia d'Aragona's (*c*.1510–56, herself a character in Speroni's *On Love*) *On the Infinity of Love* (1547) and, posthumously and pseudonyously, Modesta Pozzo (a.k.a. Moderata Fonte) *The Worth of Women* in 1600 (Burke 1989: 9–10; V. Cox 2000: 393; Smarr 2005: 16, 102, 106).

The sixteenth century also saw a remarkable intensification and broadening of the *quattrocento*'s innovatory literary evocations of female friendship and female conversation. Women continued to write letters, frequently for publication – not only gentlewomen in France and Italy such as Helisenne de Crenne (1510–52), Madeleine and Catherine des Roches (*c*.1520–87; 1542–87), Olympia Morata (1526–55) and Chiara Matraini (1515–1604), but also courtesans such as Camilla Pisana (*fl*.1515), Alexandra Fiorentina, Tullia D'Aragona and Veronica Franco (1546–91) (Bassanese 1996; Smarr 2005: 131). In England, sixteenth-century women practised the rhetoric of friendship by means of writing letters of recommendation; the *amicitia* of useful alliance preparing the way for *amicitia* more *vera* (Daybell 2007). The Elizabethan poetess Isabella Whitney (*fl.*1566–73) incorporated the rhetoric of friendship into her poetry with sophisticated flexibility, invoking it both as useful alliance and as counsel (A. Johnson 2011). More broadly, rising female literacy increased the potential audience for these literary evocations and articulations of female friendship and conversation. As a register of this increasing female literacy and of its effects, we may note that in sixteenth-century England an increasing number of books were written for female readers, with an especially sharp rise upward in the number of such books from the 1570s (Hull 1982: 1–30, esp. 1). In Italy, meanwhile, the 1570s and 1580s also saw a significant uptick in female participation in various literary environs, although female publication remained rare (Rosenthal 1992: 87). Female presence in all these cultural realms was still unusual but no longer the rarity it had been in the *quattrocento*.

We should note particularly here the appearance of women in actual sixteenth-century Italian mixed-sex social circles. We will explore this appearance further in the next chapter, in the narrative of the Italian Renaissance court, but I will mention here the development of the applicability of courtly ideals to female gentle behaviour – not merely *modestia*, which emphasised rather the withdrawal of women from male company, but that bolder *courtesy* that tempered modesty sufficiently so as to sustain a mixed-sex environment (Knox 2000: 8–9). Women began to interact with men – and against the normalising background of mixed-sex courtesy, women and men began to engage regularly in the actual practice of rational conversation. Women who conversed so included not only exceptional figures such as the courtesans Tullia d'Aragona and Veronica Franco, whose positions were inescapably precarious, but also more normal elite women, whose intellectual daring remained socially impeccable. Campbell lists among those Italian women who appeared in *cinquecento* proto-*salons*, besides d'Aragona and Franco, the noblewomen Vittoria Colonna (1492–1547), Veronica Gambara (1485–1550) and Laura Battiferri Ammannati (1523–89) as well as the *virtuosa* Gaspara Stampa (1523–54) (Campbell 2006: 27; Robin 2007: 172, 174, 184). To all this, we may add Robin's note that a significant number of Italian dialogues with female characters – those of Bernardino Ochino (1487–1564), Tullia d'Aragona and Juan de Valdes (*c.*1500–41) (possibly in part by his putative translator, Giulia Gonzaga (1513–66)] – reflected the actual conversational milieu of the Italian proto-*salons* (Robin 2007: 163–4, 176). Campbell likewise notes that Tullia d'Aragona and Sperone Speroni both presented the character Tullia in their dialogues within a proto-*salon* setting (Campbell 2006: 21–49). Robin also notes that the sixteenth-century Italian poetry anthology – the *réseau*, the web of linked poems – acted as the poetic simulation of a *salon*: 'The *réseau* form imitates the salon, whether real or imaginary, in its interactivity, face-to-face style, variety of actors and themes, and mix of personalities' (Robin 2007: 62–71, esp. 62–3). The proto-*salon* was the setting for the literary evocation of female social inter-action as much as for its actuality.

Siena appears to have been unusually open to the social mixture of men and women. Scipione Bargagli (1540–1612), recollecting the founding of the Sienese literary academy the Intronati in 1525, recollected that 'in the happy days of their youth they used to mix more often and with greater freedom with the beautiful and virtu-ous women of Siena than happens in these present wretched and corrupt times' (S. Bargagli 1594: 220–1, translated in Fahy 2000: 440). Girolamo Bargagli (1537–86) in his *Dialogo de Giuochi* (1572) further noted that at the mid-century extramarital friend-ship was possible between men and women of the Sienese elite; the men 'as a rule were accustomed to visit one or another woman with the liberty with which one visits a sister today. So that leaving the university, or the Academy exhausted, they went as to a peaceful harbor to converse with some woman or other' (G. Bargagli 1572: 21, translated in Robin 2007: 127–8). Bargagli further described a give-and-take of male and female conversation at the mid-century Sienese *veglie* (*salons, avant la lettre*) remarkably egalitarian among the sexes, if still weighted toward male discourse (G. Bargagli 1572: 184–5, translated in Robin 2007: 129–30; Robin 2007: 129). The effect, to contemporaries, was remarkable for the scope it offered women; thus the Venetian travel writer Celio Malespini (1531–1609) in his *Ducento novelle* (1609):

> The *veglie* the Sienese attended in this ancient city, especially those where men and women of rank met for the purpose of conversation, were universally valued for the pleasure of the talk they afforded. Those who came to these gatherings plunged into the consideration of difficult propositions whether it was prudent or not, and often one was left red-faced ... since in these beautiful games they heard and offered mar-velous propositions and questions and clever traps and inventions as erudite as they were subtle, since it was in the women's power as well as the men's to propose that which pleased them most ... But it was necessary to press on with the finest understanding, since all those ladies were extraordinary and divine; and they were similarly endowed in their

inventiveness, which caused every man of great intellect to marvel and to be awestruck. (Malespini 1609: fols. 86ᵛ, 88ʳ, translated in Robin 2007: 130; Robin 2007: 129–30)

If Italy was the model of female conversational practice for Europe, Siena was the model for Italy.

The parallel literary emergence of women from silence in the sixteenth century was encapsulated in Castiglione's *Courtier* and Erasmus' *Colloquies* (1518–33). In the *Courtier*, the presence of women, of speaking women, was itself a fact of some significance. What was conceivable in Italy was not elsewhere; as noted above, the Portuguese and Polish translations of the *Courtier* deleted them from the book. Castiglione made this argument of female capacity explicit: the court lady's speech was also supposed to be conversational, and such speech made her 'perhaps worthy to stand comparison with our courtier as regards qualities both of mind and body' (Castiglione 1976: 213–14 [Bk. 3]). Put another way, Castiglione's court lady now could aspire to excellence as a rule and not as an exception: as Battisti puts it, 'il prototipo di Donna perfetta riscatta la figura femminile dai supposti difetti connaturati e assorbe dalle eroine celebri alcune delle virtù attribuite ora no all'eccezione ma alla natura stessa della donna' (Battisti 1980: 245). Now, as against this near equality, the role of the man was to educate and the role of the woman to be educated: 'the lover should . . . be at pains to keep her from going astray and by his wise precepts and admonishments always seek to make her modest, temperate and truly chaste; and he must ensure that her thoughts are always pure and unsullied by any trace of evil' (Castiglione 1976: 266 [Bk. 3], 335 [Bk. 4]). But women could be educated, cultivated, to virtue: 'And thus, by sowing virtue in the garden of her lovely soul, he will gather the fruits of faultless behavior and experience exquisite pleasure from their taste. And this will be the true engendering and expression of beauty in beauty, which some say is the purpose of love' (Castiglione 1976: 335 [Bk. 4]). Here, as in *quattrocento* antecedents and *cinquecento* contemporaries, women's conversational role, and ability to attain to reason and virtue, was definitely present, if still conceived of as distinctly limited.

But Castiglione also placed women directly into his political imagery, and thus implicated women in the political world. In so doing, his imagery was not entirely consistent. On the one hand, women were the image of powerlessness. Therefore, as Javitch notes, Castiglione associated oratory, the speech of power, with men and highlighted women's role in the powerless realms of the court and conversation (Javitch 1978: 27–8). It was with this association in mind that one should consider Castiglione's worries about making the prince a powerless conversationalist; to do so was to risk emasculating him. On the other hand, women were the image of ignorance. To some extent this reinforced their association with conversation: Castiglione esteemed conversation in good measure because he took it to be the necessary means to appeal to an audience of women, whose gendered intellectual incapacity rendered them hostile to reason (Javitch 1978: 30). At the same time, their ignorance identified them with that other icon of ignorance and hostility to reason – the prince. The passages on the cultivation and education of women above, after all, were metaphors for the education of the prince – and that metaphor inescapably associated women with the world of power. Yet if thematic female ignorance was the bridge associating women with power, the association with power lingered even when the mention of ignorance was dropped. So the visible representatives of princely authority in the *Courtier* were the Duchess and Emilia Pia and Castiglione explicitly associated their authority with Urbino's status as an exemplary court (Castiglione 1976: 42–3 [Bk. 1]). Castiglione, moreover, articulated a significant portion of his (occasionally subversive) meditations on political action through his laudatory tales of women (Castiglione 1976: 229–53 [Bk. 3]; Trafton 1983; and see also Freccero 1992). The imagery of women, therefore, linked conversation, powerlessness, the court, the ignorant multitude, the educable prince, and power and political action: the realm of conversation's claim to capacity and power received its incarnation in the image of the woman.

Finally, one should note that the relationship between men and women was thematic in Castiglione. The relation of lover and beloved, educator and educated, reason and passion, were all a relation of man and woman. In all these, the woman had the passive role – but beloved woman also took on the role of passionate inspiration. Castiglione noted of beloved women that 'in our understanding of great issues far from distracting us they awaken our minds, and in warfare they make men fearless and bold beyond measure'; love generally, by analogy, both sharpened knowledge and tied it to action (Castiglione 1976: 255 [Bk. 3]). Friendship had inspired the search for truth; friendship had increased its bounds to include both men and women – but in this shift from friendship toward love, the affectionate association of men and women ceased to be one of women approximating a male status and became one of women and men distinctly, dissimilarly and thematically themselves. The search for truth, for a better world, became now in Castiglione (and thus for the tradition he would inspire) one composed of men and women, and motivated in no small measure by the love of men for women and of women for men.

In Erasmus' *Colloquies*, meanwhile, written over several decades in the early sixteenth century, women became a stronger presence from edition to edition. In *The Godly Feast* (*Convivium religiosum*, 1522), the exclusion of women from the feast – the philosophy, the dialogue – was thematic. The characters stated that they excluded the host's wife from the feast, since 'What would she be now but a mute? As a woman, she prefers to gossip with women, and we philosophize more freely [in her absence]' (Erasmus 1965: 60). On the other hand, the host stated that his wife kept him company while he conversed with himself in the garden, or when a friend accompanied him (Erasmus 1965: 77). But women began to appear in the colloquies written in 1523 and thereafter. Erasmus now included female-stereotyped subjects such as *Courtship* (*Proci et puellae*, 1523), nunnery (*The Girl with No Interest in Marriage*, *Virgo μισόγαμος*, 1523) and *Marriage* (*Coniugium*, 1523) (Erasmus 1965: 86–98, 99–111, 114–27). Female characters also begin to appear: not only the repentant harlot Lucretia in *The Young Man and the Harlot* (*Adolescentis et scorti*, 1523) but also Margaret the pert maid in *The Poetic Feast* (*Convivium poeticum*, 1523), the Innkeeper's Wife (briefly but feistily) in *The Well-to-do Beggars* (Πτωχοπλούσιοι, 1524), the Learned Lady in *The Abbot and the Learned Lady* (*Abbatis et eruditae*, 1524), the new mother Fabulla in *The New Mother* (*Puerpera*, 1526) and so on, in numbers sufficient to provide a sense of variety and individuality within the sex (Erasmus 1965: 153–8, 158–76, 203–17, 217–23, 267–85). Erasmus now also began to provide judgements such as that a woman could improve herself in conversation with another lady: in *The Girl with No Interest in Marriage* he stated that 'if you see some lady or unmarried woman of outstanding moral excellence, you can improve yourself by her conversation' (Erasmus 1965: 110). He also argued in *The Abbot and the Learned Lady* that women should read (Erasmus 1965: 217–23), while in *The Lower House, or The Council of Women* (*Senatulus, sive Γυναικοσυνέδριον*, 1529), Erasmus even hypothesised (albeit with somewhat patronising satire) a debate among women, translating women into the realm of oratory (Erasmus 1965: 441–7). His evocation of a proper love was deeply respectful of women: in *Courtship*, Pamphilus said to Maria that, 'You don't appear to me as you do because I love you; I love you because I've observed what you're like.' And later he spoke with love of 'Your mind, whose beauty will forever increase with age' (Erasmus 1965: 94–5). As much as Castiglione's *Courtier*, Erasmus' *Colloquies* registered a sea change in the status of women upon the page.

This sixteenth-century literary progression should not be over-stated: Renaissance arguments for and articulations of female equality produced only limited changes to traditional patriarchal modes of thought (Jordan 1990). Women did now speak in dia-logues – but frequently as near-silent auditors, the self-abnegating but stimulating helpmeets to the conversation of their male inter-locutors, whose participation depended on the willingness of men to engage them in conversation. So in the *Courtier* the ideal of female participation in conversation echoed faintly in the actual dialogue Castiglione rendered: as Zancan puts it, 'La donna, come interlocutore attivo, nel testo non esiste: non «forma» con parole, e le parole del testo non sono a lei direttamente destinate.' Moreover, any shift in mode from conversation to the jousting of dispute, in dialogues and doubtless in real life as well, tended to exclude women from a presumptively male form of discourse (V. Cox 2000; Finucci 1992: 29–45; Smarr 2005: 7, 11–12, 14; Zancan 1983: 53). Meanwhile, dialogues such as Sperone Speroni's 'Della dignità delle donne' (early 1530s) argued the case against women rather more vigorously than the case for them (Smarr 2005: 17). These serious reservations noted, the progress of women in the dialogue tradition was clearly perceptible.

A point is worth dwelling on here: the status of women – their capacity for reason and virtue – had become an explicit topic of dis-cussion. This topic effectively dates back to Christine de Pizan, early in the fifteenth century, but during the sixteenth century the contro-versy over the status of women, the *querelle des femmes*, became increasingly prominent throughout western Europe (Hull 1982: 106–26; MacLean 1977: 25–63; L. Warner 2011: 93–119; Wood-bridge 1984: 13–136).[3] Within that controversy, one may note early and forthright defences of women's mental capacities, such as Pietro Bembo's in *Gli Asolani* (1505) (Bembo, *Gli Asolani*: 3.1.458–9, cited and translated in Smarr 2005: 13). In Leone Ebreo's (*c*.1465–*c*.1523) *Dialoghi d'amore* (1535), the reason of the intellectual Sophia, partly an allegory of wisdom and partly a real person, might even be supe-rior to her lover's (Ebreo 2009; Smarr 2005: 16). Perhaps most to the point, the argument was made with increasing fervour that women might partake in the friendship of the mind that was the basis of conversation. So the eponymous Tullia in Tullia d'Aragona's *On the Infinity of Love* (1547):

> I should still like to know why a woman cannot be loved with this same type of love. For I am certain that you don't wish to imply that women lack the intellectual soul that men have and that consequently they do not belong to the same species as males, as I have heard a number of men say.

Tullia's interlocutor, Varchi, responded in the affirmative: 'The difference between men and women is not one of essence. And I myself maintain that not only is it possible to love women with an honest and virtuous love, but that one ought to' (D'Aragona 1997: 97; Smarr 2005: 116). Late in the sixteenth century, Montaigne in 'Of friendship' still doubted women's capacity for friendship: 'The ordinary capacity of women is inadequate for that communion and fellowship which is the nurse of this sacred bond; nor does their soul seem firm enough to endure the strain of so tight and durable a knot' (Montaigne 2003: 167; Broad 2009: 75). Yet Montaigne followed up this passage with the fascinating hypothetical:

> And indeed, but for that, if such a relationship, free and voluntary, could be built up, in which not only would the souls have this complete enjoyment, but the bodies would also share in the alliance, so that the entire man would be engaged, it is certain that the resulting friendship would be fuller and more complete. (Montaigne 2003: 167)

The influential Montaigne, harbinger of the new age, now took friendship of men and women as superior in stipulating theory, even though he doubted that it could be achieved in fact.

To sum up the changed conception *c.*1600 of the capacity of women for friendship, we should pair Montaigne's Janus-faced doubt and vision with the radical reconception of Moderata Fonte's *The Worth of Women* (1592; posthumously published *c.*1600). Fonte claimed not merely that women were capable of friendship, but that friendship pertained especially to women and their domestic realm, free of the corruptions of the masculine, public world:

> Women make friends with other women more easily than is the case with men, and their friendships are more lasting . . . But it is very uncommon to find this kind of rare, inseparable friendship arising between two men or between a man and a woman, because men's innate malignity stands

in the way, even where these points of compatibility exist. For, as we've already noted, men are by nature little inclined to love. They also have a natural tendency toward pride and vanity. The upshot is that they are so ridiculously obsessed with their reputations, and with gaining the respect of those around them, that they behave very stiffly and formally in the pretense that courtesy demands it, whereas in fact their behavior is dictated by artifice. Indeed, instead of honoring their friends by behaving in this way, they are dishonoring friendship and breaching its sacred laws, which banish all affectation. And they are revealing themselves as not only cold and lacking in affection, but also as ignorant, since they are apparently incapable of distinguishing between the behavior that is appropriate with someone you want to have consider you a real friend, and the kind of behavior we reserve for mere acquaintances . . .

'There are many,' said Corinna, 'who do not make these distinctions, because they are incapable of real affection. They do not know how to treat their friends, because they are not real friends themselves. For a man who is a true friend to another must behave toward him in an absolutely frank and open manner: there must be no artifice in his behavior, no polite scruples, no hidden object or secret agenda. He should treat his friend just as he would a brother, a father, a son: that is, he should be as free and easy in all his dealings with him as he might be with a blood relative, even feeling at liberty to command favors when he needs them, and he should give his friend license to behave just as freely in return, never denying him anything he asks. And, believe me, anyone who doesn't take – and give – these liberties has no right to call himself a friend, but rather an acquaintance or a fair-weather friend.' (Fonte 1997: 123–4)[4]

Fonte preserved the traditional link between virtue and friendship; her subversion of the trope was to posit that male friendship had become untied from virtue and that such friendship and virtue adhered particularly to the female world. Indeed, Fonte elaborated, with brio, that it was not merely that the public world corrupted, but that men were innately more vicious than women, and that their virtues derived solely from contact with women (Fonte 1997: 58–9). Fonte's description of men was in point of fact a redescription of the image of the tyrant onto the male sex, and of the free man onto the female sex. As Rinuccini's garden had been an image of escape from the Tyrant Medici, so the female garden was now an image of escape from the Tyrant Man:

These women would often steal time together for a quiet conversation, and on these occasions, safe from any fear of being spied on by men or constrained by their presence, they would speak freely on whatever subject they pleased – sometimes, their womanly labors, sometimes, their seemly diversions . . . The third [iconic statue in the garden] is Liberty and her device is the sun, which stands free and alone, giving light to itself and sharing its light with the whole universe, to show that my aunt, living free and alone as she did, won a shining renown through her many fine and respected qualities, and also that she shared the treasures of her mind with every person of refinement with whom she came into contact – something she might not have been able to do under the rule and command of a husband. (Fonte 1997: 43, 54–5)

Fonte's revolutionary vision does not appear to have been immediately influential, but it prefigured both the radical strand of feminist writing of later centuries – and the separate spheres argument, that associated female virtue precisely with female domesticity, and whose implications those later radical feminists would come to regret. But Fonte was as important for what lay behind as for what lay before. Her dialogue registered an extraordinary culmination in the Renaissance humanist transformation in the conception of the status of women – from present to absent, from inferior to superior, from incapable of friendship and conversation to particularly capable of both. As women, Fonte's female characters would scarcely have been spoken to or allowed to speak in 1400; in 1600, they took such speech as peculiarly a woman's birthright.

Intimate friendship with women

The Montaignean shift to intimate friendship significantly furthered both the idea of friendship between women and men and the idea of friendship among women. This reconceived conception of intimate friendship with and among women extended itself into an ever wider variety of social matrices of communication, and now became associated with rational discussion and the search for truth. Reconceived upon a basis of intimacy, the friendship that included women and the friendship that discovered truth intertwined.

Let us return to the slow conceptual alignment of women with friendship – which, for all the extraordinary changes registered in the fifteenth and sixteenth centuries, was still very much a work in progress. Putting aside Fonte's *Worth of Women* for the moment as somewhat atypical of the age, the conception of friendship at the time of Montaigne was still primarily that of men to men. Montaigne wrote his essays to the cherished memory of Étienne de La Boétie (1530–63). The conceptual association of women with friendship was largely confined to the institution of marriage – and at the beginning of the seventeenth century even this marital friendship remained a significantly limited conception. Pierre Charron wrote that in 'matrimoniall friendship . . . the weaknesse and insufficiencie of the wife . . . can no way correspond to that perfect conference and communication of thoughts and judgements: her soule is not strong and constant enough to endure the straightnesse of a knot so fast, so strong, so durable' (Charron n.d. [after 1612]: 458 [III.7]). A wife could be thought of as a friend, but she was still generally conceived to be a weak one. Moreover, the emergence of the idea of friendship with women was slowed by the traditional perception, and possibly reality, that friendship and marriage were rival relations (Chaplin 2001: 269). William Shakespeare's (1564–1616) and John Fletcher's (1579–1625) Emilia in *Two Noble Kinsmen* (*c*.1612–14) preferred same-sex friendship to marriage (Luxon 2005: 26; Shannon 2002: 112–22); Edmund Spenser's (1552–99) *Faerie Queene* (1590–6) conceived of male friendship and cross-sex love as rival relations (Spenser 1909: 127–8 [4.10.26–8]; Chaplin 2001: 267–8); Katherine Philips (1632–64) lamented to Charles Cotterell (1615–1701) in her letter of 30 July 1662 that 'we may generally conclude the Marriage of a Friend to be the Funeral of a Friendship' (Philips 1992: 43 [Letter 13]; Andreadis 2006: 532); and Abel Boyer (*c*.1667–1729) wrote in *The English Theophrastus* (1702) that '*Love* and *Friendship* do reciprocally exclude one another' (Boyer 1702: 199). Male friendship and marriage were tense as well, but the greater importance ascribed to female commitment to marriage made the acceptance of the idea of female friendship significantly more problematic. The emergence of mixed-sex and female friendships was so fraught, both as concept and as practice, because women were doubted to be capable of friendship, because female friendship was reinscribed within marriage, and not least because these new conceptions of friendship emerged in tension with the conception of the marital relationship.

Yet now the conception of friendship with women began to expand further still. A notable seventeenth-century expansion of the expression of friendship outside marriage came in the genre of love letters (*lettres passionnées*) – which, as in the medieval courtly romances, counted more as a passionate prelude to marital friendship (or its adulterous or fornicative shadows) than as an alternative to marriage. The seventeenth-century love letter, therefore, did not stretch the definition of friendship much beyond its marital bounds. It came, however, to be prized as a form of communication whose spontaneity was eminently sincere, whose authenticity could only be degraded by practice, and whose genre status as a written half of a conversation rendered it eminently suitable as the carrier of friendship. So La Fevrerie wrote in 'Du style épistolaire' (1683) that

> Je croy mesme que l'Amour a esté le premier Inventeur des Lettres . . . La grande affaire a toûjours esté celle du coeur. L'amour qui d'abord unit les Hommes, ne leur donna point de plus grands desirs que ceux de se voir & de se communiquer, lors qu'ils estoient séparez par une cruelle absence. (La Fevrerie 1683: 30–1; Goldsmith 1988: 33–5)

The love letter remade female friendship along Montaignean lines, even if it did not expand the range of friendship much beyond its marital bounds. Perhaps as importantly, the increasing attention paid to such love letters registered the continuing displacement within French noble culture of male friendship by male-to-female intimacy. The image of the communication of sentiments was coming to be more a *lettre passionnée* than a Montaignean *essai*.

At the same time, although 'Outside marriage, friendship between men and women was generally believed to be more difficult,' the idea of such extra-marital inter-sex friendships slowly naturalised itself in seventeenth- and eighteenth-century France (Garrioch 2009: 176). Madeleine de Scudéry wrote in the first volume of *Clélie* (1660) of a Map that showed the way to a '*Nouvelle Amitié à Tendre*' – 'une Amitié tendre', a tender friendship. The character Clélie was qualified to describe the way to Tender Friendship because 'ne pouuoit choisir personne à dire des douceurs d'amitié, qui connust mieux la veritable tendresse que Clélie la connoissoit.' Scudéry described various routes on her map, among them the way by:

> Grands seruices: & que pour marquer qu'il y a peu de Gens qui en rendent de tels, ce Village est plus petit que les autres. En suite, il faut passer à Sensibilité, pour faire connoistre qu'il faut sentir iusques aux plus petites douleurs de ceux qu'on aime. Apres il faut pour arriuer à Tendre, passer par Tendresse, car l'amitié attire l'amitié. En suite il faut aller à Obeïssance: n'y ayant presques rien qui engage plus le coeur de ceux à qui on obeït, que de le faire aueuglément: & pour arriuer enfin où l'on veut aller: il faut passer à Constante Amitié, qui est sans doute le chemin le plus seur, pour arriuer à Tendre sur reconnoissance. (Scudéry 1660: 390, 402–3; Garrioch 2009: 176; Morlet-Chantalat 1994: 321–41)

Charles Sorel (*c.*1602–74) less elliptically defined 'l'Amitié Tendre' in 'Pour L'Amitie Tendre, Hors le Mariage' (1663) as 'the honest affection between two people of different sex, which makes them glad to see each other and to converse, and to do each other service whenever they have the opportunity' (Sorel 1663: 133, translated in Garrioch 2009: 176). Three generations later, Anne Thérèse de Marguenat de Courcelles, the Marquise de Lambert (1647–1733), similarly wrote in *On Friendship* (1736):

> It has been asked, if friendship can subsist between persons of different sexes? This is indeed rare and difficult, but it is the kind of friendship which affords the highest delight; most difficult, because it requires most virtue and circumspection. Women who have only the common ideas of love, are not worthy of it: and men who only seek in women the ordinary pleasures of the sex, without supposing that they may possess qualities of the mind and heart more attractive than those of beauty; such men are not formed for the friendship of which I speak. Let us therefore attach ourselves by the ties of virtue and of personal merit; connections of this kind sometimes begin in love, and terminate in friendship. When women are faithful to the virtue of their sex, friendship being the recompence of virtuous love, they may flatter themselves with the hopes of it. From the manner in which love is treated at this time, it frequently terminates in an open quarrel, shame being generally the punishment of vice. When women oppose their duty to their affection, and offer you the charms and sentiments of friendship; when, moreover, you discover in them the same merit as in men, can you do better than connect yourself with them? It is certain, that of all unions it is the most inchanting; there is always a degree of vivacity, which is not to be found between persons of the same sex – above all, the failings that disunite, such as envy or competition, of whatever nature in [*sic*] may be, is not to be found in this sort of connection. (Lambert 1780: 86–9; Garrioch 2009: 176)

Scudéry, Sorel and Lambert registered the slow and hesitant normalisation of the possibility of friendship between men and women, more or less on the model of the old friendship between man and man.

Yet both the agreeableness and the difficulty of such friendships arose not least in the shadow of the *lettre passionnée*. The reconception of friendship as intimate facilitated its extension to the relationships of men and women, but such intimacy also threatened or invited the dangerous slip toward loving passion. Scudéry's Map to Tender Friendship mentioned an alternate destination, down 'la Riuiere d'Inclination', that led to 'vne Mer qu'on apelle la Mer dangereuse; parce qu'il est assez dangereux à vne Femme, d'aller vn peu au delà des derneieres Bornes de l'amitié' (Scudéry 1660: 405). In Lambert's telling, although she thought that mixed-sex friendship was superior to same-sex friendship when it could be achieved, it was attended by the constant danger of a decay into mere mutual passion – from which it often enough had sprung. In such circumstances, it is not surprising that men and women were still rarely represented as friends for much of this period.

From a relatively brief examination of the extension of the conception of intersex friendship, we may now turn to a somewhat longer discussion of that slenderly precedented phenomenon – the idea of friendship between women. Such precedents as existed were frequently literary: just as the model of the Learned Woman provided conceptual space for actual Italian women to enter into humanist society, so the literary representation of women's friendship in Renaissance and early modern Europe preceded and modelled its actual flourishing. Shakespeare's works, at any rate, provided a remarkable panoply of friendships among women, including, among others, Rosalind and Celia in *Love's Labour's Lost* (*c.*1594), Helena and Hermia in *A Midsummer's Night Dream* (*c.*1595), Emilia and her female friends in *Two Noble Kinsmen*, Mistress Ford and Mistress Page in *The Merry Wives of Windsor* (*c.*1597) and Paulina and Hermione in *The Winter's Tale* (*c.*1610). In the seventeenth century, the writings of Madame de Scudéry and her circle portrayed and articulated female friendships. So in Scudéry's *The Story of Sapho*, embedded within her *Artamène* (1649–53), Scudéry depicted the friendship of Sapho and Cydnon (Scudéry 2003, esp. 17–18; Wahl 1999: 109, 114, 183–93). Female friendships on the page were becoming increasingly common. They also became inflected with some of the emotional intensity that inflected *lettres passionnées* – at least in Scudéry's anonymously published *Lettres Amoureuses* (1641) (Scudéry 2004: 44–55).

These literary friendships among women now found accompaniment in real life – above all, in mid-seventeenth-century England. There the influence of Christian *caritas* on the idea of friendship, now more than a milennium old, appears to have facilitated this expansion: so John Norris (1657–1711) in 'A Letter concerning Friendship' (1687), "that Friendship is nothing else but *Benevolence* or *Charity* under some certain *Modifications* or accidental circumstances' (Norris 1687: 450). Female friendship, whether within or without the marriage bond, could be conceived of more easily as *caritas* than as *amicitia* (Herbert 2014: 24–7). Whatever the precise admixture of *caritas* and *amicitia*, women in real life – and not just as wives – now could be conceived of as friends. Extraordinarily, the poetess Katherine Philips ('Orinda') elicited from Jeremy Taylor

(1613–67) in *A Discourse of the Nature, Offices, and Measures, of Friendship, with Rules of Conducting It, in a Letter to the Most Ingenious and Excellent Mrs. Katharine Philips* (1657) an explicit acknowledgement that women were capable of friendship, without constraint within the bonds of marriage (Taylor 1657: 86–91). Whether or not Taylor primarily had marital friendship in mind, in effect his treatise acted to justify Philips' friendship with other women – Anne Owen ('Lucasia') and Mary Aubrey ('Rosania'). Philips' practice provided a model of female friendship to her contemporaries, and her poetry modelled that friendship for her future readers, which included both Mary Astell (1666–1731) and future Bluestocking Margaret Harley Bentinck (1715–85). Such friendship, moreover, now was regarded as the equal of men's friendship. John Norris' 'Letter concerning Friendship' (1687) registered the drift in thought: while he wrote only concerning marital friendship, he wrote of it as an equal friendship, between two people equally capable of friendship, even though men remained superior to women and husbands to wives (Norris 1687: 453–5). The application, however, hardly confined itself to marriage. If women now were considered to be as capable as men of friendship, they did not need a man to partake in friendship's joys (Anderson 2012: 74; Andreadis 2006; Broad 2009: 73–9; Lanser 1998/9; Myers 1990: 23, 61).

By the eighteenth century, the idea of women's equal capacity for friendship even began to be used as part of the polemic claiming general equality of women and men. So the Marquise de Lambert wrote to her daughter in *Avis d'une mère à son fils, et à sa fille* (1728) that, 'A woman of quality (*une honnête femme*) possesses the virtues of men: friendship, probity, fidelity in the fulfillment of her duties' (Lambert 1728: 121, translated in Garrioch 2009: 201; Garrioch 2009: 200–1). To claim equality in the capacity of friendship was to lay claim to virtually all the catalogue of traditionally masculine virtues.

As Taylor and Norris wrote, and Philips pioneered, an increasing number of Englishwomen made their literary and their social practice from the late seventeenth century onward. At the top of the social scale, the writings and practice of both the royal daughters of James II (1633–1701; r.1685–8) testify to female friendship – and in Anne's (1665–1714; r.1702–14) case, her friendship with Sarah Jennings Churchill (1660–1744) would help determine the high politics of England for nearly a decade (McClain 2008; Somerset 2013: 50–5). At a less rarified level, Anne Dormer (*c.*1648–95) wrote letters to her sister Elizabeth Turnbell between 1685 and 1691 in the language of both love and friendship, while Mary Astell possessed a great many friendships with women, including Ann Coventry, Elizabeth Hastings, Elizabeth Hutcheson and Catherine Jones (Broad 2009: 67–8; Herbert 2014: 21). Eighteenth-century England appears to have seen the practice of friendship among women become a widespread fact as opposed to merely a literary trope. The Bluestockings – female intellectuals attuned to the old ideals of friendship linked to reason, virtue and inquiry toward learning and truth – practised friendship extensively, not only in correspondence but also in the flesh. Such friendships, both face to face and epistolary, were linked especially to the spas such as Bath that figured so highly as locales of gentle sociability. The spas brought women together from their disparate domestic (frequently country house) locales to be able to meet face to face, provided a model for the sociability of their correspondence and also provided for these women's friendly correspondence the subject matter of 'Bath chat' – news that partook both of the feminine and the public. Figures such as Margaret Harley Bentinck, Frances Burney (1752–1840), Jemima Campbell (1723–97), Elizabeth Carter (1717–1806), Hester Thrale Piozzi (1741–1821), Elizabeth Montagu Robinson (1718–1800) and Catherine Talbot (1721–70) wrote, conversed but above all became friends with one another (Eger 2008; Herbert 2014: 117–41; Hurley 2006; Myers 1990). In eighteeenth-century England, the idea of female friendship became a widespread social practice.

The portrait provided by current scholarship suggests that the concept of friendship between women was slower to develop in France than in England, either theoretically or in social practice. The Marquise de Lambert's claim that women were capable of friendship did not extend to any great belief that women could be friends with other women (Lambert 1780: 89–90). As late as the middle of the eighteenth century, Jean-Jacques Rousseau's (1712–78) *La Nouvelle Heloise* (1761) appears to have provided a powerful model for female friendship in his portrait of the affection between Claire and Julie precisely because there were still so few such models for female friendship, in literature or in real life (Roulston 1998/9: 215–16, 219). Dalton examines the lives of various late-eighteenth-century French and Italian female participants in the Republic of Letters, including the role of friendship in that participation; her sketches give the impression that both the idea and the practice of female friendship were more shallowly rooted among these female intellectuals of the Continent than they were among their Bluestocking contemporaries (Dalton 2003). The notion of friendship between women remained sufficiently exceptional in France that Marie Antoinette's (1755–93) friendships aroused deeply hostile and sexual criticism before the Revolution, and after the Revolution received gruesome comment in the pageantry surrounding the execution of Marie Antoinette's friend the Princess de Lamballe (1749–92) (Roulston 1998/9: 224–36). Among the divides between French and English culture, the apparently quicker acceptance in England of the idea and practice of female friendship may be among the most significant.

As the reference to Rousseau's *La Nouvelle Heloise* suggests, female friendship continued to be a subject matter in the literature of the period, in the works of Pierre de Marivaux (1688–1763), various English works of the eighteenth century, including Samuel Richardson's (1689–1761) *Clarissa* (1748), Eliza Haywood's (*c*.1693–1756) *The Surprize* (1724) and *The British Recluse* (1723), and in further works in Italian and German (Garrioch 2009: 177–9). Todd provides a catalogue of the types of female friendships that appeared in the eighteenth and early nineteenth centuries: Samuel Richardson's *Clarissa* (sentimental), John Cleland's (1709–89) *Fanny Hill* (1748) and Denis Diderot's (1713–84) *The Nun* (1796) (erotic), Jean-Jacques Rousseau's *La Nouvelle Heloise* and the Marquis de Sade's *Juliette* (1797–1801) (manipulative), Mary Wollstonecraft's (1759–97) *Mary, A Fiction* (1788) and *Maria: or, The Wrongs of Woman* (1798) and Madame de Staël's (1766–1817) *Delphine* (1802) (political), and Jane Austen's (1775–1817) *Mansfield Park* (1814) and *Emma* (1815) (social) (Todd 1980). Perhaps the most important conclusion to draw from this catalogue is that the idea of female friendship had become sufficiently commonplace that anatomising a particular example was becoming more important than establishing the bare possibility of such friendship's existence.

We should at this point note the complicated relationship of lesbianism, perceived and actual, to female friendship. The background to the conceptual association is that women's association with passion, especially erotic passion, therefore served to tinge perceptions of their friendships with passion, to lend them an erotic charge. Women's friendship with other women thus could be dismissed polemically as lesbian attraction. At the same time, such friendships may actually have disguised such attraction – the evidence for a type of relationship then so widely condemned must necessarily be ambiguous, and if we should discount some polemical accusations of lesbianism, we should also give significant weight to ambiguous implications. It is difficult to assess, for example, women calling one another 'husband' or 'wife': since marriage still was considered the highest form of female friendship, such language could indicate true friendship, an erotic/domestic relationship or both. What we can say is that the passionate shadow of lesbianism inflected early modern conceptions of female friendship – as, indeed, the passionate shadow of male homosexuality likewise inflected the age's conception of male friendship. That the increase in the cultural importance of these passionate shadows paralleled the shift toward a passionate conception of friendship suggests that the conflation of friendship with homoerotic attraction, as polemic, disguise and actuality, played a significant role in realigning the conception of friendship away from reason and toward passion, as both cause and register (Andreadis 2006; Bray 2003: 196–201; Crawford 1995; Herbert 2014: 27–8; Lanser 1998/9; Legault 2012; Wahl 1999: 121, 157–8, 183–93).

The establishment of a conception of friendship with and among women brought with it the corollary idea that women could partake in those modes that depended upon friendship – intellectual inquiry and conversation. This, it should be emphasised, was conceived of as a notable innovation. Madame de Scudéry, after all, wrote feelingly in 'De la Conversation' (1680) via her character Nicanor of the absolute dullness of an all-female conversation limited to dress:

> I found myself engaged against my will with a troop of women (whom you may easily guess), who employed the whole day in nothing but speaking well or ill of their clothes, and in lying continually about the price that they cost them . . . I passed the entire day in hearing such shallow and senseless matters that it makes me still a little embarrassed.

Men by themselves might be pedantically dull, but women by themselves talked without the leaven of reason (Scudéry 2002: 84; Harth 1992: 50–1). Mary Astell's argument in *A Serious Proposal* (1697) that female education would make possible a proper conversation among women took as its predicate the general lack of such rational speech among the female sex: 'What is it but the want of an ingenious Education, that renders the generality of Feminine Conversations so insipid and foolish, and their solitude so insupportable?' (Astell 1697: Part I, 48). Female conversation would be new.

Let us continue our examination of Astell's *A Serious Proposal* (1697), wherein the female appropriation of inquiry and conversation now received an explicit articulation. In this work, Astell delineated an educational institution for women where 'we shall have opportunity of contracting the purest and noblest Friendship.' This friendship was to be a narrowing and intensification of the love one should bear toward mankind in general: 'For Friendship is nothing else but Charity contracted . . . But yet, as in Heav'n that region of perfect Love, the happy Souls (as some are of opinion) now and then step aside from more general Conversations, to entertain themselves with a peculiar Friend' (Astell 1697: Part I, 81, 83, 85–6). Astell, in other words, adapted that *caritas*-inflected conception of friendship that had helped establish female friendship in mid-seventeenth-century England and applied it to the conditions for inquiry. In this search, conversation (and not *disputatio*) would allow women's various interests, capacities and insights to bear jointly upon the common search for truth (Astell 1697: Part II, 87–90, 98, 108–9). This search for truth would also involve that supension of judgement characteristic of the whole tradition derived from *sermo* (Astell 1697: Part II, 114; cf. Boyer 1702: 222). Indeed, Astell gave to truth itself the character of a good conversationalist, albeit not of a courtier: 'There's in her that which us'd to be the Character of our Nation, an honest Plainness and Sincerity, Openness and blunt Familiarity: She cannot mould her self into all Shapes to be rendred agreeable, but standing on her Native Worth is regardless of Out-side and Varnish' (Astell 1697: Part II, 117, 161–2). This distaste for the courtly mode registered Astell's preference for conversation in a narrowly uplifting mode – but this emphasis on improvement, if somewhat straitlaced, lay squarely within the contemporary range of possibilities for conversation (Astell 1697: Part I, 52). Astell's dream of female education was, more precisely, the dream of a female academy, where friendship, virtue, variety and conversational inquiry joined in a harmonious whole.

Conclusion

The development of the conceptions of intimate friendship and of friendship with and among women went hand and hand in Renaissance and early modern Europe; together, they came to associate women as women rather than as imitation men, with conversation and the inquiry into truth. This association radically differentiated the idea of conversation from that of oratory and philosophical reason, which would still be conceived, respectively, as the modes of speech of wrangling and disputatious men. The feminisation of the concept of conversation, via the feminisation of the concept of friendship, went hand in hand with conversation's triumph over oratory. Conversation's ascendancy and conversation's feminisation were yoked aspects of the same intellectual transformation.

Yet this twin transformation only proceeded in certain mixed-sex social *milieux* – notably that of the court and of the court's successor, the *salon*. Both the Republic of Letters and the world of the newspaper, those inheritors of the humanist letter, although they articulated variants of the conversational inheritance, by notable contrast eschewed both the intimate variants of friendship and conversation and the embrace of women within their realms of discourse. In the next two chapters I trace the parallel and intertwining developments of these social matrices of conversation, which would provide rival models for discourse as conversation spread yet further into the intellectual life of Europe. Much of this took place in the court and the *salon*, which would provide successive homes for intimate and feminised conversation.

Notes

1. Guazzo has not been translated into English since the sixteenth century. I cite the English translation (Guazzo 1967) for the convenience of the reader and a modern Italian edition (Guazzo 1993) so that readers may inspect the original text.
2. James and Kent quote Margherita Datini to Lapo Mazzei, 10 April 1394, Archivio di Stato di Prato, Archivio Datini, busta 1089, cited and translated in James (2008: 54).
3. The *querelle* was a debate; for dialogues (annexing yet more subject matter) on the subject of women in sixteenth-century France, see L. Warner (2011: 121–42).
4. For my discussion of Fonte throughout, see Jordan (1996).

Chapter 5

Court, *Salon* and Republic of Letters

Introduction

Humanists resurrected the concept of conversation, but it did not remain confined within their social matrix. The humanist educational project to educate the elite of western Europe produced as one of its dizzy successes the application of the attributes of conversation to the speech and behaviour of noblemen at court. This development of the ideal of the courtier took both actual and literary conversation from the leisurely retreat from the ancient political world to the courtly heart of the Renaissance political world. The speech of the court was quintessentially that of men and women together, and so the conversational community of the court diverged from the Republic of Letters in its thematic incorporation of women. The speech of the court also shifted conversation's indirect orientation toward the political world to a direct address: the courtier now began to address his conversation to the prince. In his supple deference to the prince, in his friendly desire to make virtuous and rational that royal icon of the oratorical realm, the courtier's conversation provided a model for the tradition that would address conversation directly to the political world. The conversational rhetoric that had forwarded the continuance of conversation now modified itself to inculcate the conversational virtues in the prince.

This courtly transformation of the concept of conversation was expressed most influentially in Baldassare Castiglione's dialogue *The Book of the Courtier* (1528). The *Courtier*'s immense influence on early modern courtly culture derived both from its explicit discussion of the theory and practice of conversation and from its dissemination of conversational modes of thought and behaviour embedded in its prescriptions of courtesy (Burke 1996; Plett 2004: 78–80, 423–7). Machiavelli's importance in the transformation of prudence is paralleled by Castiglione's importance in the transformation of conversation: much of this chapter therefore will consist of a close reading of *The Courtier*.

The *salons* of seventeenth-century France further transformed the conversational tradition of the court. In the *salons*, the behaviour and speech of the courtier began a strange rebellion against the power of the prince. On the one hand, the power of the prince, embodied by *le Roi Soleil*, absolutely denied conversation a role in the political realm. The prince's power became so great that the *salon* shut itself off from the court and from the distorting imperatives of power. Furthermore, courtly conversation was no longer taken to inform the world of oratory, of power. Consequently, the *salon* began to challenge the prince in a subtle fashion: the subjects of *salon* conversation now were taken by the *salonier* conversationalists to be sharply independent from the prince's power. Those subjects were at first strictly apolitical – but, in principle, the conversation of the *salons* began quietly to contend with the world of oratory by addressing itself to the same worldly subject matter. When the power of the monarch at last began to recede, conversation would burst forth from its *salonnier* redoubt in all directions. This burst acquired some further power from the *salons*' brief subsumption *c.*1720 of the Republic of Letters, which gave to *salonnier* conversation all the scholarly and philosophical subject matter of the Republic – and which they retained as potential subjects for such conversation, even when a portion of the Republic of Letters resumed its traditional independence from the *salons*.

This chapter concludes with a narration of the long history of the Republic of Letters which preceded its temporary incorporation within the *salons*. The Republic of Letters provided an alternate social matrix for *sermo*, one scholarly rather than courtly – and one which migrated away from its Ciceronian roots towards the mode of Baylean critique. (This shift occurred not least as a defensive move of self-definition against a powerful rival, its impetus presumably stimulated by its sojourn in the *salons*, where some portion of the Republic of Letters remained in durance pleasaunte and perpetual.) Where the courtly and scholarly traditions of *sermo* acted as complementary modes during the Renaissance, the increasing scope of *salonnier* conversation and the increasing abandonment of *sermo* by the Republic of Letters set them more sharply at odds with one another in the eighteenth century. Both now harboured universalising ambitions, which would set these sibling modes to fierce conflict.

Alberti

Let us first look at the *quattrocento* and Leon Battista Alberti's fascinating prelude to Castiglione. We may recollect that Alberti's assimilation of the idea of true friendship (*vera amicizia*) to the more cynically political aspects of *amicitia* had tended to drain the moral content from the concept. On the other hand, it also opened up the possibility of applying the moral content of *vera amicizia* to the courtier's arts, of infusing the humanist tropes of friendship to the long-standing medieval topic of debate about the worthiness of the courtier's profession. Much of this debate had turned on the status of counsel: the advocate of the courtier justified his contortions to please the prince by reference to the good counsel such contortions made possible, while his critic (such as Enea Silvio Piccolomini in his *De curialium miseriis*, 1444) would counter that while courtiers always justified their career by claiming they provided good counsel, the corrupting court always forced them, sooner or later, to accommodate themselves to its vices (Piccolomini 1928: 52 [28]; Langer 1994: 206). In 'Dell'amicizia' (1441–4), Alberti now restated the debate about a courtier's good counsel in the language of *vera amicizia*: the courtier's return to the *amicizia* of his prince was to recommend only those friends who were fit to serve: 'I always refused to help anyone obtain a public office unless he was fully qualified through experience and character' (Alberti 1971: [Bk. 4]; Hyatte 1994: 182, 184). *Vera amicizia* between courtier and prince thus engaged good counsel in its mutuality of favour.

But this was not all: while Alberti's *vera amicizia* was in its weaker sense of practical friendship nothing more than a variation on civic and self-interested *benivolenza*, it continued to hearken to some of its ancient ambitions toward virtue and mutuality. Courtier and prince, though unequal, should aim toward true friendship – Alberti's innovation upon the concept of *vera amicizia* applied the medieval conception of friendship between unequals to the relationship of prince and courtier. While powerful men were '[e]mpty of all honest activity, lazy, and eventually not a little given to the seeking of pleasure, and sought out not by friends but by hypocrites and flatterers', Alberti's Adovardo nevertheless claimed that true friendship with princes was theoretically possible, since some princes – acid qualifier! – have loved virtue.

Furthermore, if a courtier might seek the prince's friendship, then could not – should not – the prince seek his subjects' friendship? Alberti's Adovardo said, 'Happy is that prince who wishes to acquire benevolence and be less feared than loved; they could all do so in an easy and most pleasant way, but in this matter they do not care to acquire benevolence and immortal glory in one single stroke.' Lionardo then replies, 'I am waiting to hear what this way is' – but the Albertis are called away, and the last line of the *Della Famiglia* is Adovardo's tantalising promise, 'Well, then, I shall satisfy you tomorrow.' So Alberti ended the dialogue – but in so doing, he posed to the reader some unanswered questions. Would the prince seek his subjects' *amicizia*? If he did, how should he try to gain it? And what would lead him to seek out his subjects' friendship? Implicitly, as Langer notes, it would be the courtier's function – his part of *vera amicizia* – to educate his prince to seek out the friendship of his subjects. But how precisely was the courtier to do that? Alberti did not say (Alberti 1971: 325–6 [Bk. 4]; Langer 1994: 210 (note 46); Hyatte 1994: 182, 193–4; Langer 1994: 199–200, 200 (note 26), 208–10). By implicitly raising the question he had approached tantalisingly near to Castiglione, but it would remain for Castiglione to provide the answer.

Pontano

Where Alberti posed a question about how the courtier was to educate the prince, Neapolitan humanist Giovanni Pontano (1426–1503) readied the way for Castiglione's shift of conversation to the court by reeling the old Roman *urbanitas* toward *sermo*'s conceptual constellation. Pontano's *De Sermone* (1499–1502/3, published 1509) explored the nature of relaxed, ordinary conversation rather than philosophical, truth-seeking *sermo*, and above all the nature of wit, jokes and good humour. Pontano thereby brought the old Roman *urbanitas* to the fore once more, in a work about conversation. Pontano's conversationalists were Neapolitan humanists at an Academy rather than Roman elites at a villa, but they shared with their forebears an urbane mode of speech.

Yet Pontano did more than resurrect the old *urbanitas*. To begin with, he discussed wit as an eminently rhetorical art – something that could be practised so that one could achieve (in Quondam's summary) a refined humour that was 'temperato e misurato, secondo convenienza e discrezione' (Quondam 2007: 94). Wit also was as democratic as any rhetorical art, for it was not inborn; rather, one acquired it by a jester's *virtù*: 'Sedes autem ipsa iocandi et quasi argumentatiuncula posita est in usu atque peritia, quando in artificio quocunque' (Pontano

2008: 233 [4.3.17]; and see Quintilian 1920–2: II, 443 [6.3.11]). Wit furthermore was an art of life, the operation of reason (*ratio*) on impulse (*impetus*) to give the impression of spontaneity, an artfully artless *sprezzatura*, a very few years *avant la lettre*. By describing wit in rhetorical terms, Pontano facilitated the more precise convergence of urbane wit with the rhetoric of conversation.

Pontano's Aristotelianising reformulatation of *urbanitas* as *facetudo* (facetiousness) – wit as a social virtue – then served to make the idea of wit not just broadly rhetorical, but also narrowly conversational. To begin with, wit to Quintilian and Cicero had been both a matter of urbane conversation and a technique of orators to forward the serious work of persuasion; now Pontano applied wit quite firmly to the conversations of ordinary educated men putting up their feet in their off hours. So far Pontano followed the ancient association of urbane wit and conversation. Yet the old *urbanitas* had shared *sermo*'s style, but not *sermo*'s ethical content, which derived from its aspiration to discover truth and inform the actions of public life. Pontano's new *facetudo* – following up on implications scattered through the thought of Aristotle, Cicero and other ancient writers – now partook of that ethical content: 'Facetudinem uirtutem esse' (Pontano 2008: 173 [3.2]). In the first place, the wit of *facetudo*, aligned with both *veritas* (truthfulness) and *comitas* (courtesy), was virtuous because, by *ratio* (reason) and *mensura* (measure) it made from the laughter it produced something that could stablise friendship and make it endure, and thus provided the preconditions for the search for truth. In the second place, wit relaxed gentlemen in their leisure, and by that relief refreshed them for the duties of public life: 'altera quidem quae susceptorum laborum honestum sit leuamen relaxatioque maxime laudabilis a curis ac molestiis (Pontano 2008: 81 [1.7.2]). (Such wit was a secularised, externalised variation of the soul-solacing conversation in Petrarch's *Secretum*.) *Facetudo* thereby made the smiling art of wit a handmaid to the twin virtues of leisure and public life.[1]

Castiglione certainly drew upon Pontano for the *Courtier* (Pontano 2008: 59) – and Pontano's concept of *facetudo* apparently informs Castiglione's portrait of the courtier, aligning that graceful gentleman's urbanity with the virtues of conversation. The Renaissance courtier already drew on a medieval heritage that aligned courtly speech at least loosely with the rhetorical strictures of decorum and urbanity (Jaeger 1985: 113–26); now Pontano's witty humanists modelled for the court a mode of urbanity that was both conversational and virtuous. Pontano's ethic of *facetudo* would allow Castiglione's courtier to aspire to these conversational virtues, rather than satisfy himself with urbanity and conversational style. *Facetudo*'s alignment with *veritas*, the truthfully sincere expression of his self, made him more than a mere dissimulating orator of the court.

Castiglione

Let us put to one side more immediate predecessors such as Alberti and Pontano: Castiglione's *Courtier*[2] drew in greatest measure upon an alloy of Ciceronian and Platonic thought. The form of the book largely imitated Cicero's *De oratore* (55 BC). Both works took the form of a private conversation among an elite discussing a particular excellence – Cicero's oratory and Castiglione's courtiership – where the nature of that excellence was to be discovered from the works' exemplary conversations themselves rather than by the provision of fixed rules. Yet Castiglione also imitated Plato, not least in his search for 'the Idea . . . of the perfect Courtier'. The very structure of the book proceeded from largely Ciceronian thought in the first three books to quite Platonic thought in the fourth and last book (Castiglione 1976: 35–6 [Preface]; V. Cox 1992: 47–60; Javitch 1978: 18–49; Kinney 1989: 128; Rebhorn 1972; Richards 2003: 47; Rigolot 2004: 7–10). In this oscillation from Ciceronian to Platonic thought, we should recollect the dialectic between Ciceronian and Platonic conceptions of knowledge of the *quattrocento* humanists (especially the circle of Marsilio Ficino), and the idea of conversation as a means to acquire sure knowledge of philosophical universals, with application upon the flux of the world. Castiglione's *Courtier* transposed this dialectic to courtly conversation.

The discussion of conversation was at the heart of the *Courtier*, for the courtier was in good measure defined by the way he spoke. The perfect courtier was supposed to speak with decorum, fitting his words to the occasion, the subject and the listeners (Castiglione 1976: 77–8 [Bk. 1]). His speech, however, was not only supposed to be decorous in general but also to be conversational in particular:

[H]e should be so constituted that he never lacks for eloquence adapted to those with whom he is talking, and that he should know how to refresh and charm the minds of his listeners, and move them to merriment and laughter with his agreeable pleasantries and witticisms, in such a way that, without ever being tedious or boring, he is always a source of pleasure. (Castiglione 1976: 151 [Bk. 2])

The courtier's speech adapted most of the attributes of the Ciceronian *sermo*. It took place in leisure among a small and elite group, among equals to the extent that it took place among courtiers, where friendship and familiarity underpinned a civil and considerate knowledge of one another's particular characters so as to elicit free and full speech from all participants. Where the courtier's conversation differed from its Ciceronian model was that, at first glance, such conversation aimed merely at mutual delight rather than at mutual inquiry into indefinite truth. This shift to delight partly registered a *quattrocento* shift in rhetoric: Marsh takes Lorenzo Valla's *De vero falsoque bono* (1431), for example, to associate practical experience and rhetoric with *voluptas* (pleasure, although used by Valla in an elevated Epicurean mode) and the aim to delight (Marsh 1980: 75–6). More generally it registered that courtiers were not precisely humanists and mutual delight was more their métier than mutual inquiry. Their conversation initially appeared to be a hollow simulation of the forms of *sermo*.

Castiglione's discussion culminated, however, in a higher justification of the courtier's conversation. The courtier, after all, did not only interact with other courtiers, with his equals. He also interacted with the prince – his superior, the embodiment of oratory, of power and passion, of lordship and will. The Ciceronian *sermo* did not conceive of such an interlocutor; the leisured conversation of Cicero's companions knew no lord. Yet the prince was present in Castiglione's court – and the courtiers' conversation did not include an equivalent function to the mutual inquiry of Cicero's time, or even of their humanist contemporaries. Castiglione, brilliantly, made the presence of the prince a solution to the absence of purpose in courtly conversation. The courtier would now engage the prince in conversation, and by so doing his behaviour and his speech would lead toward the moral education of the prince.

> In my opinion, therefore, the end of the perfect courtier (which we have so far left untouched) is, by means of the accomplishments attributed to him by these gentlemen, so to win for himself the mind and favour of the prince he serves that he can and always will tell him the truth about all he needs to know, without fear or risk of displeasing him. And, if he knows that his prince is of a mind to do something unworthy, he should be in a position to dare oppose him, and make courteous use of the favour his good qualities have won to remove every evil intention and persuade him to return to the path of virtue . . . Therefore I consider that just as music, festivities, games and other agreeable accomplishments are, so to speak, the flower of courtiership, so its real fruit is to encourage and help his prince to be virtuous and to deter him from evil. (Castiglione 1976: 284–5 [Bk. 4])

Since the prince embodied the realm of oratory, the courtier's desire to influence the prince recapitulated the Ciceronian justification of conversation as oriented toward action in the world, as meant to 'amend our lives, purposes and wills'. Yet the relation of conversation to oratory was now radically changed. Conversation had been at a remove – the speech of leisure, meant to inform public speech only indirectly. This new courtier's conversation addressed itself directly to the prince, directly to the realm of oratory. The villa's detachment from the Forum had been replaced by the courtier's propinquity to his sovereign lord.

Castiglione's formulation registered or paralleled several other shifts discussed above. The dialogue genre had seen a shift toward addressing political subject matter: the reorientation here of the courtier's speech toward the prince personified this address. Guicciardini had spoken of flattering the people: here the courtier flattered the prince. More's *Utopia* had hinted at the use of conversation as a means to bring about the best state: here conversation was also to be the means to improve the state. Friendship had splintered into Albertian and Montaignean alternatives: here a distinctly Albertian friendship toward the incarnation of the political world was meant to produce political virtue. These similarities underline how embedded Castiglione's conception of the courtier was in the humanist innovations on the traditions of the *sermo*.

Several aspects of this new conversational mode oriented toward the prince are worth noting in detail. First, as Castiglione uneasily acknowledged, it shifted the conversational mode from the Ciceronian assumption that it occurred between equals toward one that created the *appearance* of equality among unequals: 'I know that to talk of a courtier being conversant with his prince in this way implies a certain equality that can hardly exist between a ruler and his servant; but for the time being we shall let this go' (Castiglione 1976: 125 [Bk. 2]; Javitch 1978: 26–7). The medieval development of Christian friendship between unequals had presaged the development of conversation between unequals, as had Alberti's explicit conception of a friendship between courtier and prince – but these suggestive precedents now became an actuality. As oratory always had been, conversation now was to be a speech among unequals – although conversation's insistence on an appearance of equality had a powerful dynamic that would shift it far away from oratory's assumptions.

Yet conversation now had to encompass an inequality far greater than that of the Forum, a radical inequality between the powerless and the powerful that rendered the speech of truth to power (to coin a phrase) itself virtually impossible. The power of princes, possessed of unbridled will, had both corrupted them and rendered them unwilling to listen either to counsel (persuasive rhetoric) or to reason (philosophy) (Castiglione 1976: 285–88 [Bk. 4]). Indeed:

> [I]f some of our rulers were to be confronted by a strict philosopher, or indeed anyone at all who openly and candidly might wish to show them the awesome face of true virtue, teach them a good way of life and how a good prince should conduct himself, I am sure that as soon as he appeared they would loathe him as if he were a serpent or mock at him as if he were dirt. (Castiglione 1976: 287–8 [Bk. 4])

Nor was the princes' wilful deafness incidental to their vices, for it was precisely the princes' isolation from communication with other human beings that made them sinful: '[P]rinces lack most of all what they must have in the fullest measure, namely, someone to tell them the truth and remind them of what is right' (Castiglione 1976: 285 [Bk. 4]). The Renaissance prince had inherited from the Ciceronian multitude not only their oratorical function but also their hatred of philosophy. We may note that Castiglione's revision of this theme shifted that hatred from the realm of sociology to that of psychology and the mental faculties, abstracted it into a natural revulsion of the will toward reason.

The prince's hostility toward rational speech in consequence positively deterred their inferiors from counselling them, from fear of punishment, and fostered among those inferiors, out of self-preservation, the resort to mere flattery (Castiglione 1976: 285–6 [Bk. 4]). This fear was quite justified, for princes could react with hatred should a courtier even make a request of a prince – i.e. recommend policy based on reason and virtue.

> For very often when lords have refused to grant a favour to someone who has been seeking it importunately they imagine that the person who has been so insistent must be very anxious to get what he wants and therefore, when he is baulked, must be ill-disposed towards the one who has denied him; and this belief breeds in them a hatred of the person concerned, whom subsequently they can never see without distaste. (Castiglione 1976: 126–7 [Bk. 2])

The prince even loathed the exercise of independent judgement, as Castiglione suggested via the story of an engineer tortured to death because he substituted his own better judgement for his prince's (Castiglione 1976: 131–3 [Bk. 2]). The courtier had to assume that his conversation must aim to improve a wicked lord, who might kill him if he realised the courtier was playing the schoolmaster. Castiglione emphasised the general vice of princes by a pointedly half-hearted demurral: 'that would be too plainly to argue that the rulers of our time are all wicked and evil; and this is not so, since we find some good princes among them.' A pious exclamation then pointed out what must be expected: 'We must pray God . . . to grant us good ones, for once we have them we have to put up with them as they are' (Castiglione 1976: 130 [Bk. 2]). Castiglione's advice, as Machiavelli's in *The Prince* (1532), was for the world as it is. The courtier's conversation should improve the prince, but he faced the almost insuperable task of how to address that conversation to a prince who personified the corruptions of power, will, isolation and passion, and who was likely to lash out and destroy any would-be and self-appointed tutors.

The fable of the *Courtier* described the courtiers' behaviour and speech throughout as conditioned by a desperate powerlessness. On the one hand, the necessary freedom to engage in the conversation that generated *The Courtier* proceeded from the withdrawal of Urbino's prince, Duke Guidobaldo, whose authority had been deputed to the relatively powerless Duchess, and further subdeputed to the court lady Emilia Pia. Duke Guidobaldo's infirmity had in any case constrained him, even when present, to substitute the exercise of (conversational) taste for the lordly (oratorical) action that was his proper métier (Castiglione 1976: 42–3 [Bk. 1]; Hanning and Rosand 1983: xi–xii). Yet even if he was absent in person, the prince's power was pervasive: 'Castiglione's speakers obfuscate but never ignore the prince's decisive influence while they fashion their model individual' (Javitch 1983: 18). The courtiers' speech to one another was governed by prudence and discretion, those attributes of a world governed by power and will (Martin 1997: 1324). In the presence of the prince, the courtier needed to bend himself in all indifferent circumstances to his whims: 'I would have our courtier try to act in this manner, even if it is against his nature, in such a way that whenever his prince sees him he believes that the courtier will have something agreeable to say' (Castiglione 1976: 125 [Bk. 2]). His art of decorum was formed entirely by the desire to please his prince. So was the courtier's *mediocrità* (moderation, temperance), since earnestness was intolerable to the prince, and so too were his modesty, reticence and nonchalance, since these were the best means by which to gain favours and preferment from the prince. The courtier would always behave toward the prince with 'reverence and respect'. He could not be distinguished from a mere flatterer by his behaviour, but only by his motivation to pursue an ultimately virtuous end (Castiglione 1976: 55 [Bk. 1], 125–7 [Bk. 2]; Javitch 1983).

The courtier's conversation and conversational behaviour likewise had to accommodate the need to please the powerful prince, even as he sought to lead the prince to virtue. The courtier would use all his flattering decorum to entice the prince toward 'continence, fortitude, justice and temperance . . . and with all the means these gentlemen have suggested, he will be able to keep the prince continually absorbed in innocent pleasures, while also, as I have said, always accompanying these beguilements with emphasis on some virtuous habit' (Castiglione 1976: 288 [Bk. 4]). Castiglione justified this procedure by arguing that

> the irrational part of the soul precedes the rational . . . So we must take care for the body before the soul, and the instincts before the reason . . . moral virtue is perfected by practice. First, therefore, the prince should learn through practice, which will make it possible for him to govern the instincts that are not yet susceptible to reason and through this commendable discipline direct them towards a worthy end. (Castiglione 1976: 305 [Bk. 4])

The courtier's *sprezzatura* – artful artlessness, nonchalance – also helped to lull the prince's suspicions. (*Sprezzatura* will play a crucial role in the ensuing narrative; the concept will appear again and again, the perpetual sign of the presence of the conversational mode.) The ancient orators had 'tried hard to make everyone believe that they were ignorant of letters . . . For if the people had known of their skills, they would have been frightened of being deceived'; neither must the prince suspect that the courtier played upon him (Castiglione 1976: 67 [Bk. 1]; cf. Shakespeare 2008: *Hamlet*, 1744 [III.2.322–3, 329–31, 334–41]). The courtier's conversational style was governed throughout by the need to make the prince virtuous unawares.

We should also note that the virtues that the courtier sought to instill in the prince were his own conversational virtues. The similarity began with the means by which such virtues were to be acquired: just as the courtier's virtues could be acquired by practice, so the virtues the courtier sought to instill within the prince required 'skillful practice' in addition to 'reason' (Castiglione 1976: 55–7 [Bk. 1], 291–2 [Bk. 4]; Richards 2003: 52–5). The prince, moreover, should be taught particularly to value temperance, which 'is wholly perfect and especially appropriate for men who rule, for it gives rise to many other virtues' (Castiglione 1976: 295 [Bk. 4]). Among these associated virtues Cicero had included decorum, which embraced 'the exercise of restraint and self-control on the one hand, and the deportment of a free spirit on the other'. Cicero also explicitly had applied temperance to conversation:

> Just as throughout our daily lives the golden rule is to avoid mental disturbances when excessive emotions fail to obey the reason, in the same way our conversation ought to steer clear of such feelings. We should not allow anger to obtrude, nor any grasping or world-weariness or any such attitude to surface. Above all we should demonstrate our apparent respect and affection for those with whom we are to converse. (Cicero 2000: 34, 46 [1.96, 1.136])

The prince, in other words, was to be taught those quintessentially conversational virtues of decorum and temperance (Richards 2003: 55–64). Furthermore, he was to be taught temperance in preference to continence – and the contrasting descriptions of the two virtues paralleled precisely the relationship of peaceful, rational conversation to violent, passionate rhetoric (Castiglione 1976: 294 [Bk. 4]).

The courtier's conversation began by simultaneously appearing to treat the prince as an equal while actually bending in all ways to the prince's superior will. Yet the skilful courtier reversed these terms so as to make the appearance a reality: while appearing to bend he led the prince to acquire the courtier's conversational virtues and speak to his courtiers as an equal. By doing so, the prince became amenable to reason and willing to act upon its dictates. Reason, the icon of the courtier, insinuated itself into the compelling power of sovereignty, for the prince would 'follow wherever reason may lead with the utmost docility'.

Castiglione recognised a danger here: to endow the prince with conversation, the rational speech of the powerless, risked making him powerless by removing the passions that motivated his will to act. 'And if they [the emotions] were killed altogether, this would leave the reason weak and languid, so that it would be ineffectual, like the captain of a ship that is becalmed after the winds have dropped' (Castiglione 1976: 295 [Bk. 4]). Castiglione's analysis of temperance, however, provided an answer to this danger:

> I did not say that temperance completely removes and uproots the emotions from a man's soul, nor would it be well to do so, since there are good elements even in the emotions. But what it does do is to make what

> is perverse and opposed to right conduct in the emotions responsive to reason . . . So when they are moderated by temperance the emotions are conducive to virtue, just as wrath strengthens fortitude, hatred against wicked men strengthens justice, and the other emotions strengthen other kinds of virtue. (Castiglione 1976: 295 [Bk. 4])

The prince's passions were not to be killed off; rather, just as reason should inform the passions so as to inform the will, so conversation would moderate the prince's passions so that they motivated him to act according to reason. Castiglione reinforced this parallel with his advice that the prince should choose both a council of nobles and a council of the people to counsel him; the shift from counsel to councils restated in terms of political structure the conception that (noble) reason and (popular) passion should inform the (princely) will (Castiglione 1976: 306 [Bk. 4]).

Castiglione also provided the motivation that led the courtier to try to improve the prince. Let us recollect that the friendship of equals underpinned conversation and its search for truth. Yet the courtier and the prince were not equals and not friends. The prince, moreover, was a monster of power, who might well destroy the courtier if the courtier misstepped for a moment in his conversation with the prince. Duty and the love of good might well motivate an exceptional courtier to engage in conversation with the prince:

> He himself will know great contentment, when he reminds himself that he gave his prince . . . what is doubtless the greatest and rarest of all human virtues: the manner and method of good government. This alone would be enough to make men happy and restore to earth the golden age which is said to have existed once, when Saturn ruled. (Castiglione 1976: 296 [Bk. 4])

Yet what of the ordinary courtier, the courtier as he was?

Castiglione's conception of (Platonising) love provided the answer. Love was the ultimate of all virtues, but some in particular were conversational: 'You join together the things that are separate, give . . . likeness to the unlike, friendship to the hostile . . . make us so attuned to the celestial harmony that there is no longer room within us for any discord of passion' (Castiglione 1976: 342 [Bk. 4]). In general, to 'be in love' was among the preferred 'accomplishments of the courtier', and in particular, the courtier was supposed to love his prince: 'I want the courtier . . . to devote all his thought and strength to loving and almost adoring the prince he serves above all else, devoting all his ambitions, actions and behaviour to pleasing him.' This met with the immediate counter that this was nothing more than flattery, but Castiglione insisted that this was a true love. The courtier 'can obey and further the wishes of the one he serves without adulation, since I am referring to those wishes that are reasonable and right, or that in themselves are neither good nor bad' (Castiglione 1976: 125 [Bk. 2], 322–3 [Bk. 4]). The courtier's love was bound up centrally with the conversational complex of apparent obedience grounded in reason and virtue. Indeed, the contrast with flattery indicated that the courtier's love was tied to the education to virtue. Flatterers corrupted the prince 'by telling lies that foster ignorance in the prince's mind not only of the world around but of himself. And this can be said to be the greatest and most disastrous falsehood of all, for an ignorant mind deceives itself and lies to itself' (Castiglione 1976: 286 [Bk. 4]). The truly loving courtier – a flatterer transformed into a friend, a man seeking power transformed into a man seeking truth – presumably should instead enlighten his prince.

That the courtier's love should proceed toward the prince's education and virtue found support in Castiglione's other discussions of the nature of love. While Emilia Pia early described love as the lover's submission of his will to his beloved's, Bembo's later exaltation of Platonic love gave this submission of the will an admonitory cast:

> [T]he lover should honour, please and obey his lady, cherish her even more than himself, put her convenience and pleasure before his own, and love the beauty of her soul no less than that of her body. He should, therefore, be at pains to keep her from going astray and by his wise precepts and admonishments always seek to make her modest, temperate and truly chaste; and he must ensure that her thoughts are always pure and unsullied by any trace of evil. (Castiglione 1976: 266 [Bk. 3], 335 [Bk. 4])

Such true love again was described as an education to virtue: 'And thus, by sowing virtue in the garden of her lovely soul, he will gather the fruits of faultless behavior and experience exquisite pleasure from their taste. And this will be the true engendering and expression of beauty in beauty, which some say is the purpose of love' (Castiglione 1976: 335 [Bk. 4]). The courtier's love also sparked in the prince himself the courtier's accomplishment of being in love. Castiglione praised the reciprocities of virtuous love between a courtier and a lady, and he likewise praised the reciprocal love of the prince and his people: the prince 'should love his country and his people', and as a result he would 'be not merely loved but almost adored by his subjects' (Castiglione 1976: 260–4 [Bk. 3], 307–8 [Bk. 4]).

Bembo's discourse of Platonic love generally identified the beautiful with the good and the ugly with the evil (Castiglione 1976: 324–42 [Bk. 4]). What was attractive in the prince was the innate virtue he already possessed. This loveable virtue was an innate potentiality, but it must be educated: 'although the potentiality for these virtues is rooted within our souls, it often fails to develop unless helped by education' (Castiglione 1976: 291 [Bk. 4]). In this education, 'skillful practice and reason . . . purify and enlighten the soul by removing from it the dark veil of ignorance, which is the cause of most human errors.' The ignorance that reason pruned was the passions: 'removing the thorns and tares of our appetites which often so darken and choke our minds' (Castiglione 1976: 291–2 [Bk. 4]). The courtier, using an identical agricultural metaphor, cultivated the prince's soul (Castiglione 1976: 296 [Bk. 4]). It was the beauty of the prince's soul, moreover, that inspired the courtier to dare to cultivate it further:

> Certainly, once the flame of love is burning in a man's heart, cowardice can never possess it. For a lover always wishes to make himself as lovable as possible, and he always fears lest some disgrace befall him which can make him less esteemed by the woman whose esteem he craves; neither does he flinch from risking his life a thousand times a day in order to deserve her love. (Castiglione 1976: 255 [Bk. 3])

This love, in marked contrast to those passions and appetites that made men ignorant, led toward enlightenment: love proceeded from, united and proceeded to 'beauty, goodness and wisdom' (Castiglione 1976: 341 [Bk. 4]). Castiglione noted of beloved women that 'in our understanding of great issues far from distracting us they awaken our minds, and in warfare they make men fearless and bold beyond measure'; love generally, by analogy, both sharpened knowledge and tied it to action (Castiglione 1976: 255 [Bk. 3]). We divested ourselves of the earthly dross of passion as we ascended toward the highest and most abstract of loves, angelic and divine – but we were not reduced to the cold bones of reason, but rather burnt and consumed by love's fire (Castiglione 1976: 336–42, esp. 340 [Bk. 4]). We kissed a monster, with our flesh and spirit, and hoped that a prince would return our kiss: 'a kiss is a union of body and soul . . . but the rational lover knows that although the mouth is part of the body nevertheless it provides a channel for words, which are the interpreters of the soul, and for the human breath or spirit' (Castiglione 1976: 336 [Bk. 4]).

Yet not all princes had the virtue that both inspired such love and rendered them capable of being instructed to further virtue by the courtier: some 'are like barren soil and by nature so alien to good conduct that they can never be taught to follow the right path' (Castiglione 1976: 318–19 [Bk. 4]). Even Plato, that icon of philosophy, could not educate every prince – and Castiglione explicitly suggested this as a model.

> And subsequently when Plato found the tyrant Dionysius to be like a book full of lies and errors, and so in need of complete erasure rather than any change or correction, he decided that it would be useless to use the method of courtiership in this instance, because Dionysius was so soaked in tyrannical habits that there was no remedy for it. This example should be followed by our courtier too, if he happens to find himself in the service of a prince whose nature is so degraded that he is completely sapped by evil, like consumptives by their disease. In such a case he should withdraw his allegiance in order to escape blame for the misdeeds of his master and not experience the anguish felt by all good men who serve the wicked. (Castiglione 1976: 322 [Bk. 4])

Love could motivate the courtier, but only where the prince was loveable, capable of virtue. This love would not always operate and would not always succeed. This caution was the counterpart to Castiglione's rhapsodies of love, and to their application to the courtier's speech to the prince. Conversation led naturally to the reciprocities of love and virtuous political action – but not inevitably. We will consider the implications of this 'not inevitably' as our narrative progresses.

Castiglione thus articulated the maximum possible pessimism about human nature that could overlap with any belief that eloquence and wisdom, speech and truth, could be united. The power of Castiglione's conversational *exemplum* was that it showed how speech could motivate reason and virtue under the worst possible circumstances, and still aspire toward the ideals of speech and action. Furthermore, this conversational mode could motivate precisely because it remained a mode of rhetoric, aimed at the passions, albeit in the service of reason.

Castiglione in this fashion united into a new synthesis the different aspects of the Renaissance humanist conception of the relationship between conversation, oratory and political action. In part, Castiglione recapitulated the shift between the (relatively) free late Roman Republic and the despotisms of Renaissance Europe by reassigning to conversation the persuasive function Cicero had assigned to oratory. Where a free man used oratory to persuade a mixed public, the constraints of despotism now required a courtier to use the blandishments of conversation to persuade his prince: '*delectare* [delight] assumes the functional priority in courtiership that *movere* is granted in oratory' (Javitch 1978: 40). Thus far Castiglione articulated the Renaissance humanist impulse to have conversation speak *instead of* oratory. But Castiglione, as he provided the basic motivation for the courtier's speech, also made the relationship of the courtier to the prince, of conversation to oratory, a loving relationship – *vera amicitia* in Platonic accent. Here Castiglione articulated the parallel Renaissance humanist impulse to have conversation speak *to* oratory. Castiglione's synthesis rested on the power of loving conversation to make oratory itself more conversational in nature: oratory remained, but conversation lovingly burned away its vices.

Castiglione's thought articulated the Renaissance humanist thematising of the oscillation between Cicero and Plato, between the particular and the universal, between the exemplary and the ideal. Just as Castiglione set up a dialectic between the exemplary realm (Urbino) and the ideal one (Plato's Republic in Renaissance garb), so his exemplary conversation acted as the mode of inquiry by which to discover and link the ideal speech situation and proper political action. 'So let us first try to discover him [the perfect courtier], since I defer to him as regards both this subject and all the other matters that concern a good ruler' (Castiglione 1976: 301 [Bk. 4]). He did so with his usual irony, of course, and embedded doubt of the effectiveness of conversation within *The Courtier* itself: 'If I had the favour of some of the rulers I know, and were to speak my mind freely, I imagine I would soon lose it again' (Castiglione 1976: 302 [Bk. 4]). And, as noted above, some unlovable rulers were so steeped in vice that even conversation was useless. Nonetheless, the dynamic created by conversation's loving speech to oratory remained the sole means Castiglione offered as a way to approach the yoked ideals of proper speech and proper action.

This Castiglionean solution would offer challenges as well as models to the future. One aspect was the nightmare: what of the prince so incapable of virtue that the blandishments of conversation would not make him good? This was a vision of a political world that could not be wooed by reason. The silent alternative, of course, was for the loving courtier to force the beloved world to virtue – for conversation to dictate to reason, if somehow a means to power could be found. Another challenge lay in Castiglione's reliance on the motivation of a Platonic love to activate his system. This Platonic motivation sat uneasily in an intellectual construct so largely constructed among the amoralities of prudence and decorum – an ungrounded element among the grounds of self-love and will. What if there were no such Platonic love? Then one must either reconstruct the activation of the passions on different grounds, or motivate conversation without recourse to love at all. Both of these solutions would be considered in later centuries. The Platonic goal would remain the distant ideal that justified the terrified obsequies of conversation with the world, but the means would all become worldly.

Those worldly means offered a final challenge to the Castiglionean solution – that they would decay into worldly ends, mere oratory. Consider *sprezzatura*. Canossa in the *Courtier* cites his model Antonius in Cicero's *De oratore* for the concealment of artistry, but, as Richards notes, Canossa also followed Antonius in saying that the way to acquire such an art is by making it so habitual a practice as to be indistinguishable from nature (Cicero 1967: I, 241–3 [2.14.59–60], 305 [2.34.147], 309 [2.36.153]; Castiglione 1976: 66–8 [Bk. 1]; Richards 2003: 48–55). Just as for Machiavelli the reputation of power was the thing itself, so for Castiglione (by this reading) the appearance of spontaneity was the thing itself. Yet (as noted above) Petrarch's epistolary model of spontaneity by its polish encouraged a slip back toward the manipulations of oratory, while *sprezzatura* also could be taken as merely the dissimulative appearance of spontaneity, no more than a Renaissance variation on the old oratorical conceal-ment of art (*Rhetorica* 1954: 251 [4.7.10]; Burke 1996: 30–2; Plett 2004: 78, 193, 453, 457). *Sprezzatura*, as indeed the entire model of courtly speech and behaviour proffered by Castiglione, could aspire to and embrace a conversational ethic – but it could also forward a mere oratorical style. Indeed, Castiglione's conception of courtly behaviour also drew upon Cicero's prescription to the orator on how to dispose of his body while speaking (Cicero 1967: III, 177–79 [3.59.220–3]; Rebhorn 1993: 251–2). The polemical dismissal as mere dissimulation of the Castiglionean courtly tradition, described below, registered its characteristic weakness: the courtier who did not aim to be a true conversational friend to the prince perforce decayed into a mere oratorical flatterer.

The courtly art of conversation

In the centuries following the publication of the *Courtier*, Casti-glione's book would provide an enduring model for the behaviour of the nobility across more than half of Europe. The *Courtier*'s influence was exerted both directly and indirectly – the latter via republications, translations, imitative courtesy-books such as Giovanni della Casa's (1503–56) *Galateo* (1558) and collections of maxims on proper conversation and decorum such as the anonymous *Maximes de la bienséance en la conversation* (1618). As Burke notes:

> Castiglione's *Courtier* . . . was translated into French and Spanish in the 1530s, and later into Latin, English, German and Polish. By 1620 more than fifty editions of the text had appeared in languages other than Italian. By the early seventeenth century, Della Casa had been translated into German, Spanish, and twice into Latin, and Guazzo into English, Latin, Dutch and twice into French. (Della Casa 2013; Burke 1993: 102–3; 1996)

More generally, Mee describes how handbooks of conversation flourished

> in sixteenth-century Italy, seventeenth-century France, and eighteenth-century England. In the first half of the eighteenth century, more than fifty works on conversation were published in Britain alone . . . Although they often translated continental treatises, where the British handbooks and essays differ most from their Italian and French antecedents is in their aversion to 'ceremony and compliment'. (Burke 1993: 98–112; Mee 2011: 5)

The *Courtier* and its derivative successors together disseminated a culture of noble decorum, positively described as manners and negatively as hypocrisy, dissimulation and unscrupulous ambition. While Castiglione thus influenced the nobility throughout western Europe, and would begin to attract an audience among a broader social range, we shall focus here particularly upon the evolution of the Castiglionean tradition in seventeenth-century France. It was within France that the Castiglionean tradition would mutate and ultimately provide the matrix for the development of the *salons* and all the traditions of conversation that would flow therefrom.

Castiglione's influence at first spread slowly in France, for it did not align easily with several entrenched attitudes toward speech. To begin with, a more martial conception of speech still held sway in French manuals of behaviour at the opening of the seventeenth century. Nicholas Pasquier (1561–1631) in *Le Gentilhomme* (1611) divided his section on speech ('Parler') into warnings to be moderate in one's speech, to control one's words, not to speak ill of other gentlemen – and followed up on that last injunction with later sections on

'Injures', 'Desmenti', 'Combats', 'Querelles', 'Seconds' and 'Duelz' to itemise what might follow upon speaking ill of another.[3] 'Parler' only briefly descanted upon the pleasantries of conversation:

> La reputation ne s'acquiert seulement par la candeur de nostre parler et de noz actions: mais encore par gentillesse, qui par une bien-séance des choses bien composées en soy leur rend une beauté parfaite. Quand il procedera en sa conversation de ceste grace, nul ne pourra mal parler de luy, ains donnera subject à tous d'en bien penser. (Pasquier 2003: 188–90, 203–13; Goldsmith 1988: 17–18; Goodman 1994: 115)

Pasquier's focus upon speech that might offend – how to avoid it, how to respond to it with honourable violence – told of a French nobility less domesticated than their Castiglionean equivalents, whose later addiction to rapier wit would reflect an earlier addiction to the rapier itself. The association of conversation with reputation and speech more broadly with the duel – the subjects of opinion, in the world of rhetoric and power – likewise reflected a nobility retaining power, an ability to act in the world of power, and hence a concern for the effect in that sphere of words, actions and appearances. The shift away from a martial conception of speech would parallel the taming of the nobility in seventeenth-century France.

Indeed, in tandem with the absolutist progress, Castiglione's influence on French manuals and practice became pervasive during the seventeenth century. We should note, however, a dual inheritance: Castiglione's influence extended itself both in the hierarchical mode of civil behaviour focused upon the court and in the more egalitarian mode focused upon the *salons*. Gordon exemplifies these contrasting approaches by reference to Antoine de Courtin's (1622–85) *Nouveau traité de la civilité que se practique en France* (1671) and Dominique Bouhours' (1628–1702) *Remarques nouvelles sur la langue française* (1675). Courtin provided directions for all permutations of civil interaction within the hierarchy: 'We are not to take snuff before any person of honour (who has priviledge to take it before us) unless he presents it himself; in that case it is lawful; and though we have an aversion to it, we are bound to accept, and pretend to make use of it.' Bouhours, meanwhile, mocked Courtin's elaborations, concluding with the *bon mot* that 'This new master even teaches a method for paying compliments in all kinds of encounters, and the only thing that is left for him to do is to give rules for how to laugh correctly' (D. Gordon 1994: 86–9; Courtin 1671: 54; Bouhours 1675: 34, translated in D. Gordon 1994: 87). In the court, Castiglione's influence

spread via guides that emphasised how the properly amoral courtier should bend himself to the king's will, among them Eustache de
Refuge's (1564–1617) *Traité de la cour* (1616) and Faret's *L'honnête
homme* (1630) (Refuge 1622: II, 13–51 [5–11]; Faret 1632: 169–97;
D. Gordon 1994: 120–2). Refuge epitomised this advice by repeating the '*Maxim*, which is not onely knowne, but too much practised by those, who frequent the Courts of Princes, insomuch that
whosoeuer will bee welcome to them, must conforme himselfe to
second their inclinations and passions' (Refuge 1622: II, 13–14 [5]).
We shall not here focus on this tradition, which would produce no
such revolutionary fruit as its *salonnier* rival. In the *salons*, however,
Castiglione's thought began a radical and enduring transformation
in rebellion against this courtly mode.

The salons

The *salons*, although they received their classic articulation in
seventeenth-century France, had roots tracing back to sixteenth-century
Italy – whose mixed-sex social gatherings, proto-*salons*, I have noted
above. In the first instance, the widening of Italian literary *accademias*
to allow for female presence, however peripherally and intermittently,
provided a first precedent for mixed-sex gatherings devoted to conversational inquiry. In Siena, the home of the *veglie*, the all-male literary
academy called the Intronati included women (albeit only as an audience) for the performance of plays and for public lectures, especially
vernacular lectures performed during Carnival with a female audience in mind, on topics such as love. The interest of some Intronati
in fostering the the talents of literary minded Sienese women, such
as the poetess Laudomìa Forteguerri, also registered some parallel
willingness to include women in joint literary endeavour. The Paduan Infiammati academy had a similar relationship toward women –
although the Florentine Fiorentina academy, since quasi-official, more
rigorously excluded women. Looking forward a little, the highly literary and learned actress Isabella Canali Andreini (1562–1604) was
a member of the *Accademia degli Intenti di Pavia* from 1601 to her
death in 1604. In the latter half of the *cinquecento*, various Italian
literary academies continued the pattern of rare female membership,
of limited social integration with women and of very limited literary
outreach toward female authors. Yet these academies' core concern
remained the classics, and their meetings frequently were conducted in
Latin; given the gendered access to classical learning, these attributes

in themselves placed women on the margins (Campbell 2006: 51–2; Fahy 2000; Robin 2007: 128).

In France, meanwhile, Henri III's Académie du Palais included some women during its brief existence, but this provided no precedent for widening female participation in future French academies after its decease (Harth 1992: 17). Academies in sixteenth- and seventeenth-century France remained largely male institutions, housed in libraries rather than *ruelles*, and often bearing the approving stamp of royal charter (Beasley 2006: 76–88; Harth 1992: 16). The quasi-official nature of the French academy, as with the Florentine one, would seem to correlate with greater exclusion of women.

The more direct forebears of the *salons* were those mixed-sex gatherings that were more largely populated by women and themselves hosted by women – also called *accademias* and *académies* to begin with, but soon to diverge sharply in their membership and their mode. Through the 1530s and 1540s, several Italian noblewomen linked by blood or friendship – Vittoria Colonna, Costanza d'Avalos (d.1560), Giulia Gonzaga Colonna (1513–66), Renata di Francia, the Duchess of Ferrara (1510–74) and Maria d'Aragona d'Avalos (1503–68) – hosted or cohosted circles of men and women whose discussions, albeit more theological in subject matter and tone than would be typical of Paris, prefigured the form of the *salon* (Robin 2007: 3, 14, 17–18, 27, 31, 35–39). As a register of the expanding social matrices of these Italian *accademias*, the Jewish Sarra Copia Sulam (1592–1641) hosted an *accademia*, a literary salon, about 1620 in Venice (Harrán 2009: 34). More generally, courtesans such as Tullia d'Aragona and Veronica Franco were explicitly attested as taking part in proto-*salon* social settings. Overall, the ideal of the silent woman was on the decline in *cinquecento* society, and the articulate woman, participating in a discussion of both men and women, was at an increasing premium – if often as a diversion rather than as a seriously regarded interlocutor (Smarr 2005: 99–101, 104–5).

In sixteenth-century France, meanwhile, Louise Labé (*c.*1524–66) (possibly a courtesan, certainly a published author of poetry and literary polemic) appeared in Lyons' proto-*salon* literary society, Catherine des Roches and her mother hosted what the historian Sçévole de Sainte-Marthe (1571–1650) called an 'Académie d'honneur' in Poitiers, and Catherine des Roches also articulated the tone of the proto-*salons* in her writings (Campbell 2006: 97–122; Harth 1992: 17–18; Smarr 2005: 99). Early in the seventeenth century, the Vicomtesse d'Auchy (1570–1646) and Madame Marie des Loges (1585–1641) hosted highly academic (in the modern sense) *salons*, sites of serious debate, not least on literary topics (Beasley 2006: 22; Timmermans 1993: 71–84). Catherine de Vivonne, the Marquise de Rambouillet, fleeing from Henri IV's (1553–1610; r.1589–1610) goatish barracks of a court, set up the first proper *salon* (*ruelle*) in 1608; thenceforward the *salon*, genteel, conversational and *honnête* – a term whose meaning and significance we will examine shortly – may be said to form a continuous tradition. Aside from the Marquise, there were more than fifty *salonnières* hosting *salons* in sevententh-century Paris alone (Beasley 2006: 22–3, 27; Maland 1970: 45).

Although the *salons* diverged from the academies, they were regarded in seventeenth-century France as complementary rather than as rival institutions, with significantly overlapping member-ships – at least so far as the men were concerned, for academicians frequented *salons* even if *salonnières* found scant welcome in the academies. Not incidentally, *ruelle* and *académie* were used more or less interchangeably to refer to *salons*; Saint Simon referred to the Hôtel de Rambouillet as 'une espèce d'académie de beaux-esprits'. The *salon* and the academy (in the modern sense) did not as yet claim to be more than the appropriate locations and milieux for different modes of discourse (Saint Simon 1890: 385; Beasley 2006: 24, 27–8; Harth 1992: 16–18, 20).

For all that they were complementary, however, the gendered delimitations retained great force. As noted above, *salonnières* were little welcomed in the academies, and *salonnières* were not meant to intrude upon the discussion appropriate to academies. The Vicom-tesse d'Auchy attempted to be a *femme savant*, *erudit* rather than *honnête*, with a *sénat feminine* to play the role of an academy; for her pains she was attacked savagely for unwomanly aspiration. Marie de Gournay's (1565–1645) similarly academic *salon* would likewise meet with ridicule and hostility. A *salon* that confined itself to general discussion of literary subjects was acceptable; a female academy, detailed and erudite, and aspiring to the mode of rational-ity gendered as male, was not. Jean Chapelain's (1595–1674) praise to Guez de Balzac in 1638 of the Hôtel de Rambouillet contrasted with his critique of the Hôtel d'Auchy:

> People there [at the *salon* at the Hôtel de Rambouillet] don't speak with erudition, but with reason and there is nowhere else in the world with more good sense and less pedantry. I say pedantry, Monsieur, which reigns at court as well as in universities, and which can be found among women as well as men . . . the hotel de Rambouillet is the antithesis of the hotel d'Auchy. (Chapelain 1638: 215–16, translated in Beasley 2006: 25; Harth 1992: 28, 33; Pekacz 1999: 83, 139)

Madeleine de Scudéry, via her literary alter ego Sapho, found it necessary to warn that an educated women needed to conceal her learning
(Scudéry 1972: 359; Harth 1992: 52).

These gendered limitations of the role of women noted, the role
of women in the *salons* was central – as was the role of conversation
with women. Faret in *L'honnête homme* (1630) already dedicated a
substantial portion of his work to conversation with women. Faret
noted both the allure and the difficulty of such conversation:

> [I]t is the sweetest and most pleasing, so it is the most difficult and nice
> of all others. That of men is more vigorous and free, and therfore for
> that it is commonly fild with more solid and serious matters, they doe
> lesse obserue the faults which are committid, then women, who hauing
> more actiue spirits, and not charged with so many things, do presently
> dicouer the least errours, and are more eager to lay hold of them.

Such conversation civilised: 'The first care that he must haue that will
frequent the Cabinets and companies, and accustome himselfe to the
entertainment of women, is to make his presence pleasing.' But Faret
also noted that the presence of various unpleasant people at court
meant that the best conversation with women was often to be found
elsewhere:

> [M]any times wee are forced to fixe vpon such a person whose encoun-
> ter out of that place we would fly, as from a pestiferous person. We
> must then descend vnto the City, and obserue who are those amongst
> the women of quality which are esteemed the most honest women and
> where are the best assemblies, and if it may be, draw himself into their
> companies to the end they may haue an interest to do vs good offices,
> with all those that come to visite them. (Faret 1632: 338–60, esp. 338–9,
> 347–8, 349–50; MacLean 1977: 146)

Jacques Du Bosc (d.1664) in *L'honneste femme* (1633) – and it is
worth noting that the *honnête femme* made her appearance in print
almost immediately after the *honnête homme* – likewise stated that
'I know many of them [women], who can judge so well of things
of this nature [history, philosophy, poetry, etc.], and are so eminent
in them, as their conversation serves as a School to the best wits,
so as many excellent Authors consult with them, as with Oracles,
holding themselves happy in their approbation and praises' (Du Bosc
1639: second pagination, 25; MacLean 1977: 149). The anonymous
author of the first part of 'Si la conuersation des Femmes est vtile
aux Hommes', published in *Recueil General des Questions Traitees*

dans les Conferences du Bureau d'Adresse (1646), wrote of the high character and the usefulness (for men) of mixed conversation:

> Ainsi voyez-vous que le discours de deux hommes finit souue[n]t par vne facheuse contestation, l'vn ne voulant point ceder à l'autre en pointe d'esprit, comme le parler des femmes aboutit ordinairement à vn caquet inutile: Mais ceux des hommes auec les femmes sont volontiers pleins d'vn respect, d'vne douceur & d'vne defference mutuelle . . . Comparez-moy la rusticité honteuse d'vn païsan qui n'ose leuer les yeux deuant vne fille auec la gentillesse d'vn courtisan accoustumé à cajoler les dames, & vous connoistrez par là si leur conuersation est inutile aux hommes. (Recueil 1646: 111–12; MacLean 1977: 146)

Étienne Martin de Pinchesne (1616–80), in his Preface to Vincent Voiture's *Oeuvres* (1650), wrote that, 'This beautiful half of the world, with the ability to read, also is able to judge as well as we are, and today is the master of men's glory' (De Pinchesne 1654: sig. õ^r, translated in Beasley 2006: 21). The Marquise de Lambert, in her *Sur les femmes* (1727), said that, 'A very respectable author [Nicolas Malebranche (1638–1715)] endows women with all the attributes of the imagination: that whch concerns taste is, he states, within their competence, and they are judges of linguistic perfection. This advantage is not a minor one' (Lambert 1746: 18, translated in Beasley 2006: 36). The emergence of women as full partners in the world of *salon* conversation may be measured in two images: the Italian iconographer Cesare Ripa (1555–1622) depicted Conversatione in his *Iconologia* (1603) as a good-humoured young man, but Cesare Orlandi's updated edition of *Iconologia* (1765) depicted 'Conversazione Moderna' as a young male and female couple in a *salon*. As Miller notes, 'The woman is being helped on to a throne by the man, and holds a scepter in her right hand topped with an all-seeing eye' (Ripa 1625: 132; Ripa and Orlandi 1765: 64; Miller 2000: 62, 74). Conversation here was the Queen of the World – as Rhetoric had been, as Opinion would also be – and it was the female partner in conversation, pre-eminently the *salonnière*, who was the avatar of conversation, *regina mundi*.

Before proceeding with the narrative of the *salons*, we should pause to examine the concepts of *honnêteté* and the *honnête homme*, to which we have already made multiple references. Slightly before the extraordinary spread of the term that was to come in the ensuing generations, Montaigne in 'Of three kinds of association' provided a late-sixteenth century usage much in accord with the later connotations of the term:

The men whose society and intimacy I seek are those who are called talented gentlemen [*honnestes et habiles hommes*]; the idea of them spoils my taste for the others. It is, if you take it rightly, the rarest type among us, and a type that is chiefly due to nature. The object of this association is simply intimacy, fellowship, and conversation: exercise of minds, without any other fruit. In our talks all subjects are alike to me. I do not care if there is neither weight nor depth in them; charm and pertinency are always there; everything is imbued with mature and constant good sense, and mingled with kindliness, frankness, gaiety, and friendliness. It is not only on the subject of lineal substitutions or the affairs of kings that our mind shows its beauty and strength; it shows it as much in private confabulations . . .

If learning is pleased to enter our conversation, she will not be turned out; she will not be magisterial, overbearing, and troublesome, as she usually is, but subordinate and docile. We seek only to pass the time; when it is time to be instructed and preached at, we will go and find her on her throne. Let her stoop to our level just for once, if she will; for, useful and desirable as she is, even so I suppose that in a pinch we could perfectly well get along without her completely, and do our business without her. A wellborn mind that is practiced in dealing with men makes itself thoroughly agreeable by itself. Art is nothing else but the list and record of the productions of such minds. (Montaigne 2003: 758–9)

These terms, *honnêteté* and *honnête homme*, became far more current about the beginning of the *salon* tradition. We may especially note the importance of Faret's *L'honnête homme* (1630), which widely disseminated Castiglione's prescriptions under the term *honnêteté* – *honestas*, appropriate behaviour, given sufficient diacritical marks to pass muster as naturalised in France. Faret detached gentlemanly conduct both from the martial vocation and from military imagery, redefined it to include social interaction and conversation between men and women, and promoted a more conversational mode of sociability, marked by egalitarian reciprocity and the supple yielding to one's interlocutor. This conversational mode, however, took place only within a confined social milieu of *honnête gens*, separate from the sphere of studied *complaisance* at the court and attractive precisely because it offered nobles a temporary escape from the pressures of courtiership:

Without doubt it is a troublesome constraint for a free minde to be often among such different humours, and so contrary to his own, and how sufficient and pleasing soeuer he be, it is a difficult thing, but in the end it will ingender waywardnesse, to counterfeit himselfe in this manner, and to torture himselfe so often. But when he finds himselfe in the company of honest men, who, like himselfe, shall haue all the parts of generosity, he may fully recompence his bad houres. He may there with all liberty suffer his inclinatio[n] to work, and open his minde vnto the bottome, without any feare that his apprehensions shold be crossed: for that virtue being generally equall, it makes the opinions of those which follow it comformable. O what a pleasure doth a good minde feele, when he encounters others of the same temper; and how imperfect are all other ioyes in regard of his, which is so much the more pure and sweet, for that he knowes better then any man, that the contentment which he inioyes, is the soueraigne good of life. (Faret 1632: 267–70 and *passim*; Fader 2003: 10–11; Goldsmith 1988: 19–22)

The Guazzian note of civil conversation as a pressure, which we will discuss below, found a notable resonance here. Here also was a first attempt to find a place from which to escape from the pressure of courtiership, to escape from the court.

Honnêteté not only was an attribute of the *honnête femme*, as noted above, but also centrally involved the relation of men to women. The *honnête homme* had to know how to talk and to behave with women. The perfection of this orientation of the *honnête homme* to his female counterparts was the ideal of *galanterie*, which came to signify particularly refined *honnêteté*, and in particular the exercise of these manners toward women, often with a sense of refined love. By the time Bishop Pierre-Daniel Huet (1630–1721) wrote his *Traité de Pierre-Daniel Huet sur l'Origine des romans* (1669), he ascribed the comparative excellence of the French novel

> to the Refinement and Politeness of our Gallantry; which proceeds, in my Opinion, from the great Liberty which the men of *France* allow to the Ladies . . . in *France*, the Ladies go at large upon their Parole; and being under no Custody but that of their own Heart, erect it into a Fort, more strong and secure than all the Keys, Grates, and Vigilance of the *Douegnas* [*Dueñas*]. The Men are obliged to make a Regular and Formal Assault against this Fort, to employ so much Industry and Address to reduce it, that they have formed it into an Art scarce known to other nations.

Yet *galanterie* also retained as an undertone its original connotation of trickery and deceit, often with the signification of seduction or other behaviour intended to entice women into sexual relations. The double meaning of *galanterie* conveyed the fragility of women's place in the world of conversation: even in the *salons* that were the redoubt of such female speech, to speak with men exposed women to rut masqued as reason (Huet 1715: 138–40; Viala 1998).

Returning to the main narrative of courtly conversation and the *salons*, Courtin's *Nouveau traité de la civilité* (1671), whose focus upon court civility presupposed the court's distinctly inegalitarian hierarchy, elaborated upon this Castiglionean *mentalité* by allowing polite conversation to take place among social unequals speaking as equals and by defining the emerging concept of civility in terms largely synonymous with decorum – albeit with an emphasis on free and natural manners as against the stiffly formal (Courtin 1671, esp. 6–7, 146–7; Goodman 1994: 116–17; Goldsmith 1988: 22–3). Courtin's innovations proceeded from his broadening of his intended audience beyond Faret's narrow and homogenous elite closely associated with the court, and his parallel broadening of civility to constitute a pleasing style that the *honnête gens* could use in any milieu: although it was prudent to give the greatest men the highest civilities, 'we must retain in our memories these general precepts of Civility; that thereby we may be enabled to pay every man his due respect upon all occasions, and do all things according to our own choice and discretion.' Conversation itself, which now became the most prominent of the arts of civility, was now defined by the exchange of words itself rather than (as in Pasquier) by those who spoke: 'all humane conversation passes betwixt Equals, or Superior and Inferior' (Courtin 1671: 18, 144–5; Goldsmith 1988: 22–4). Perhaps the most important thing to note here is the abstraction of the idea of conversation from a circle of homogenous noblemen. This conceptual shift rendered conversation universally accessible, but also required in tandem the supposition of social unequals speaking as equals – the supposition that such could be done. Such an achievement therefore became a problematic of the realm of conversation: if it could be done at all, how was it to be done? We may note that this *speaking as equals* is similar to, but not identical with, that Guazzian civil conversation we will examine below, where unlike spoke to unlike.

In this increasingly conversational milieu, French manuals of conversation now began to focus upon the *salons*, whose guests included select nobles and, increasingly, members of the bourgeoisie, and which would become the social nexus for this egalitarian mode of *honnête* conversation for much of the seventeenth and eighteenth centuries (Craveri 2005). In Méré's *Les conversations* (1668), for example, Méré parted from his contemporaries who identified *le grand monde* with the court and its milieu, and instead defined it as a separate world of the best people and the best conversation, self-generated by its own speech and sociability, and, as distinct from Castiglione, self-contained rather than oriented toward the prince

(D. Gordon 1994: 101–2; Goldsmith 1988: 24–5; Méré 1930: 111, translated in D. Gordon 1994: 102). Clear, conversational language accommodated itself to its listeners so as to promote their mutual understanding, so as in turn to produce a refined pleasure in the conversation itself. Both a distinctly Castiglionean nonchalance and the exercise of spontaneity (in contrast to the rigidities of court hierarchy and ceremonial) likewise were intended to promote such conversational pleasure (Méré 1930: 105; D. Gordon 1994: 102–4).

Madeleine de Scudéry, who herself ran a polite and conversational salon, likewise theorised about salon conversation in works written from the 1640s to the 1680s. Scudéry also preferred a socially exclusive (if not exclusively aristocratic) homogenous elite; she took conversation between unequals to decay into unsociably practical ends. Their mode of conversation, as with Méré meant to promote the pleasures of conversation, aimed to sustain the conditions of conversation, not least by the mutual compliments that defined and preserved the conversational elite's cohesion. So Amilcar caps Valeria's definition of conversation in 'On Conversation' with a compliment: 'without giving you the trouble of speaking any more upon conversation or making rules for it, it is enough to admire your [conversation], and to do as you do, to merit the admiration of all the earth' (Scudéry 2002: 90). Yet while Scudéry promoted conversation as a rhetoric especially appropriate and congenial to aristocratic women, socially disjunct both from professional (practical) affairs and from politics, she also thought that any topic – including politics – might be discussed, so long as the discussion was handled in an appropriately conversational tone, to the enjoyment of all (Donawerth 1998: 184–6; Goldsmith 1988: 26, 41–75; D. Gordon 1994: 107–10). In this ideal conversation, Scudéry wrote in 'On Conversation':

> I think that nothing is precluded; that [conversation] ought to be free and diversified, according to the times, places, and persons with whom we [converse]; and that the secret is to speak always nobly of small things, very simply of great things, and graciously of the subjects of polite [conversation], without transport and affectation. Thus, though the conversation ought always to be both natural and also rational, I must not fail to say, that on some occasions, the sciences themselves may also be brought in with a good grace, and that an agreeable silliness may also find its place, provided it be clever, modest, and courteous. So that, to speak with reason, we may affirm without falsehood that there is nothing that cannot be said in conversation, provided it [is managed with] wit and judgment, and one considers well, where one is, to whom one speaks, and who one is oneself. Notwithstanding that judgment is

absolutely necessary in order never to say anything inappropriate, yet the conversation must appear so free as if we rejected not a single one of our thoughts, and all is said that comes into the fancy, without any affected design of speaking more often of one thing than another. For there is nothing more ridiculous than those people who have certain subjects on which they talk wonders, and otherwise say nothing but foolishness. So I would have it appear that we do not know what we are going to say, and yet that we always know well what we are going to say. For if this course is taken, women will not be inappropriately learned, nor ignorant to excess, and everyone will say only what ought to be said to make the conversation agreeable. But what is most necessary to make it sweet and entertaining is that it must have a certain air of civility, which absolutely precludes all bitter retorts, as well as anything that might offend decency. (Scudéry 2002: 89)

Scudéry significantly contrasted her description of *salon* conversation with the court-centred alternative. In 'De la Politesse', Scudéry praised *politeness*, that new refinement upon civility, for its reciprocity so unlike the speech mode of tyrants, of monologic power:

It [politeness] is never to express a rude or uncivil word to anyone. It is to say nothing to others that you would not wish them to say to you. It is the absence of a wish to be the tyrant in conversation, to be always speaking without letting those to whom you are speaking speak themselves. (D. Gordon 1994: 110; Scudéry 1684: 1: 126–7, translated in D. Gordon 1994: 110)

On the one hand, this contrast presented a very subdued challenge to the sovereign, by arguing the value of those conversational virtues that took place outside the sovereign's political realm (D. Gordon 1994: 110–12). On the other hand, Scudéry did not (unlike Méré) take the conversational world to be self-contained. Rather, just as Duke Guidobaldo's offstage presence generated the conversation of the *Courtier*, so the king's offstage presence, as perfect model and lodestar, generated the conditions that made *salon* conversation possible. (Scudéry 1684: I, 181, 184–5; Goldsmith 1988: 54–62, 66). Scudéry's acknowledgement of *salon* conversation's debt to the king took the form of the most gross flattery: 'Pour moy, repliqua galamment Celinte, ce que fait LOUIS LE GRAND m'occupe si agreablement & j'en ay l'esprit si remply, que je ne m'informe point de ce qui s'est fait avant luy.' Speech appropriate to the despot's court was still the necessary boundary condition to the reciprocal autonomy of *salon* conversation (Scudéry 1693: 129; Goldsmith 1988: 62–4).

Méré and Scudéry were not alone (although neither were they uncontested) in their praise of 'anticourtly and egalitarian' conversation and manners; theorists of this mode also included Jean-Baptiste Morvan de Bellegarde (1648–1734) and François de Callières (1645–1717) (Bellegarde 1688, 1707, 1717; Callières 1692, 1717; D. Gordon 1994: 95–100, 105–7). Bellegarde, the author under Louis XIV (1638–1715; r.1643–1715) of numerous and influential guides to *politesse*, associated politeness with the personal merit of good manners – especially skill in conversation – rather than with blood or rank: 'We decide upon any one's merit according as he acquits himself in common conversation: We do not always take the pains to search into his good or bad qualities, but we are apt to judge of him according to his personal recommendations of himself to the world' (Bellegarde 1765: xi–xii; D. Gordon 1994: 95–7). Bellegarde defined politeness in terms that continued the association with decorum, as '*a certain Attention, that both from our Words and Behaviour, makes others satisfied with us and themselves*' (Bellegarde 1717: I, 28). Bellegarde likewise valued free and easy conversation that promoted the pleasure of conversation itself, mutually supportive rather than competitive, egalitarianly reciprocal and spontaneous (Bellegarde 1688: 242, 269–70; 1765: xiii–xiv; D. Gordon 1994: 97–9). Bellegarde echoed Scudéry as he opposed conversation to the image of tyrannical monologue – although unlike Scudéry, Bellegarde affirmed the independence of conversation from sovereign authority:

> This is, however . . . the privilege of conversation: everyone is permitted to say his sentiment, and we must suffer with good grace those who contradict us. It would be an insupportable tyranny to wish to fix the thought of others under one's own opinion. Kings, with all their authority, have no jurisdiction over the sentiments of their peoples, and individuals should not claim to be more absolute than kings. (Bellegarde 1688: 285–6, translated in D. Gordon 1994: 98–9)

At the very apogee of the Sun King, a veritable manifesto for the independence of the sphere of conversation was now in print.

This crystallisation of the *salons* from the court and separation of conversation from the basilisk presence of the Prince enlarged to *Roi-Soleil* was not simply a continuation of the sixteenth-century parlementary elite's opposition to the royal court. Some of the elegance of seventeenth-century court style indeed derived from the chaste Atticism of the court's old enemies, the defeated and now much assimilated *parlementaires*. Guez de Balzac in particular played a notable role in transmitting and transmuting the old *parlementaire* eloquence to the *honnêtes hommes* of the court and *salon*, and the Attic note was reinforced from the 1650s onward, as the French shifted from the Italianate models of Castiglione and della Casa to imitations of ancient Rome (Borgerhoff 1968: 22–4; Carr 1990: 7–8; Fumaroli 1983: 270–2; Viala 1998: 22–3; and see Borgerhoff 1968; Croll 1969; Maland 1970: 202–26). Yet as we shall see below, the *parlementaires* were more directly influential upon the parallel evolution of the Republic of Letters. To the extent that France's courtiers and *parlementaires* can be distinguished from one another, the *salons* were more the creation of the former than the latter.

Yet if the *salons* were not precisely oppositional as the *parlementaires* had been, their emergence still registered deep anxiety about the unchecked sovereign, who was the realisation of the nightmare adverted to in Castiglione. What if the prince did not listen to the courtier at all? In absolutist France the *Roi-Soleil* monopolised power to an extraordinary extent: the courtier had – 'no power at all' is perhaps a simplification, but 'remarkably little power' is accurate enough. The nobility's ability to utter political speech had been increasingly constrained as monarchs gained power through much of early modern Europe; in late seventeenth century France, it scarcely existed at all.

As always, such a sweeping statement requires qualification. We may note, for example, that Pierre d'Ortigue, sieur de Vaumorière (*c*.1610–93), in *The Art of Pleasing in Conversation* (1688) played delicately with the idea that freedom of speech actually existed in Louis XIV's France. His character Belise even argued that one could discuss first principles of the polity:

> *Philemon.* Have you not apprehension that your Policy will make us exceed the bounds which our Entertainments prescribe?
> *Belise.* Why fear it? Do we not grant the liberty of talking on all sorts of subjects? And would you have the principles of a Science omitted, which places a man above multitudes of others? I hope the Company will punish you, and oblige you to speak the first your opinion on the Monarchical State. Do you prefer it to other Governments?
>
> (Vaumorière 1691: 319–20)

Yet even if we set aside the distinctly tactful nature of the ensuing conversation (Vaumorière 1691: 320–3), to speak more concretely of domestic politics remained dangerous. Vaumorière rationalised the reserve necessary for conversing on such subjects:

> *That State affairs must be discoursed of with great reservedness* . . .
>
> Dorante.   We may speak our opinions touching the Government of other Nations with as much boldness as *Belise* does, supposing we understand the Interests and Maxims of them. But when we are pleased to discourse on the State under which we live, we should never extend our conjectures too far, nor affect to appear too penetrating. [Because things need to be done secretly, without 'uncertain conjectures'.] Persons of good sense never talk of these matters but with great modesty, and for my part I can only forgive this imprudence in Persons who are incapable of making any reflexion. How many do we hear every day censuring that Government which they do not understand, they make War and Peace according to their Fancy, and wholly busie themselves in hearing News, and modelling the affairs of State, when their Families at home are perhaps ready to starve for want of Bread.
>
> (Vaumorière 1691: 314)

The rationalisation, however, retained the nub of the matter: 'Persons of good sense never talk of these matters but with great modesty.' Even flattering counsel was, if not absolutely fruitless, cast upon extraordinarily stony ground. As Fénelon noted in 1713:

> RHETORICK has no such Influence [as it had among the ancient Greeks] now among us. Publick Assemblys meet only for Shows, and Ceremonys. We have scarce any Remains of a powerful Eloquence, either of our Old Parliaments, or our General States, or our Assemblys of Chief Persons [De Notables]. Every thing is determin'd secretly in Cabinet-Councils, or in some particular Negotiation. So that our People have no Encouragement to use such Application as the *Greeks* did, to raise themselves by the Art of Perswasion. The publick Use of Eloquence is now almost confin'd to the Pulpit, and the Bar. (Fénelon 1722: 215)

Let Fénelon be our witness: the political realm, the realm of oratory, was extraordinarily (if not absolutely) circumscribed in Louis XIV's France.

Louis' courtiers turned to the *salons* to talk to one another not least because there was no longer any point to speaking at a court where the absolutist state claimed a monopoly of political deliberation. And if they could not speak to any purpose of politics – although, as Scudéry noted, politics remained a potential topic of conversation – then they would focus on other spheres: as Gordon notes, 'reason and speech turned toward philosophical, aesthetic, and moral concerns that were unrelated to the direct exercise of sovereign authority' (D. Gordon 1994: 40–2, 51–73). As early as 1663, François Hédelin, the abbé d'Aubignac (1604–76) in his *Troisième Dissertation concernant le Poème dramatique en forme de remarques* framed the divide between politico-religious constraint and freedom of mind in all other spheres:

> I know very well that as regards the truths of Religion which are mat-
> ters of faith and the maxims of Politics which concern the Sovereignty
> of our Kings there is no liberty for the individual to challenge or even to
> entertain doubts; one must maintain a humble belief and an inviolable
> respect; silence itself does not suffice; one must always bring to such
> matters a submission of the heart. But everything else is a quarry open
> to the force of our minds; one can write everything one thinks, including
> even the most extravagant visions. (D'Aubignac 1663: 15, translated in
> Kaiser 1989–90: 186)

'Everything else' soon found its home in the *salons*. *Salons* become the home of collaborative literary criticism, associated with common sense (*sens commun*), (female) taste (*goût*), *plaisir, sentiment naturel, sensibilité, bon sense* and *je ne sais quoi* (Lambert 1748: esp. 146; Beasley 2006: 31–6). Moral self-improvement became part of the point of conversation: René Bary (d.1680) in the 'Advis av Lectevr' of his *L'Esprit de cour, ou les conversations galantes* (1662) justified by its moral end his sometimes all-too-gallant garland of conversations (Bary 1662: [iv–v]; Goldsmith 1988: 26). And in this realm of con-versation, the conversationalists insisted that some last inch remained to them. Let us recollect Bellegarde: 'Kings, with all their authority, have no jurisdiction over the sentiments of their peoples . . . This is, however, the privilege of conversation: everyone is permitted to say his sentiment.' The *salons* were a far redoubt from the power of the court, but one from which new campaigns could be begun.

And, indeed, the counter-offensive began as soon as the Sun King passed away. The conversational culture of the *salons* and the aris-tocracy had maintained itself throughout in their various redoubts – and it made a vital conquest in the person of Philippe d'Orléans (1674–1723), Regent for the young Louis XV from 1715 to 1723. Not only did the grip of the court culture relax with the death of Louis le Grand, along with the extraordinary royal monopolisation of discourse and judgement, but also the Regent's court itself began to patronise the *honnête* culture of the *salons* (Crow 1985: 39–41, 72). The pretentions of the prince were still great thereafter, but even in Versailles the tide had begun to turn.

The Republic of Letters

We must now shift our focus to that great conversational alternative to the court, the Republic of Letters, and go back some centuries. Let us recollect that the medieval world had institutionalised friendship within the corporate structure of Christianity, and also revived the practice of personal friendship; *trecento* and *quattrocento* humanists combined these precedents with their own revival of a classical conception of friendship. So (Hyatte concludes) Giovanni Boccaccio (1313–75), Laurent de Premierfait (*c*.1370–1418) and Leon Battista Alberti all conceived of friendship as 'a like-minded group within a quasi-institutional structure', rather than just a pair of friends, or a pair of friends with God (Hyatte 1994: 194–5, summarising 137–94). Such institutionalised forms of friendship came to include the *Respublica literaria*, the *quattrocento*'s new collective term to refer to the community of leisured friends engaged in humanist pursuits.

Fumaroli summarises the early history of the Republic of Letters thus: Franceso Barbaro apparently coined the phrase *Respublica literaria* in a 1417 letter to Poggio Bracciolini – an exercise in epideictic praise – congratulating him for discovering Quintilian's *Institutes* and other manuscripts. It seems to have been conceived of as a variation of the Augustinian *Respublica christiana* – a community of reason and love working toward the common good, rather than (as in the earthly *res publica*) the satisfaction of passion and interest. Certainly a great many humanists themselves held clerical benifices, and hence membership in the *Respublica christiana*: this too likely would have furthered the identification of the *Respublica literaria* as a scholarly aspect of the *Respublica christiana*. That Barbaro coined *respublica literaria* in 1417 may also indicate an association with the egalitarian and anti-papal emphasis that the Conciliarist movement, then at a high point, gave to the authority in the *Respublica christiana* of the clergy and laity in universal council. On the other hand, *literaria* necessarily implied membership in an elite – the literate, whose literacy was the prerequisite for that productive, studious leisure (*otium*) capable of forwarding the common good (Fumaroli 1988: 136–41).

Together, these last two associations would appear to have given to the *respublica literaria* the social and genre characteristics of *sermo*: leisured, elite and internally egalitarian participants in a joint inquiry into truth. Meanwhile, the word *respublica* emphasised the orientation toward the *res publica* that this new articulation of humanist *sermo* inherited from *Respublica christiana*.

The collective *Respublica literaria* of the Italian *quattrocento* was linked in part by letters in a humanist mode, practised by ever-wider circles as the humanism of Petrarch and Salutati institutionalised itself as an educational programme first in Italy and then north of the Alps. These letters associated the *Respublica literaria* with both *sermo* and oratory, since the *quattrocento* humanist letter, inheritor of both the classical letter and the medieval *ars dictaminis*, retained affiliations to both modes. The *Respublica literaria* was also constituted by the reborn academies (Burke 1993: 114–15), whose conceptual associations reinforced the linkages between the *Respublica literaria* and *sermo* (Fumaroli 1988: 135). These academies were modelled ultimately upon Plato's Academy, itself a gathering of *philoi* (friends), guided (as etymology would suggest) by *philia* (Hutter 1978: 93, 99). The *quattrocento* academies thus in their very name drew on ancient notions of friendship, albeit perhaps with a Platonic cast. The *quattrocento* academies acquired further associations at least as Ciceronian as Platonic: leisured discussion among learned – scholarly – friends, in 'a villa in the country, equipped with a library.' In a medievalising touch, academies also drew upon the example of the pious confraternity, with its banquets and feasts to honour God by pastime with good company: the *quattrocento* academy was as much a confraternity of learning as a Greek Academy reborn. At the end of the *quattrocento*, Marsilio Ficino gave the Academies a new and persistently Platonising cast, but their procedures and methods of communication generally retained the *quattrocento* reliance upon the Ciceronian matrix of leisured conversation. For the *Respublica literaria* as a whole, constituted both by letters and by academies, the Ciceronian *sermo* in its various modes remained the dominant element, albeit with strong elements of Platonism and of the *ars dictaminis* (Fumaroli 1988: 135–6, 145–6).

The *Respublica literaria*, not least in the academies, had remained a creature of actual conversation as much as of letters during the *quattrocento*. Charles VIII's (1470–98; r.1483–98) invasion of Italy in 1494, however, played havoc with the functioning of the Italian academies, and generally served to disrupt the Italian scene. Of necessity, the *Respublica literaria* fled from physical, private sites – and reconstituted itself as a reborn Republic of Letters within the abstracted and necessarily public world of print, of printshops, printers and readers of printed books (Fumaroli 1988: 147–9). The Republic of Letters severed its close association with the actual conversations of gentlemen at leisure in their gardens; from now on, its primary 'conversation' would be the written and printed communications of scholars dispersed across the breadth of Europe.

Here we may turn to Erasmus, who nearly re-created the Republic of Letters in his image. Erasmus' influence was ambiguous in the extreme. On the one hand, as Remer notes, Erasmus applied the conventions of *sermo* to his scholarly correspondence and learned discussion, and thereby not only deepened the association of *sermo* with the Republic of Letters but also helped expand the scope of the Republic to become more nearly coterminous with all scholarly and philosophical communication. Remer particularly notes the implications of Erasmus' choice of examples in his discussion of scholarly letters in *De conscribendis epistolis* (1522), which 'permit Erasmus to imply something about the *decorum* of scholarly discussion, implications that echo the Ciceronian model of *sermo*' (Remer 1996: 87–90).

On the other hand, as Struever points out, Erasmus' indiscriminate use of *sermo* to all his correspondents in the Republic of Letters – his calculating simulation of familiarity, whose manipulative ends were by definition unfriendly – to a considerable extent dessicated the Petrarchan mode of shared, friendly inquiry, making of it a routine communication within an academy also hardening, and by this transformation further hardened, into an institution whose annealing friendship was pro forma. The Erasmian *sermo* now also emphasised its political function, a polemical tool to forge a humanist party against the scholastic establishment more than a universal invitation to join in a mode of shared inquiry (Struever 1992: 46–7, 51–5). The connotation within the Republic of Letters of the *consensio studiorum* altered in tandem with this shift. Where for Petrarch consensus had emphasised the common feeling of friendship that underpinned the search for truth, the Erasmian consensus emphasised the already formed common opinions of the humanist intellectual party (Kaufman 1981: 148–51; 1987: 29; Struever 1992: 28, 54). *Sermo* now permeated and constituted the Erasmian Republic of Letters, but it was a conversation where, behind the pro forma protestations of friendship, was an ever colder love of truth wielded polemically by a learned faction.

The Republic of Letters so far had proceeded at some distance from the political world; this now would change. Rinuccini and Guicciardini had formulated a conception of free conversation in exile from the tyrannical city. This conception now became a model available to both the intellectual and the rural gentleman in their several retreats, by way of the tradition of Erasmus, Lipsius and Montaigne. This tradition, which prescribed both style and substance, united anti-Ciceronian stylistic restraint (a plainness allied with that of conversation) to the autonomy shared by those whose distance from kingly power allowed them a modicum of independence from that power. Lipsius' neo-Stoic dialogue *Constantia* (1584), for example, echoed Rinuccini and Guicciardini as it articulated a tense dialectic between leisured conversation and the ordinary world of politics. Yet in Lipsius' rendition, the garden, the traditional home of conversation and friendship, was a refuge from the world of politics, a place to practise constancy against inevitable misfortune, without even Rinuccini's or Guicciardini's hopes of a return to the city (Lipsius 1594: 66–7 [2.3]). The tyrant monarch's triumph was total, and the gentleman would have to abandon politics more or less completely. In this retreat from political hope, from the realm of oratory, the gentleman came closer to the scholar in the character of his conversation and friendship. The courtier bent to the monarch's will; the country gentleman and the scholar alike retreated from it.

In sixteenth-century France, as Fumaroli summarises matters, these traditions became even more closely united. The Parlement of Paris' rearguard aspiration to deliberative powers and a political role found articulation in a chastely, austerely eloquent style, deliberative rather than epideictic, forceful rather than pleasing, whose contrast with the court's Ciceronian style was the literary register of the Parlement's resistance to the court's encroaching power. *Parlementaires* thus aligned with the *érudits* of the Republic of Letters in France in this anti-courtly simplicity – and, indeed, sponsored them as well. The *parlementaire* simplicity was oratorical and the *érudit* simplicity conversational – but this distinction became less relevant as the *parlementaires* were driven from power. The fragile and vulnerable Republic of Letters in self-defence generally had allied itself with powerful rulers up until this point – and scholar-courtiers would never go out of style – but the centre of gravity of the Republic of Letters' French chapter now shifted toward the *parlementaire* redoubt. Bound together by a sincerity and a plain style the antitheses of courtly ignorance and flattering dissimulation, at the end of the sixteenth century French scholarship and science found themselves the *foederati* of the *parlementaires* (Burchell 2007: 59–70; Fumaroli 1988: 150; 1983: 259–60, 262–4, 268–9; Yeo 2009: 13).

This alliance was not entirely fortunate for the French Republic of Letters, for the reduction of Parlement to a judicial role in the seventeenth century swept up the plainly conversational scholars in the wake of the decline of the plainly eloquent *parlementaires* (Fumaroli 1983: 269–70). Seventeenth-century French scholars, as the *parlementaires*, perforce made measured obeisance to the style of the court. The new scholarly style synthesised an elegance and a taste that combined scholarly force with courtly *douceur* – and indeed looked to the court for the ultimate judgement as to whether a scholar had achieved true style or remained a mere pedant (Fumaroli 1983: 270–2). Scholarly civility likewise came to be embedded within the matrix of noble sociability – the *honnêteté* of the *salons* – albeit scholarly civility retained a greater emphasis on self-improvement and a more Stoic cast (Miller 2000: 68–70). The effect of this transformation was all the greater on the French Republic of Letters because it truly was becoming a *French* Republic: the old Latin-speaking *Respublica litteraria* was splintering, transforming into overlapping, but increasingly distinct, literary republics of Latin, French and local vernaculars (Yadav 2004: 55–109). France's Republic of Letters, increasingly isolated within France, orbited ever closer to the immense attraction of the court and the nobility. The milieu of the *salons* revived in new guise a home for the French Republic of Letters that preserved a certain distance from the court and its tyrannies of action and speech – but at the price of subordinating the Republic of Letters to noble conversational norms instead.

This incipient union of the *salons* and the Republic of Letters received a check in the two generations between 1680 and 1720, when the Republic became in some measure an opponent of France and the French court. A significant portion of the animating spirit of the Republic of Letters in these decades derived from the Protestant opposition to Louis XIV's France, with the prominent role played by the Huguenot exiles – Pierre Bayle (1647–1706) being the archetypal example – and the prominent locus of the Netherlands both reflecting this general Protestant opposition (Marshall 2006: 469–501; Ultee 1987: 104–5). Various aspects of the Republic of Letters therefore now became charged as attributes in increasingly explicit distinction to the practice of the absolutist court. Toleration, for example, inherited by this generation from Erasmus via its revival by seventeenth-century Arminians, now became almost a weapon against obscurantist foes, an abstraction of those conversations that cured prejudices. The enduring aspects of the Republic of Letters (Dibon 1978; Goodman 1994: 15–18; Marshall 2006: 501–2, 509–14) – its very status as a republic, its egalitarianism – likewise were emphasised for their sharp contrast to the theory and practice of the court (Marshall 2006: 507, 514, 519). This sense of opposition between the Republic of Letters and the court was not unprecedented: earlier in the seventeenth century, Agostino Mascardi (1590–1640) had argued that tyrants feared academies because they instituted conjoined wisdom and friendship, whence came a solidarity that the tyrants took as threats to their rule (Miller 2000: 64). But this topic became a pre-eminent theme *c.*1700, in the generation of Bayle, as did a polemical orientation against the claims of the court and the absolutist state.

At the same time, the hollowing out of friendship and familiarity became even more noticeable in the Republic of Letters than it had been at the time of Erasmus. As early as the middle of the seventeenth century, it was a commonplace – and an all-too-accurate one – that in the Republic of Letters *amicitia* was variously utilitarian, hollow, dissimulating, Machiavellian and treacherous – in a word prudential, and so unfitting a home for *vera amicitia* that it was no wonder that such friendship ultimately took refuge in the sincere exchange of sentiments rather than the scholarly exchange of thoughts (Keller 2011). The increased size of the Republic of Letters, to some low thousands of readers across Europe, eliminated neither actual personal contacts nor the reciprocal exchange of letters – but it did attenuate their importance, as the Republic of Letters became something closer to an anonymous public (Marshall 2006: 506, 508; Ultee 1987: 98, 100–1). The new Republic of Letters was becoming ever more impersonal.

The Republic of Letters, as such, was at its most influential between 1680 and 1720, perhaps precisely because it did maintain so hostile and distinct an identity from the French monarchy and court (Ultee 1987: 96). Its influence began to wane again precisely with the coming of European peace: as the wartime generation that sustained the separation of *savants* from the court of Paris came to an end, the Republic of Letters rapidly collapsed once more into the rule of the *salons* (at least by comparison with the anti-court polemics of the pre-1720 and the post-1750 generations) (Ultee 1987: 104–8).

For a generation, the Republic of Letters would submit itself to *salon* requirements of civility – and indeed, civility and politeness now more than ever became virtues in the Republic of Letters (Marshall 2006: 516–18). Seen from a different perspective, the conventions and the judgements of the *honnêtes gens* and the *salonnières* expanded by way of the realms of manuscript news letters and printed journalism to absorb and to regulate the Republic of Letters (Goldsmith 1988; Goodman 1994: 117, 119). The mixture of the spirit of the Republic of Letters and of the *salons* found marvellous expression in the 'Preface' to the *Bibliothèque italique* (1728), where one could read 'that justice, equity & politeness, whose rules people of Letters must follow, more exactly than anyone, are so opposed to partiality, that an Author delivered over to this base passion is surely sullied in the spirit of *honnêtes* people of all Communions' (*Bibliothèque* 1728: xxii, translated in Goldgar 1995: 99).

Yet this confluence of the *salons* and the Republic of Letters was uneasy and partial: the oppositional Republic of Letters could not be submerged entirely within the *salons*. Bayle, following his own practice and (presumably) preference, emphasised discourse as contention. In '*the Common-Wealth of Learning* . . . The Empire of Truth and Reason is only acknowledged in it; and under their Protection an innocent War is waged against any one whatever'. Likewise, Bayle wrote:

> Every body there [in the Republic of Letters] is both Sovereign and under every-body's Jurisdiction. The Laws of the Society have done no Prejudice to the Independency of the State of Nature, as to Error and Ignorance: in that respect, every particular Man has the Right of the Sword, and may exercise it without asking leave of those who govern. (Bayle 1735: 389; Marshall 2006: 519–21)

Bayle, in other words, conceived of discourse, and the search for truth, in agonistic or martial terms rather than in terms of the mutual search for truth in conversation. We may see in this a translation of the Hobbesian state of nature, *sans* Leviathan, to the Republic of Letters; we may also see a sublimation of the martial imagery of rhetoric prevalent in early modern Europe, an echo of *disputatio* and a revival of the wary friendlessness and impersonality of the seventeenth-century Republic of Letters. Furthermore, we may perceive in the contrast between the *salons* and Bayle a reiteration of the complex sixteenth-century oscillation between, and mutual interpenetration of, Ciceronian and Platonic conceptions of dialogue – although with *critique* substituting for Platonic dialogue in the polarity.

What is most to the point is that the Baylean tradition of *critique* ultimately would be unharmonisable with the assumptions of *salon* discourse (Koselleck 1988: 103–18). As Koselleck summarises the Baylean conception of critique:

> In Bayle, reason forever weighed the *pour et contre* against one another and ran up against contradictions; thus reason disintegrated, as it were, into a constant exercise of criticism. If criticism is the ostensible resting point of human thought, then thought becomes a restless exercise in movement. Criticism is the activity that marks reason as a factor of judgment, a constant goad to the process of pro and con. (Koselleck 1988: 108)

Or as Bayle himself put it, 'Human reason . . . is a principle for destroying not for building. It is fit only to start doubts, and to turn on all sides, in order to make a dispute endless' (Bayle 1738: 401; Koselleck 1988: 108 (note 28)). Baylean annihilations did not a pleasant *salon* conversation make.

Indeed, in its high road to the Physiocrats, the Republic of Letters would ultimately attempt to dispose entirely with the Ciceronian conception of *sermo*. The Baylean branch of the Republic of Letters would re-emerge from its Babylonian Captivity among the *salons*, to revive the old polarity in the new guise of the competing judgements of *philosophes* and *salonnières*. In this revived struggle, not incidentally, the *philosophes* would deal strongly in anti-feminine polemic, for the Republic of Letters in all its guises remained pre-eminently an association of men, in contrast to the mixed-sex *salons* (Marshall 2006: 508).

But if the world of the *salons* had subordinated the Republic of Letters to its judgements, some part of the Republic of Letters remained to animate the *salonnier* world, and the old complementary relationship between the two would no longer suffice. Consider the all-seeing eye of Conversation in Cesare Orlandi's updated edition of Ripa's *Iconologia* (1765). Miller takes the image to indicate 'that conversation demanded wisdom and prudence' (Ripa and Orlandi 1765: 64; Miller 2000: 74), but conversation's Sauronic gaze may also be understood as a universally applicable mode of inquiry. The mixed-sex world of the *salons* and the male world of the *philosophes* now contested for the same territory, Ciceronian conversations and Baylean critiques that both sought to make subjects of all the world.

Conclusion

The speech of the *salons* was in some ways a step backward from the speech prescribed by Castiglione: as in Cicero's time, conversation inhabited a realm distinct from that of oratory, where leisured aristocrats spoke of non-oratorical subjects at a distance from the the locus of power. Yet the *salons* had preserved or even intensified much of the Castiglionean constellation of innovations: the conversation of the *salons* was conducted between men and women, the purposes of these conversations included both moral improvement and delight, the characteristic style of these conversations was *nonchalance*, that Gallican *sprezzatura*, and the participants of these conversations were unequals speaking to one another as equals – although the unequals were no longer prince and courtiers, but rather aristocrats and the bourgeois. Furthermore, as Renaissance dialogue had become increasingly tense and challenging in its relation to the realm of oratory, so the conversation of the *salons* had also developed a rivalry with the king's tyrannising monologue: *salonnier* conversation now was a separate sphere from that of kingly oratory rather than a complementary mode. The hints that such conversation could address any subject at all therefore promised an open conflict with the realm of oratory such as had never existed in all of *sermo*'s long history.

The *sermo* of court and *salon* had been accompanied throughout by a competing social matrix of *sermo*, the Republic of Letters. In the Republic, conversation early had become more friendless and polemical than in the courts or *salons* – and the old *parlementaire* hostility to the court had infused the French Republic of Letters in particular with an open and polemical hostility to the French monarchy. Yet court, *salon* and Republic had coexisted passably well until the long crisis *c*.1700, when the Republic of Letters had gyrated between utter collapse into *salon* culture and utter rebellion from all conversationality, by way of the pure sword of reason, Baylean critique. One fraction of the shattered Republic remained within the *salons*, to infuse them with its spirit; another fraction revived in Baylean mode; both *salons* and Republic would enter the Enlightenment with ambitions to conquer the world of oratory, quarrelling fiercely over the division of the spoils.

But what would be the medium of communication by which *salons* or Republic would discourse upon this brave new world? To answer this question, we must go back to examine the humanist letter and its descendant, the newspaper.

Note

1. For the above paragraphs on Pontano, see Pontano (2008: esp. 81–2 [1.6–1.7], 87–91 [1.10], 92–7 [1.12–1.13], 120–2 [1.26], 134–42 [2.2], 173–8 [3.2–3.4], 191–2 [3.15], 224–6 [4.2], 231 [4.3.13], 233 [4.3.17], 266 [5.2.7]), Luck (1958: 115–20), Quondam (2007: 35–131).
2. Throughout this analysis of the *Courtier*, I assume a broad unity in Castiglione's thought, despite his deliberate resort to speaking through different characters, many of them mutually contradictory.
3. For the duel as the counterpart of civility, see Peltonen (2003).

Chapter 6

Letters

Introduction

Renaissance humanists happily classicised their letters so as to approximate more closely the familiar style of *sermo* – but Renaissance humanists also inherited the medieval tradition of *ars dictaminis*, which had shifted letters toward the public realm. Humanist letters therefore continued to depart from familiar style in practice – and in Erasmus' theory, he explicitly acknowledged that letter-writing was no longer entirely a genre of familiar communication. The Renaissance humanist letter became a mode of communication mediating between conversation and oratory, and firmly oriented toward the public world.

One descendant of the humanist letter would be the newspaper – that genre that Habermas took to constitute the public sphere. The newspaper, by way of the news letter, preserved aspects of the style of familiar communication, but, as it shifted in medium toward print, transformed into a distinctly persuasive communication between anonymous correspondents and anonymous recipients. Conversation had shifted in theory to be able to address the public world; the newspaper would become the genre that embodied a familiar conversation, universal and anonymous, that discussed all the subjects of the world.[1]

Humanist letters

Let us return to Petrarch. Petrarch had advocated a private, contemplative variation on humanist ethics, and this infused his letter-writing practice, but Salutati's discovery of further letters by Cicero (*Epistulae ad familiares*) in 1392 reoriented much of humanism, and not least the humanist letter genre, around the Ciceronian conception of the active life (*vita activa*) and civic virtue (Grendler 1989: 121; Moss 1996: 56; Witt 2003: 224–7, 244, 260, 265, 326–34). This civic ethos does not seem to have affected Salutati's own private correspondence, but in the following generations it slowly insinuated itself into the genre. In the early fifteenth century, the Ciceronian private letter, civic and humanist, began to be disseminated beyond its initial coterie of humanist devotees. Gasparino Barzizza (1360–1431), Vittorino Ramboldini da Feltre (1378–1446), Guarino Guarini da Verona (1374–1460) and their generation of north Italian educators created an enduring programme of humanist education centred upon an unprecedentedly intense study and imitation of the style, grammar, rhetoric and ethics of classical speeches and letters (Grendler 1989: 125–32; Mercer 1979: 1–2). Their schools continued to teach the dictaminal art of letter-writing, but in a heavily classicised format, in which Cicero and the familiar letter replaced the medieval authors (*auctores*) and the official letter as the model for imitation. Guarino assembled an anthology of fifty of Cicero's letters for his syllabus, while Barzizza's own collection of model letters, *Epistolae ad exercitationem accommodatae*, consisted of Ciceronian pastiches set in Republican Rome, which included discussions of a wide variety of affairs of state (Grendler 1989: 122–3; Mercer 1979: 94–7). In the mid and late fifteenth century, humanist education, Ciceronian familiar letters and the Ciceronian ideal of the active life would expand together throughout Italy and into northern Europe. Barzizza's *Epistolae* constituted a particularly influential vector of influence: they were much copied and much printed throughout the fifteenth century, both north and south of the Alps, incorporated into other influential works such as Carolus Virulus' (*c.*1419–93) *Epistolarum formulae* (Louvain, 1476) and Albertus de Eyb's (1420–75) *Margarita poetica* (written by 1459, printed 1472), and used as a textbook north of the Alps in the late fifteenth century (Grendler 1989: 133–5, 221; Mercer 1979: 6, 97–8; Monfasani 1988: 192–3, 198; Moss 1996: 56–7, 67–8).

To this influence we may add the humanists' tradition of publishing their own letter collections. Petrarch began this custom, and it became increasingly common throughout the *quattrocento*. The end of the *quattrocento* saw two shifts within the genre: from manuscript into print, and from Latin into the vernacular – the Italian familiar letter an innovation of Aretino's, at least by Aretino's account. Printed vernacular Italian letter collections were published in massive quantities during the *cinquecento*; Montaigne apparently owned nearly one hundred volumes of them. The popularisation of these letter collections, and their translation into print and the vernacular, constitute another area of the spreading influence of *sermo* in Renaissance culture (Eden 2012: 69–70; Rosenthal 1992: 119–20, 122).

By these metamorphoses, the Renaissance humanist private letter was established by about 1500 across Europe as a genre with a Ciceronian, civic imperative to engage in public affairs (Grafton 1991: 11–14); by 1600 it would be a pervasive presence in Europe's intellectual world. This was a radical change: in antiquity, the practice of a Cicero was not taken as the model of the multitude, and it was understood that private letters were generally intended to be limited in their subject matter to private concerns. Demetrius wrote that 'we should realize that there is not only an epistolary style, but also epistolary content. Aristotle, who seems to have been a most successful letter-writer, says in one of them: 'I am not writing to you about this; it is not a suitable subject for a letter.' A letter was supposed to express 'a simple topic in simple language', and simple language (and therefore, implicitly, the letter) was not appropriate for public matters: 'The faulty style which is akin to the plain is called aridity . . . Aridity of diction occurs when an important subject is described in trivial words, like Gadêreus' description of the battle of Salamis' (Grube 1961: 113–14). Practice might not exactly follow theory, particularly when a public man wrote private letters; both in antiquity and in medieval times, private letters often discussed public matters. Cicero went so far as to write that 'letter-writing was invented just in order that we might inform those at a distance if there were anything which it was important for them or for ourselves that they should know' (Cicero 1927–9: I, 101 [2.4.1]) – but this left ambiguous the crucial definitions of what was important for whom, and was in any case written in a private letter, not in a manual of rhetoric. Yet now Cicero's letters were the model for letter-writing, and every humanist letter-writer was taught to conceive of himself as a Cicero reborn. As a matter of theory as well as of practice, the Renaissance private letter came to be seen to have both the capability and the duty to include public affairs among its subject matter; by the sixteenth century, Juan Luis Vives put it explicitly that:

> Letters concerning others recount what has been done in some one else's home, or in another country, what someone said, did or thought. I use the word alien or foreign in the meaning, now too much accepted and approved by us, that was current among the pagans, who considered all public matters outside of their own affairs and those of their friends and of the state to be alien to them. How much more correct and closer to

nature the words of the old man in the play to the self-tormentor: 'I am a man. Nothing that pertains to man is alien to me.' (Vives 1989: 39)

Renaissance epistolary rhetoric not only tacitly allowed but also positively encouraged public subject matter within the confines of the private letter.

Renaissance epistolary rhetoric, in other words, inherited the *ars dictaminis*' conflation of the personal and the public letter, but in a more classicising mode. This inheritance was not foreordained: the revival of the familiar letter by Petrarch and his successors had suggested the distinct possibility that letters should forswear public and persuasive purposes. Yet this option would be largely foreclosed by the effects of Erasmus' *De Conscribendis Epistolis* (1522). This, the most influential of letter-writing manuals in the sixteenth century, solidified the tie of the classicising familiar letter to the realm of oratory.

Let us examine Erasmus' theory in detail. To begin with, Erasmus was aware of the definition of the ancient letter as a conversation *in absentia* and the stylistic prescriptions that followed from this definition:

> Even if the name 'letter' be restricted to interchanges between friends on private matters, it would still not be possible to settle on any fixed form. Nevertheless, if there is something that can be said to be characteristic of the genre, I think that I cannot define it more concisely than by saying that the wording of a letter should resemble a conversation between friends. For a letter, as the comic poet Turpilius skillfully put it, is a mutual conversation between absent friends, which should be neither unpolished, rough, or artificial, nor confined to a single topic, nor tediously long. Thus the epistolary form favours simplicity, frankness, humour, and wit. (Erasmus 1985: 20)

Nevertheless, Erasmus was aware that the actual contemporary uses of the letter – even, and notably, by humanists themselves – were not confined to the private realm, and were often used as a means of persuasion: he wrote that 'to them [letters] as to well-tried servants we entrust all our moods; to them we confide public, private, and domestic affairs', and that a letter for public purposes 'plays the part not of a speaker or messenger but of an advocate'. Simply by classifying letters into four types – persuasive (deliberative), encomiastic (demonstrative), judicial and familiar – Erasmus broke with the conversational definition of the letter (Erasmus 1985: 20, 71; Henderson 1983b: 339–40; 1992: 275).

But Erasmus not only said that letters could be public and persuasive but also that the art of persuasion applied likewise to familiar letters. As regards the introduction of a letter, he wrote that

> the freedom of a letter is such that one can take anything at all as one's starting-point as long as it is of such a nature as to prepare the recipient for what you have in mind . . . In a letter . . . an indirect introduction may be used whenever it seems desirable . . . [and] the introduction of a subject by artful dissimulation will not seem a faulty approach but a separate part of the letter. (Erasmus 1985: 75–6)

Erasmus concluded these strictures with the explicit statement that 'A proper beginning is determined according to precisely those principles which writers on rhetoric have handed down concerning the judicial class . . . modified to suit the peculiar characteristics of the letter' (Erasmus 1985: 76). Likewise he advised young students to 'be well acquainted with the nature, character, and moods of the person to whom the letter is being written' (Erasmus 1985: 74), and wrote of the letter of friendship that 'The conciliatory letter is that by which we insinuate ourselves into the good graces of a person previously unknown' (Erasmus 1985: 203). Erasmus' entire approach to letters was persuasive, both explicitly and implicitly.

Erasmus' letters persuaded by recourse to the rhetoric of Castiglione's perfect Courtier: Erasmus used the Castiglionean language of *artful dissimulation* and *insinuation*, and his advice to the young student was to approach correspondence as a courtier would approach his relationship with his prince. Furthermore, just as the ancients themselves applied the artful persuasions of rhetoric to their apparently plain and artless letters, 'in the end it is better for letters which seem at times to have no order at all, even where they are in fact carefully constructed, to conceal rather than reveal their order' (Erasmus 1985: 65; Henderson 1992: 277). *Sprezzatura*, in other words, also applied to letters. The letter was to be rhetoric that disclaimed rhetoric, a flatterer in the guise of a friend.

Erasmus opposed the ultra-Ciceronians' inappropriate and rigid insistence on applying the genre characteristics of private conversation, of *sermo*, to letters that were meant to be public and/or persuasive. Erasmus granted that Ciceronian style was still generally appropriate, and also that 'as a rule a certain simplicity of expression, provided it be elegant, is appropriate'. Yet in crucial distinction to the ultra-Ciceronians, those 'rhetoricians [who] have certain forms laid down, so that they believe not even a stroke can be altered without great peril to things human and divine,' Erasmus thought that epistolary style rather should adapt itself to both the 'subject matter and the circumstances and personalities of the correspondents'. Erasmus argued that 'one must consider the recipient. Some interpret a casual and unelaborated letter as a mark of contempt . . . there is no kind of ornament and elevation of style that is not proper to a letter, depending upon the recipient's personality and the content' (Erasmus 1985: 14–15, 72; Henderson 1983b; 1992: 276, 278). Where adaptation to recipient and subject matter conflicted with simplicity, Erasmus explicitly preferred the former: 'What one man finds obscure is perfectly intelligible to another . . . One must but take into account the subject and recipient of the letter' (Erasmus 1985: 18). To write a letter in Latin, after all, was to write in a language that had become the preserve of a limited elite; obscure, unknown or positively disliked by the multitude. 'Plain style' and Latin no longer plausibly overlapped, and to champion simplicity in Latin was oxymoronic (Erasmus 1985: 16–17).

Very significantly, Erasmus used the Plutarchian imagery of polypian flexibility and mutability (see Chapter 1 above); a letter's style

> should be flexible, and, as the polyp adapts itself to every condition of its surroundings, so a letter should adapt itself to every kind of subject and circumstance . . . At the same time the style will also keep in mind the writer and not merely the recipient or the purpose for which it was sent. Therefore it will play the part of a Mercury, as it were, transforming itself into every shape required by the topic at hand, yet in such a way that amid great variety it retains one feature unaltered, namely that of being always refined, learned, and sane. (Erasmus 1985: 19)

This polypian prescription had a further implication: when the letter was sent to an unknown recipient, one should use the model of oratory rather than of conversation. As Erasmus put it:

> [T]he orator cannot fully know the inclination and character of the judge, and when proceedings take place before several magistrates there is the added difficulty that what wins over one person may put off another because their dispositions differ. On the other hand, one who sends a letter to a specific individual can easily have certain knowledge of the things that usually influence him; even if, as is often the case, there is no close friendship between them, he may find out by diligent inquiry . . . Yet if one must write to someone of whom he has very little knowledge, the position of the orator will be more advantageous than that of the letter-writer. (Erasmus 1985: 74)

In effect, the rhetorical address to mixed audiences was the best approach to a letter to an unknown recipient, and the polypian letter-writer – the mutable, flexible equivalent of Machiavelli's Prince and Castiglione's Courtier – therefore should use that rhetorical form in any such letter. In an age of anonymity and print, where the address to the unknown reader(s) was rapidly becoming the norm – and would become characteristic of genres descended from the Renaissance letter such as the newspaper, the scientific article (Hall 1965; Kronick 1976: 53–76) and the novel (Watt 1964: 189–96) – Erasmus' advice argued that an oratorical style was appropriate to all such communications.

Erasmus thus bequeathed to the later Renaissance and beyond a tradition of epistolary rhetoric that fused together the oratorical and the conversational conceptions of the letter (Henderson 1992: 291, 300–2). He also gave to his posterity a prescription that letters to unknown recipients should adopt the forms of oratory as well – advice that would indeed influence the more anonymous successor genres to the letter. So the news letter was firmly embedded in a rhetorical context:

> Thus we will mention in particular the kind of letter in which we tell a friend of any news that he ought to know or that will bring him pleasure, whether it be of a public or a private nature . . . No fixed method can be laid down for this class, because of its great variety. I shall only say in general that the information should be straightforward and clear, as well as short and precise, and should sometimes include congratulation or consolation. It consists of narration. (Erasmus 1985: 225)

To the news letter, and its descendant the newspaper, we will now turn.

The newspaper

The newspaper genre occupies a particularly important place in this book for it was the keystone of the historical narrative in Habermas' *Structural Transformation*. There Habermas argued that the printed newspaper provided the medium of rational discussion through which the public sphere was constituted – its master genre, so to speak (Habermas 1991: 16–26). It matters very much for the broad rhetorising critique of Habermas to establish that the newspaper was a transformed descendant of epistolary rhetoric rather than some coagulation in print of disembodied reason. Within the narrative of conversation and oratory, it matters as much that the newspaper partook of both modes – a form of conversation that took in all public affairs as its subject matter and a form of persuasion that used the conversational style. The newspaper was the means by which conversation acquired the means to subsume oratory – but also a way for the persuasive imperatives of oratory to disguise the putative intent of the newspaper to inquire conversationally after the truth of public affairs. Here we will examine this ambiguous genre by way of a case study of the emergence of the newspaper in England.

The *ars dictaminis* provided the model – in structure, elegance and style – for the vernacular English private letter (Camargo 1995: 33 ['Introduction']; Richardson 1984). It is no coincidence that the dictaminal Chancery English written by the clerks of the English royal government gave birth to the modern English language, nor that the fourteenth-century literary English derived from Chancery Standard was the creation of authors themselves employed in, or associated with, the civil service – Geoffrey Chaucer (1343–1400), John Gower (*c*.1330–1408), Thomas Hoccleve (*c*.1368–1426), and their cohort (Fisher 1977: esp. 896). More particularly, Malcolm Richardson has established that the birth of private letter-writing in English correlated very closely with the early fifteenth-century transition of the English government under Henry V (1386–1422; r.1413–22) to writing in English, and that the first English private letters, increasing in tandem with the increase of official letters in English, were written in dictaminal style in Chancery Standard dialect (Richardson 1984: 210–13, 219–26; 2001). As a result of the slippage facilitated by Englishmen's indiscriminate use of dictaminal form in their public and private letters, dictaminal rhetoric provided the model for the structure and the diction of English late medieval and early Renaissance private letters.

This slippage of form particularly affected the English private news letter, since it emerged directly from the medieval and Renaissance modelling of familiar letters upon official letters. The internal communications of the state – the letters written from one bureaucrat to another – provided the content and the form for the private news letter; parallel to the letter of news they sent to other bureaucrats, government agents also began to write familiar letters of news to their friends and their kin. As David Zaret puts it, 'transmission of news by private letters evolved as a literary practice as an extension of scribal practices animated by narrowly strategic purposes: diplomatic dispatches, military intelligence, official record keeping, and business communications' (Zaret 2000: 118–19). So in October 1594 George Clarke, who was employed to convey 'Letters from her Majesty to the said *Duke Ernestus*, here at *Brussels*', wrote from Ostend to Richard Bagot about the news he had heard of a Turkish victory over the Austrians near the town of Raba (Clarke 1594: fo. 2^r). The author of a news letter written in June 1622 from Mannheim appears to have been an Englishman serving on a diplomatic mission, probably as part of Lord Chichester's (1563–1625) embassy – he mentioned in the course of his narrative that 'I went from my Lord Ambassador (the Lord Chichester) at Mentz to the King of Bohemia, being in the field before a small town called Bieber' (Copy of a lre 1622). The tattling tendencies of the state's servants played an essential role in the birth of the private English news letter.

As Englishmen came to write of news in their vernacular private letters, humanist epistolary rhetoric superimposed itself upon dictaminal structure, which gave the English news letter its particular configuration, diction and persuasive arguments. Italian humanist epistolary rhetoric of the fifteenth century, communicated and reinforced by intermediaries such as Desiderius Erasmus and Juan Luis Vives (Gerlo 1971: 111–12; Henderson 1983b: 337–9; Kristeller 1970), became pervasive in England by the mid sixteenth century (Fantazzi 1989: 9–17; Jones 1998: 174–6; Ong 1971: 71–4); mid-Tudor English treatises of rhetoric generally followed humanist strictures (e.g. L. Cox 1532; Sherry 1550; T. Wilson 1553). Significantly, the letters cited as models to be imitated by the English letter manuals of the era recapitulated the intellectual lineage between fifteenth-century Italy, the Erasmian humanists of early sixteenth-century northern Europe and mid-Tudor England: in addition to the usual exemplars of antiquity (Cicero, Pliny, etc.), the second part of William Fulwood's (*fl.*1562–8) *The Enimie of Idlenesse* (1568) reproduced the letters of fifteenth-century Italian humanists such as Ermolao Barbaro, Marsilio Ficino, Angelo Poliziano and Pico della Mirandola, while Abraham Flemming's (*c.*1552–1607) *A Panoplie of Epistles* (1576) reproduced the letters of sixteenth-century humanists, both Italian and non-Italian, such as Paulus Manutius (1512–74), Desiderius Erasmus, Johannes Ravisius Textor (*c.*1480–1524), Georgius Macropedius (1487–1558), Christoph Hegendorff (1500–40), Conradus Celtis (1459–1508), Juan Luis Vives and Christophe de Longueil (1490–1522) (Fulwood 1568: 91^v–104^v; Flemming 1576: 314–412). Over one half of Richard Sherry's (*c.*1506–*c.*1555) *A Treatise of Schemes and Tropes* (1550) consisted of a declamation by Erasmus, included to illustrate the proper use of rhetoric. Finally, it is worth emphasising that Tudor humanist rhetoricians, as much as their Italian predecessors, considered letters to fall within rhetoric's scope: Thomas Wilson (1524–81) in his *Arte of Rhetorique* (1553) deemed his rhetorical strictures as pertinent for writing as for speech, and the very title page of William Phiston's (*fl.*1570–1609) *The Welspring of Wittie Conceites* (1584) announced that it was 'No less pleasant to be read, then profitable to be practiced, either, in familiar speech, or by writing, in Epistles and Letters' (T. Wilson 1553: 2ᵛ–3ʳ; Phiston 1584: title page).

Thus, when Englishmen came to consider the news letter, they placed it within the traditional categories of epistolary rhetoric. In Renaissance English letter-writing manuals, themselves remote descendants of the *ars dictaminis* letter-writing manuals, model news letters were included among their various categories (Day 1592: 8–21, second pagination [*The Second Part of the English Secretory*], 66–7; Gainsford 1616: title page, 104–24). Significantly, Angel Day (*fl.*1586–92) in his *English Secretorie* (1592) categorised these news letters both as narrative letters and as familiar letters: 'Touching now our *Familiar Letters*, they also are to be drawn under their several titles, as *Narratory* and *Nunciatory*, somewhat falling into the demonstrative kind before remembered, wherein we express and declare to those far from us, the matters or news presently in hand amongst us' (Day 1592: 24). Furthermore, following Vives' ambitious statement of the scope of the letter, Day wrote in the 1586 edition of the *English Secretorie* that a letter could cover 'all occurrences whatsoever, [which] are thereby as faithfully advertised, pursued, and debated, as firmly might fall out in any personal presence or otherwise to be remembered.' More particularly, Day explicitly added that in Epistles Nunciatory, 'we advertise the news of any public or private matters unto our friends' (Day 1586: 1, 42). Day's editions of the *English Secretorie* confirm that humanist epistolary rhetoric continued to provide both the justification and the form of Renaissance English news letters. While the relationship between the theory prescribed by manuals and everyday practice is inevitably sketchy, it is worth noting that between 1553 and 1635 Thomas Wilson's *Arte of Rhetorique*, William Fulwood's *Enimie of Idleness* and Angel Day's *English Secretorie* were printed, respectively, eight times, ten times and nine times, which suggests that these works, at least, possessed a certain popularity and influence (Mack 2002: 76). Many Elizabethan news letters certainly followed these manuals' rhetorical strictures (Poulett 1593; Clarke 1594).

Now, in the late sixteenth and early seventeenth centuries, these English news letters underwent an extraordinarily rapid series of transformations. First, the form of these news letters was increasingly standardised and abstracted into a letter of pure news (e.g. Broughton 1591). Then the news letters began to be passed on from one person to another with increasing frequency, such that it became less and less likely that the correspondent and the recipient of a news letter would know one another (see Report of Cales 1596: fo. 249^r; Seddon 1983: 304). The multiplication of surviving copies of letters of news in the records is one indication of the process by which correspondent and recipient lost contact with each other;[2] another is that news letters began to acquire titles such as 'The Copy of a Letter', 'This Is a True Copy', etc., shorn of one or both of the superscriptions naming the original author and the original recipient (Copie 1589: fo. 370^r; Copy of a lre 1622). After a while, the correspondents of news simply became anonymous. In August 1629 Andrew Withers, at the siege of 's-Hertogenbosch, forwarded a letter of news to an English lord: 'Meeting with this letter above copied out, after I had delivered that other of mine enclosed to the carrier, I thought it my duty to present your Lordship [the original], though never so hastily and so raggedly scribbled' (Withers 1629: fo. 25^r). One 1621 letter, recognising the existence and the significance of this transformation, was playfully entitled 'The Copy of a Letter Written by a Dutiful Servant Nobody[.] Sent from Brussels to his Worthy Master Nemo' (Copy of a Letter 1621: fo. 20^v).

Anonymous already, these news letters continued their swift transformations. As they separated themselves from known authors and recipients, physically they also began to become 'separates' (Jornals 1589; Brief Relation 1636). As separates, these letters began to be sold, rather than simply sent from one person to another; there were commercial manuscript news letters in England by the 1590s, and the genre reached a swift heyday by the 1620s and 1630s. These commercial letters then began to be printed. The earliest printed news reports were essentially a title page attached to a single letter put in type; most of these early accounts seem to have been manuscript letters snatched for the press, and usually made anonymous if they were not already (Discourse 1569; True Reporte 1579). Finally, printers began to publish large numbers of news letters together. Pamphlets began the transition towards newspaper form at least as far back as 1589, by bundling together multiple items of news or multiple versions of the same item of news (Newes 1595; Newes 1597), and early newspapers could sometimes depend very heavily on a very few individual letters for their material (Present 1620: 5–10; Continuation 1632: 11–14). The end result was the printing of abstract 'news' collated from various news letters. News began to be divided by time and place, not by letter: the practice was increasingly common among news pamphlets,[3] and pervasive among newspapers. In 1624 one newspaper editor wrote that:

> As I have several Letters from *Vienna* concerning the troubles of *Hungary*, & watchings of *Bethlem Gabor* at this instant more especially, than any other affairs or business of *Germany*: so will I divide them asunder for you, and not huddle them together, to avoid confusion; and yet it may be you may hear of one thing twice, if I should write you every word in the Letters, as I find them: but I will be as cautelous, as I can, both to avoid repetitions, and tautology. (Affaires 1624: 5–6)

This was, in essence, the modern newspaper form. Future editors would not bother to caution their readers about their practice, but only because it was common knowledge. Apparent evidence of the newspaper's roots in the news letter dwindled generation by generation, until all that remained were odd phrases such as 'foreign correspondent'.

These rapid transformations have been referred to by historians, in shorthand, as components of the 'news revolution' that swept across early modern Europe (Dooley and Baron 2001, *passim*). While generally associated with the slow adaptation of the European news genres to the printing revolution, the specific timing of the onset of new forms of news within each country tended to correspond to upsurges in warfare – quintessentially and unceasingly newsworthy – with the exception of the *sui generis* spike in German pamphlet production in the first decade of the Reformation (Cole 1975: 96–7; Harline 1987: 3–4; Latimer 1976: 33). Thus, the dramatic increase in production of printed English news pamphlets (and the appearance of separates and commercial manuscript news letters) correlated with England's entry into the Spanish Wars in the late 1580s and 1590s (Streckfuss 1998: 87; Voss 2001: 66–75). Likewise, the coranto (an early newspaper) first appeared in the Netherlands at the outbreak of the Thirty Years War and quickly spread to England (Dahl 1950).

As this last example indicates, the international aspects of this news revolution complicate the narrative of genre transformation from English news letter to English newspaper. Sixteenth-century English news pamphlets were often imitations or direct translations of French and Dutch originals (Discourse 1569; True Report 1601), while the form of the first English corantos emerged directly from Dutch practice. From at least 1566, English ambassadors in Italy collected Italian printed *gazzette*, themselves derived from Italy's mid-sixteenth-century manuscript *avvisi* news letters, and copied them or included them in their dispatches home; these *gazzette* directly influenced the form of English diplomatic letters, and consequently of English private letters, news pamphlets and newspapers (Infelise 2002; Stephens 1988: 151–6; Lomas 1916: liii–liv). The immediate ancestry of the English newspaper was to a considerable degree continental.

As the news letter evolved into the newspaper, its rhetoric transformed accordingly. We should recollect that the dictaminal letter was relatively dependent on arguments based on the statement of social status and aural effects, and that civic (Salutatian) humanism had infused the letter with an ethical imperative to include public affairs among its subject matter. This last characteristic provided the continuing justification for the very existence of the genres of the news letter and the newspaper. Indeed, by the end of the seventeenth century the civic imperative to comment on public affairs would be expanded into a *right* to comment uncensored on public affairs: the ideal of the freedom of the press would provide an enduringly civic justification for the newspaper genre (Achinstein 1994: 27–70; Randall 2006: 309–12; 2008a: 154). The first two characteristics, however, swiftly atrophied during the news letter's transformation into the newspaper, as logical argument embedded in the narrative strengthened to the point of hypertrophy. Alongside the ethical orientation that demanded private involvement in public affairs, logic and narrative alone virtually constituted the new newspaper rhetoric.

Newspaper rhetoric's hypertrophy of the logical narrative was due almost entirely to the newspaper's anonymity. This anonymity was almost total: in his entire bibliography of more than four hundred English corantos, Folke Dahl found only two named sources for news (Continuation 1622: 3; Dahl 1952: 73, 162). The effects of this anonymity must be emphasised. The humanist Renaissance letter in general, although it lauded the individual and rejected some dictaminal forms, had remained highly aware of the social status of the correspondent and the recipient (Vives 1989: 29; Henderson 1983b: 341–4, 347, 354). Letters in early modern England between known correspondents and recipients still adhered to the dictaminal rules whereby social status governed the forms of correspondence (Fulwood 1568: sig. A7^v) – indeed, the physical space between the body of a letter and the signature conventionally indicated the social distance between the correspondent and the recipient (Day 1592: 16; Fulwood 1568: sig. A8^r; Gibson 1997). The Renaissance news letter in particular had still relied heavily upon the rhetorics of a known correspondent and a known recipient; witness the instructions for writing a news letter in William Fulwood's *Enimie of Idlenesse* (1568):

> *How to certify some news lately happened.*
> To certify some novel or new thing, the Letters must be divided into three parts. First, we must purchase benevolence to our selves, declaring that we are inclined to write unto him, as unto our friend, of news which happened, as well in public affairs as in private: for we know well that he takes pleasure to hear speak of them. Secondly, shall be declared the history, be it of Battle or other business. Thirdly, we shall say that that which we have written unto him was not to have been left behind without advertisement, promising him that we will not complain of our labor in writing always unto him like news, provided, that we know them to be acceptable unto him. (Fulwood 1568: 47^v–48^r)

Since news letters had remained so dependent upon personal knowledge and the attendant statements of social status for so much of their rhetorical authority, anonymity necessarily required a radical restructuring of newspaper rhetoric.

Newspaper rhetoric, written by an unknown writer to an unknown reader, substituted logical argument, embedded in the narrative, to replace the rhetoric of personal knowledge. This was a natural development: as noted above, news letters were narrative letters, and already derived an unusual amount of their persuasive authority from the text of the narrative. Now newspapers were forced to rely solely upon the narrative. Printed news letters began the process by emphasising such factors as claims of eyewitness and specific textual detail, embedded within the narrative, to lend credence to the information they provided (Randall 2008a: 103–9). As the newspaper developed into a collated abstract of different news letters, it shifted its claims of persuasive authority from logical examination of a single textual narrative to logical examination and comparison of multiple textual narratives (More Newes 1623: 26–7). Furthermore, each newspaper based its claims of superior credibility over *other* newspapers on appeals to its own narrative. The author of *A True Relation of the Affaires of Europe* (4 October 1622) observed:

> There are so many Letters from the several parts of the Low Countries, and so much contradiction, as men on either side favor the cause, that I know not how to satisfy the Reader: yet considering there is but one truth, and to be honest in a plain narration of the same, is allowable, therefore as near as I can, I will relate, what is most probable and worthy of your acceptation. (True Relation 1622: 17)

Likewise, the author of *Newes of Europe* (12 March 1624, no. 17) wrote that 'for the truth I refer you to the Discourse' (Newes 1624: 9). Newspaper rhetoric now grounded its persuasive authority almost exclusively upon a textual narrative based on logical argument. All other means had disappeared.

Newspaper rhetoric had also inherited the *stilus humilis*, the plain style, from the Renaissance private letter. Indeed, the plain style was stronger than ever by the time of the birth of the newspaper; Renaissance humanists' emphasis on the individual, rather than on social status, had brought with it an even greater commitment in Renaissance epistolary rhetoric to the plain style, as the clearest window of communication between one individual and another (Fantazzi 1989: 6; Henderson 1983a, 1983b). Now, however, the plain style itself acquired persuasive authority; from the sixteenth century onwards, plain language, unsophisticated but informative, was coming to be perceived as an indicator of truth in and of itself (Shapiro 1983: 227–66; 2000: 58–9, 72, 94–5, 160–5); like the medieval *cursus*, the plain style also provided rhetorical authority in its diction. The *cursus'* rhetorical authority, however, had operated extra-logically, by means of aural effects; the plain style, the clear window that made visible the logic of the narrative, instead amplified the rhetorical authority of the narrative. So we may see plain style declared a deliberate goal in writing news. In 1591 G.B., citing Roman figures iconically associated with plain style, wrote in *Newes out of France for the Gentlemen of England* that '*nothing (saith* Quintilian*) so much commendeth the person of the writer, as the truth of the subject, he proposeth to write: And certes nothing advanced so highly* Julius Caesars *history, as truth polished with Eloquence discreetly*' (B. 1591: sig. A4^r). S.W. wrote in 1622 that his *Appollogie of the Illustrious Prince Ernestus, Earle of Mansfield* was plain, 'but if it be plain, plainness best sets forth truth, as this is' (W. 1622: *iii–iv*). The plain style of the newspaper, soon to be a pervasive characteristic of the genre (Shaaber 1929: 218–21; Raymond 1996: 129–30), had rooted the genre's persuasive authority yet further in its logical narrative.

Conclusion

The newspaper's style had become that of a conversation stripped naked, familiarity yoked to nigh-exclusive dependence on plain style and logic so as to allow the newspaper to address an anonymous audience. Yet the newspaper, as any other form of *sermo*, was not stably set within the framework of conversation. On the one hand, the persuasive aspects of the humanist letter perpetually threatened that the newspaper's inquiry into the facts of the world would decay into mere persuasion – an artfully artless work of persuasive oratory addressed to a mixed audience, simulating the conversational inquiry into truth even in this discourse that avowedly eschewed all but plain and logical narration. The omnipresent propagandas of state and faction in early modern Europe, eagerly grasping the newspaper to be their tool, were the prerequisites that motivated the quixotic ideal of impartiality (Sawyer 1990). On the other hand, the nakedness of the newspaper, its great dependence on logic, gave prima facie plausibility to the ambition of practitioners of the genre, and its derivatives, to write with complete impartiality and objectivity, to inform without persuasion – to make of the newspaper what Habermas conceived it actually to be, a sort of Platonic dialogue concerned with the facts of the world. The newspaper, that medium of discourse that addressed itself to all the facts of the realm of oratory, could be with equal plausibility a medium of oratory, of conversation or of Platonic dialogue. In its instability, it encapsulated the larger instability of all the genres of conversation.

The newspaper, indeed, not only encapsulated the perpetual instability of conversation in Renaissance Europe but also pointed forward to several of the transformations of conversation during the Enlightenment. To begin with, as the newspaper would be the characteristic medium of (public) opinion, the instability of the conception and practice of the newspaper presaged a parallel instability in the conception and practice of (public) opinion, between more oratorical, conversational and philosophical variants. In the second place, the anonymisation of the newspaper's assumed audience combined with its expansion into the range of unknown multitudes to render it into something like a *public* – a theoretically universal audience, and certainly an audience that defied easy practical limitation or characterisation. This *universalisation* of the newspaper's audience relocated the question of the judgement of the reader – his ability to tell true information from false, a friend from a flatterer, a conversationalist from an orator – from the question of the sociological preconditions for judgement among a restricted elite (birth, money, education, virtue) to a philosophical question as to the presence of a universal faculty of judgement, and the consequences that would follow from such a faculty's existence. The particular questions inspired by the conversation of the newspaper, theoretically universal both in scope and participation, presaged the broader questions that would shift conversational thought toward the universalising realm of moral philosophy. The questions that would drive the Enlightenment history of both public opinion and the philosophy of conversation arose first in the history of that unstable and universalising genre of conversation, the early modern newspaper.

We shall return to public opinion and the philosophy of conversation in this book's sequel. Before we do so, we must first complete the transformations of conversation that preceded the Enlightenment. We have already finished the sketch of the exfoliations of *sermo* between the age of Petrarch and the age of Louis XIV – conversation and dialogue, friendship and women, court and *salon*, Republic of Letters and newspaper – and now it is time to return to a question posed in our discussion of Castiglione. What, if not Platonic love, could motivate conversation? Since conversation now had expanded to enormous proportions, the question of its foundations became more critical than ever. To answer this problem, we shall return to *conversatio*.

Notes

1. For a fuller statement of much of this chapter, see Randall (2008a).
2. Advertizement (1589) is repeated in Walsingham (1589). Dr Roger Marbeck's account of the 1596 expedition to Cadiz appears in Marbeck (1596a and 1596b). The same account of the 1627 expedition to Ré, albeit with significant variations, appears in Account (1627), True and Exact (1627) and Relation (1627).
3. For example, the divisions of the news by city and date in Newes (1595: sigs. A4^v–B1^r, B2^v–B3^r) and Newes (1597: 3, 6–8, 10, 13, 17).

Chapter 7

Sociabilitas

Introduction

Conversatio, mutual conduct, had possessed loose affiliations with *sermo* in ancient and medieval times. During the Renaissance, *conversatio* shifted far closer to *sermo* and its constellation of cognate concepts. Most notably, Stefano Guazzo elaborated an influential theory of civil conversation in his eponymous late-sixteenth-century dialogue, which reconceived *conversatio* in secular terms as the realm of society, the realm of manners, intermediate between the *oikos* and the political world. This Italian conception of civil conversation then received a peculiar, universalising spin from the natural law jurisprudential tradition of Grotius and Pufendorf, transforming it into an amoral disposition toward sociability shared by all humanity. The long parallel tracks of *sermo* and *conversatio* now finally converged: *sermo* became conversation as *conversatio* became sociability.

The convergence of *sermo* and *conversatio* made possible the establishment of a causal connection between the two concepts. This connection appeared via *doux commerce*, the application of sociability to the realm of economics: sociability, by the means of the universal exercise of economic self-interest, became the conceptual and historical predicate to conversation – and, as the Enlightenment progressively tied together manners with the civic humanist tradition, the predicate in turn for both virtue and liberty. Sociability thus at last substituted for Platonic love an amoral, entirely human motivation for conversation – or at any rate, a motivation that pushed the role of God farther distant from the consequent portrait of human interaction, from direct infuser of mutual human love to indirect creator of needful and sociable humanity. By this means, conversation received a coherent grounding in the merely selfish needs of humanity – the discourse of reason found its base in human passions.

Civil conversation

Conversatio, in the vernacular *conversazione*, generally preserved its traditional range of meanings deep into the sixteenth century (Robiglio 2006: 113 (note 2)). The Florentine humanist Matteo Palmieri (1406–75) did use *conversazione civile* in passing in his *Della vita civile* (1429, printed 1528), applied narrowly to cities, but this does not seem to have been immediately influential (Palmieri 1825: 74; Quondam 2007: 30). Pontano also casually used the phrase *conuersationibusque ciuilibus* in *De sermone* (Pontano 2008: 266 [5.2.7]). Robiglio notes that Castiglione used 'conversation' to connote 'a connection between political engagement and humanistic education . . . The friendship among the members of a group of more-or-less likeminded people, who share the same duties and (political) responsibilities' (Robiglio 2006: 119). These usages, however, left *conversatio* largely undisturbed.

Castiglione exerted more influence on the conception of *conversatio* by strengthening the application of *sermo* to manners. *Sermo* had had an ancient tie to *urbanitas*, and Pontano had strengthened that tie by infusing a conversational ethic into *urbanitas* as *facetudo*. Castiglione's transferral of *sermo* to the court, however, had brought it into a realm where manners were at a premium. The Castiglionean tradition thus made *sermo* a model for mutual behaviour at court – and, as we shall see, Guazzo's conception of civil conversation not only explicitly referred to Castiglione's prescription for courtly manners as a subset of civil conversation but also implicitly widened the scope of such manners to the society of mankind. The overlap was not precise: *sermo* and *conversatio* remained different concepts, and Guazzo's use of *conversazione* kept his discussion at some distance from Castiglione's. As noted above, the Castiglionean courtier also drew on the Ciceronian orator as a model for his manners. Nevertheless, Quondam is correct to see a broad unity between Pontano, Castiglione and Guazzo: Guazzo's civil conversation displayed the clear impress of Pontano's and Castiglione's innovations upon the tradition of *sermo* (Quondam 2007: 35–219).

Not least because of this new impress of the *sermo* tradition, the publication of the sixteenth-century Piedmontese writer and courtier Stefano Guazzo's (1530–93) *Civil Conversation* (1574) radically innovated upon and transformed the concept of *conversatio*. This work – as important in the development of civil conversation as Castiglione's *Courtier* was in developing the conception of the Renaissance courtier, and therefore the subject of the remainder of this section – was broadly influential throughout Europe (Lievsay 1961; Richards 2003; Withington 2005: 124–55). *Civil Conversation* 'was translated almost immediately into French, English, Latin, and German', and became a model for the friendly, private discussion of civic matters (Miller 2001: 3–4). Guazzo's great contribution was to popularise the tying together of the two terms 'civil' and 'conversation', and by so doing to yoke two constellations of concepts which had previously been at most loosely linked. *Conversatio* previously had been oriented toward the non-political world – for a millennium, characteristically oriented toward God. 'Civil', on the other hand, had pertained particularly to the world of the city, and hence narrowly to political affairs. By uniting them, Guazzo broadened the application of civil to all the areas of life previously excluded from the realm of politics, and reoriented *conversatio* to a this-worldly application – to the realm of subject matter covered by *sermo* – whose framework was political.

Guazzo stated his thesis quite plainly in his definition of his subject matter. To begin with:

> to live civilly, is not sayde in respect of the citie, but of the qualities of the minde: so I understand civile conversation not having relation to the citie, but consideration to the maners and conditions which make it civile. And as laws and civile ordinances are distributed not onely to cities, but to villages, castles, and people subject unto them, so I will that civile conversation appertaine not onely to men inhabiting cities, but to all sortes of persons of what place, or of what calling soever they are. [Paragraph.] To bee shorte, my meaning is, that civile conversation is an honest commendable and virtuous kinde of living in the world. (Guazzo 1967: I, 56 [Bk. 1]; 1993: I, 40 [1 A32])

We may note for later reference the philosophical implications of the universalising phrase 'the qualities of the minde'. Immediately, the importance of broadening the concept of civil conversation beyond the city was that the conduct of civil conversation now appertained 'to all sortes of persons': civil conversation, in contrast to both oratory and *sermo*, could take place among all mankind. At the same time, as it escaped beyond the bounds of the city walls, the subject matter of civil conversation also broadened to include:

> howe to behave our selves towardes others, according to the difference of their estates, for that it is our hap to come in companie, somtime with the young, sometime with the olde, assoone with Gentlemen, assoone with the baser sorte, nowe and then with Princes, nowe and then with private persons, one while with the learned, another while with the ignoraunt, nowe

with our owne Countriemen, then with strangers, nowe with the religious, then with the secular, nowe with men, then with women. (Guazzo 1967: I, 168 [Bk. 2]; 1993: I, 119 [2 A116]; Miller 2001: 3)

This catalogue included all the traditional and apolitical subject matter of *conversatio* – but it also now encompassed the political realm of Gentlemen and Princes, by way of the 'maners and conditions' which made the city civil. Furthermore, by this casual introductory sentence, Guazzo implicitly subordinated to civil conversation the entire realm of behaviour at court – more or less the entire subject matter of Castiglione's *Courtier*.

Yet the court was not Guazzo's main focus. It mattered far more that civil conversation engaged all the varieties of mankind – and indeed, Guazzo made thematic the diversity of mankind encompassed within civil conversation.

[P]eople differ one from another in degree, in age, in kinde, in life, in maners, and in profession . . . [and] there must bee respect had not onely to the difference which is betweene one kind and another, but to that also which is betweene persons of one onely kinde: for not onely young men differ in behavior from olde, and Gentlemen from Yomen: but even young men amongst themselves differ, as also one olde man differeth in behavior from another olde man, and one Gentleman from another Gentleman. (Guazzo 1967: I, 54 [Bk. 1]; 1993: I, 39 [1 C25])

We should note just how far this emphasis distinguished Guazzo's idea of civil conversation from its conceptual roots in *conversatio*. Ancient *conversatio* had included *familiarity* and *habitual association* among its meanings; while medieval *conversatio* had depended upon a shared Christian faith. Such *conversatio* emphasised friendship, familiarity and similarity. Guazzo's civil conversation united the unknown and the unlike as it emphasised familiarity with strangers and conduct appropriate toward the variety of mankind.

It was, moreover, precisely the diversity of mankind embraced by civil conversation that justified its practice. Guazzo approached this point by comparing civil conversation with the two great alternatives of solitude and the court. To begin with, Guazzo had his character Guglielmo Guazzo (the author's actual brother) argue a preference for the liberty of solitude to the conversation of the court: 'for I feele it a great travell to my minde, to understand other mens talk, to frame fit answeres thereto, and to observe suche circumstances, as the qualitie of the persons, and mine owne honer require: which is nothing els but paine and subjection' (Guazzo 1967: I, 17 [Bk. 1]; 1993: I, 15 [1 C4a–b]). Here we have a notable response to the forthright prescription of Alberti and Castiglione to take the flatterer's part: it is wearying and painful to be a polyp, and a relief to avoid the conditions that require such flexibility. Guazzo struck a (Rousseauian) note that would become stronger as the centuries progressed; other people were, if not hell, at least a prison. But to this initial contention, Guazzo provided a further riposte: 'who so leaveth the civile society to place himself in some solitarie desert, taketh as it were the forme of a beast, and in a certaine manner putteth upon him selfe a brutishe nature.' More to the point, to embrace such solitude was to embrace the nature of the tyrant: 'So the common saying is, that there is no other name meete for a solitarie person, but either of a beast, or a tyrant' (Guazzo 1967: I, 30 [Bk. 1]; 1993: I, 24 [1 A161]). The relief that solitude provided was deceptive: our relations with other people, no matter how wearying, were necessary to ward us from becoming a tyrant or a brute.

As for speaking in court, that conversation, paradigmatically, was the conversation between courtiers and the prince. Guazzo generally referred the reader to Castiglione; but he also provided a verse epitome of counsel to courtiers who wished 'to maintain the Prince's favor':

Before their Prince let Courtiers silent be,
Or let their words be saust with pleasaunt glee.

> (Guazzo 1967: II, 111–12 [Bk. 3]; 1993: I,
> 261–2 [3 A226–A227, 3 A228CIT])

The choice of courtly conversation was to amuse or be silent. This analysis implicitly did not speak well of the Prince who set the conditions of the court – and Guazzo's discussion of princes, guarded and indirect though it was, had real bite. The character Guazzo stipulated that evil princes exist; while Annibale Magnocavallo, interlocutor in *Civil Conversation* with Guglielmo Guazzo, although he said 'that the dooings of Princes are blamelesse, altogether without the compasse of our judgement', followed up by saying that their cruelty, avarice, etc., were really figments of their subjects' imperfect judgements. Princes actually were just, provident and so forth, when seen rightly. Annibale then allowed that ancient Princes 'were unjust, disloyall, covetous, [and] lascivious' – but modern princes, to the contrary, were lawful, Christian and sent by God (Guazzo 1967: I, 198; 203–4 [Bk. 2]; 1993: I, 141 [2 C168b], 143 [2 A174,

2 C175, 2 A175a, 2 A175d]). Annibale's indiscreet hints and osten-
tatious extenuations cannot have been intended to fool any reader.
But even the discreet Annibale allowed that Princes were especially
subject to ignorance and covetousness. The former led the Prince
either to spurn the counsel of the wise, or to be subjected to it, while
the latter led him to such evil acts that his life was 'always miserable,
full of suspicion and feare, with a sword still hanging by a haire over
his head, hee taketh at one tyme from his subjects libertie, from himselfe safetie, from both tranquilitie' (Guazzo 1967: I, 204–5 [Bk. 2];
1993: I, 144–5 [2 A176b–c, 2 A177b]). In consequence, courtly conversation with princes might be profitable for subjects, but remained
dangerous due to the fatal passions of the Prince. At best, courtly
conversation was wearying: 'The conversation of Princes in my
judgement is not to bee avoided, in any other respect, but for that
it taketh away that libertie, which is so acceptable in company, and
bringeth us into a certaine kinde of bondage, which we cannot like
of long' (Guazzo 1967: I, 209–10 [Bk. 2]; 1993: I, 148 [2 C181]).
Here the word *bondage* (*servitù*) seemed intended to resonate. Just
as a solitary person was in impulse a tyrant, so the monologic desire
was likewise tyrannical: 'to covet to speake always, and never to
heare others, is a kind of tyrannie' (Guazzo 1967: I, 151 [Bk. 2];
1993: I, 106 [2 A80a]). Courtly conversation, subject to the tyranny
of a prince, was not in any genuine sense conversation; rather it
was to be subject to the monologue, the will, of the prince. Solitude
made one a tyrant, the court made one subject to a tyrant, and
neither alternative was alluring.

Civil conversation, to be sure, was also a subjugation – a subjugation to the mass of the world rather than to a prince, but a subjugation all the same. This submission, however, was alloyed with
more than compensating advantage. Annibale articulated both the
trials and benefits consequent upon accommodating oneself to conversation with the diverse company of the world. To begin with, he
emphasised the trials:

> As if you were bounde from Padua to Venice, you will not let slip opor-
> tunitie, for that you will not imbarke your selfe in a vessel wherin there
> are sometime men, women, religious, seculer, Souldiours, Courtiers,
> Almans, Frenchmen, Spaniards, Jewes, and other of divers nations and
> qualities. And therefore wee must force our will, and make it sometime
> content it selfe with that it liketh not, whereof followeth a vertue of
> necessitie. Touching this I will tell you, that the place and time have
> sometime forced mee to be present (rather with my bodie then minde)
> in the companie of those persons, which I could verie ill away withal, as

being altogether different from my manner of life and profession: from whom neverthelesse I could not withdrawe my selfe, least I shoulde bee thought to take upon mee, either too muche gravitie, or too litle courtesie. And though at the first I was in my dumpes, yet afterward I went away well pleased and joyful: seeing that I had so well framed my selfe to the humours of others, and that I had got my selfe honestly away being verie well thought of by the companie when I was gone: so likewise, when you shall be acquainted with the course of the worlde, and when by long use, you shal be brought to abide the companie of suche manner of people, you shal perceive, that if it be not good for your health, yet at least it shal not be hurtful. (Guazzo 1967: I, 21–2 [Bk. 1]; 1993: I, 18–19 [1 A12b–c])

Thus far Annibale cannot be condemned for enthusiasm for such conversations: *vertue of necessitie, brought to abide* and *at least it shal not be hurtful* were but faint expressions of zest for the company of the unavoidable multitude. Moreover, one was forced to remain among undesirable companions not only because the world was filled with such beings but also because opinion misprized men, and forced one to tolerate the grossly imperfect: 'As a Courtier you cannot keep you from them: not so much for the great number of them, as for the error of the world, which esteemeth them in the rowe of the tolerable. To be short, wee ought to consider that our name dependeth of the general opinions, which have such force, that reason is of no force against them' (Guazzo 1967: I, 60–1 [Bk. 1]; I, 43 [1 A39]). Man's diverse nature and man's eminently fallible opinion both required one to be civil, but such civility was more to be endured than relished.

We should note here that Guazzo discussed such civil conversation in terms and phrases that invoked polypian decorum. The prescribed civility was that of a *Courtier*, and the action given for approbation was *I had so well framed my selfe to the humours of others*. Guazzo emphasised this point at length: one must not only tolerate others but also adapt one's exterior to their desires.

But to be acceptable in companie, we must put of as it were our own fashions and manners, and cloath our selves with the conditions of others, and imitate them so farre as reason will permit. And in some, touching the respect of honestie and vertue, wee ought to bee alwayes one and the same. But touching the diversities of the persons with whom wee shall be conversaunt, wee must alter our selves into an other: according to that olde saying, The heart altogether unlike, and the face altogether like to the people. (Guazzo 1967: I, 105 [Bk. 1]; 1993: I, 72–3 [1 A110b])

The person who could not so adapt himself 'shall bee driven to curse Conversation', and hence to bestial, tyrannical solitude (Guazzo 1967: I, 105 [Bk. 1]; 1993: I, 73 [1 A110b]). As civil conversation was necessary, so the polypian character of a courtier was necessary. *Reason, honestie* and *vertue* provided theoretical limits to the mutability required by company, but it was difficult to tell where exactly one would encounter these boundaries – or whether to follow these virtues too exactly would drive one, *comme Alceste*, to bestial solitude.

What imposed constraint here was that flip side of the Prince, the power of the multitude: *wee ought to consider that our name dependeth of the general opinions, which have such force, that reason is of no force against them.* As courtly conversation was a necessary response to the power of the prince, so civil conversation was a necessary response to the power of the people – whose power, very significantly, was excercised by *general opinions* of one's reputation. The rise of civil conversation registered the slippage of power from the prince to the people, who now also required from one a necessary decorum.

So far such civil conversation seemed no more than a sort of courtly decorum exercised toward the people rather than toward the prince. But Guazzo also argued that it was a positive good in itself, as the necessary means to knowledge. To begin with, while solitude exposed one to the errors of ignorance and passion, conversation helped dispel both:

> In conferring with his companions, if he have understood any thing amisse, he therby most commonly commeth to the right meaning of the matter, and cleereth his minde of many errours, and beginneth to perceive that the judgment of one alone may bee easily darkened with the veile of ignorance, or of some passion, and that amongst a multitude, it seldome falleth out that all are blinded. (Guazzo 1967: I, 43–4 [Bk. 1]; 1993: I, 32 [1 A18n])

Even scholarly isolation was insufficient, for knowledge could not be found in solitary study among books: 'neither can a learned man assure him selfe of his learning, until he meete with other learned men, and by discoursing and reasoning with them, bee acertained of his sufficiency. Whereby it seemeth to me verie cleere, that conversation is the beginning and end of knowledge' (Guazzo 1967: I, 39–40 [Bk. 1]; 1993: I, 30 [1 A18a]). Such conversation encompassed disputation, whose rivalries and emulations give zest to the search for knowledge. But such disputation was not in search of some truth that, once revealed, was self-evident: rather, 'the trueth is taken from the common consent and opinions of men, [and] those opinions can not be knowen but by conversation and companie' (Guazzo 1967: I, 41 [Bk. 1]; 1993: I, 31 [1 A18h]). Disputation was praiseworthy when Philosophers practised it with 'love and mutuall goodwill, but seeke with one accord the trueth', but it was a characteristic failing of Philosophers to dispute contentiously, distant alike from affection, reason, and truth (Guazzo 1967: I, 91–3 [Bk. 1]; 1993: I, 63–4 [1 C80a–1 A80d, esp. 1 A80b–c]). In other words, Guazzo applied to disputation the friendly framework of *sermo*, quite aware that *disputatio* had available a less pleasing mode.

Civil conversation's mode was friendly dispute in good part because it was predicated on the belief that truth had to be learned from other people. Disputation motivated a willingness to argue, but friendliness motivated a willingness to listen – and to listen in silence was an essential aid to the discovery of truth: 'one that can quietly heare an other speake, sheweth howe he liketh to have the truth evidently and quietly opened in every matter: and that he can not away with unadvised and contentious arguing' (Guazzo 1967: I, 151 [Bk. 2]; 1993: I, 106 [2 A80a]). And listening to others implied a crucial generalisation: as mentioned above, *the trueth is taken from the common consent and opinions of men*. Opinion was power that governed and constrained, but opinion was also the medium of truth; civil conversation was the necessary response to opinion's power, but it was also the means to opinion's truth. Civil conversation and opinion jointly mediated between the realms of conversation and oratory, of truth and power.

Moreover, civil conversation provided self-knowledge, which was gained by listening to other people's (epideictic) blame of oneself. The predicate to this contention was that men in general were self-flatterers, princes notably subject to this defect, and wise men distinguishable from the common ruck of mankind by their lack of a desire to be flattered (Guazzo 1967: I, 81–2 [Bk. 1]; Guazzo 1993: I, 56–7 [1 A68a–b]). To avoid such self-flatteries, to come to a proper estimation of one's own character, it was necessary to be 'content to submit our selves to the common opinion of al men, and come to acknowledge in our selves some imperfection, which wee indevour to correct after other mens judgement' (Guazzo 1967: I, 115 [Bk. 2]; 1993: I, 81 [2 A11a]). Conversation also led men to improve themselves by imitating what was praised (epideictically) according to common opinion and judgement: 'And as they learne to eschue those thinges which they see to bee unseemely in any, so they indevour to followe and appropriate to themselves those things which are commendable in others, so that by Conversation they become markers and imitatours of wise men, and such as are patternes to bee practised by' (Guazzo 1967: I, 115–16 [Bk. 2]; 1993: I, 81 [2 Allb]). But to submit oneself to opinion, to follow its strictures, one had to know it – and civil conversation was important above all as the means by which to dispel ignorance of other people's opinion: 'for want of knowing and being experienced by meanes of conversation, in the natures, manners, and dooings of others, wee offende eyther by arrogancie, or by distrust . . . the remedie . . . is civile conversation, and that chiefly which is practiced out of the house, haunting many and divers persons' (Guazzo 1967: I, 113 [Bk. 2]; 1993: I, 79–80 [2 A6b]). Contrariwise, the lack of interest men displayed in knowing 'what opinion the worlde hath of them' was a sign both of arrogance and of 'sencelesse brutishnesse' (Guazzo 1967: I, 112 [Bk. 2]; 1993: I, 79 [2 A5]). Lack of interest in other people's opinion was brutish, and aligned conceptually with solitude and tyrannical impulses – and, by implication, pertained to those princes, tyrants, who did not interest themselves in the opinion of other people. Not lightly did Guazzo suggest that a prince should practise conversation with his subjects and the conversational virtues (Guazzo 1967: I, 208 [Bk. 2]; 1993: I, 147 [2 A180a]). Nor lightly did he argue that as Christ himself conversed with all manners of men, so mankind, in *imitatio Christi*, should engage in similarly extensive conversation (Guazzo 1967: I, 30 [Bk. 1]; 1993: I, 24 [1 A16j–k]). Civil conversation was the way to knowledge, to virtue and to devotion to God.

In all the above discussion, it is worth emphasising that speech was at the heart of conversation. That speech was part of conversation, we will recollect, had been true since ancient times. That speech remained an irreducible component of *conversazione*, and perhaps latterly had been growing more important, was registered in its usage from Dante and Petrarch to the Jesuits. Guazzo, however, came close to identifying speech with conversation: 'wee winne chiefly the friendship and good will of other, by the manner of our speech, and by the qualitie of our conditions: yea I might in a certaine manner reduce al conversation, to that point of manners and behavior, wherein are likewise comprised our woordes and speech' (Guazzo 1967: I, 119 [Bk. 2]; 1993: I, 84 [2 A17a]). Speech in particular was the means by which conversation united mankind:

The same nature hath given speech to man, not to the ende to speake to himself, which were to no purpose, but to the ende it might stande in steede towards other. And you see that the tongue serveth us to teache, to demaunde, to conferre, to traffike, to counsaile, to correct, to dispute, to judge, and to expresse the affection of our hearte: meanes whereby men come to love one another, and to linke themselves together. (Guazzo 1967: I, 35 [Bk. 1]; 1993: I, 27 [1 A16w–x])

Whether this was innovation or merely influential application, in Guazzo the concept of *conversatio* began its rapid shift toward speech as a primary signification – modern conversation. Moreover, the constellation of concepts associated with civil conversation – including, as we shall see, sociability – were likewise identified with this shift; *conduct*, *way of life*, *aspiration to the good* were deeply implicated with *communication*. By this shift the conflation of *conversatio* and *sermo* accelerated markedly, for both now overlapped very heavily as modes of speech that both sought truth and existed in tense relation with a world in reaction to which they alternately wished to retreat or to act.

A register of the overlap between *sermo* and civil conversation was that Guazzo prescribed for civil conversation the same stylistic register, the plain and the simple, that characterised *sermo*. Civil conversation's preference for simplicity, however, derived from somewhat different motives than *sermo*'s. *Sermo* was an informal talk among gentlemen, but civil conversation, which pertained to 'the qualities of the minde', was directed toward the multitude of the world. For civil conversation to function, this multitude required some capacity – and indeed Annibale believed that nature had endowed among mankind a widespread capacity – understanding, rhetoric and philosophy – even among rural rustics (Guazzo 1967: I, 123 [Bk. 2]; 1993: I, 86 [2 A21]). On the other hand, he also took this widespread capacity to depend not so much on capacity among the labourers, but on the existence of 'the infinite number of persons which reach not to the degree of Gentlemen . . . but that both for the good minde they carie with them, and the good calling they live in, they are woorthie some place in company, and that they ought to bee put in the middest betweene Gentlemen and clownes' (Guazzo 1967: I, 174–5 [Bk. 2]; 1993: I, 124 [2 A129]). To this middling sort, a simple and plain style was most appropriate. Annibale prescribed 'that a man ought to proceede in common talke simply and plainly, according as the truth of the matter shal require' (Guazzo 1967: I, 123 [Bk. 2]; 1993: I,

86 [2 A21]). Philosophical jargon, incomprehensible and offputting, should be avoided in speech to the unlearned (Guazzo 1967: I, 220–1 [Bk. 2]; 1993: I, 154 [2 A197]). Civil conversation required 'purity of speech . . . a man must indevour to be a Grecian [presumably Attic] in wordes' (Guazzo 1967: I, 147 [Bk. 2]; 1993: I, 103 [2 A71–2 C72]). Civil conversation thus had some of the stylistic attributes of that oratory that aimed at a mixed or unknown audience, but where oratory had aimed to persuade its auditors, to move their passions; civil conversation sought rather to elicit truth from the multitude.

Yet there was a tension here where civil conversation indicated a preference for plainness. Plain speech was meant to be accompanied by plain manners; pure speech by 'puritie and sinceritie of manners' and Greek words by the actions of 'a Romane in deedes' (Guazzo 1967: I, 147 [Bk. 2]; 1993: I, 103 [2 A71–2 C72]). Annibale likewise cited Socrates' counsel: 'who being demaunded which was the readiest way for a man to winne honour and renowne: answered, To indevour, to bee such a one in deede, as hee desireth to seeme to bee in shewe' (Guazzo 1967: I, 147–8 [Bk. 2]; 1993: I, 103 [2 A72]). But this advice did not harmonise well with Guazzo's polypian prescriptions elsewhere, the argument that civil conversation should also be an exercise in courtiership to the multitude. So Annibale, for all that he advised plain dealing, also advised that some art improves nature, so that by artful artlessness, a sort of *sprezzatura* applied to civil conversation, a man 'bee desired, honoured, and esteemed in any honest companie hee shall come in' (Guazzo 1967: I, 123–4 [Bk. 2]; 1993: I, 86 [2 A21]). Sincerity was the avowed prescription, but the appearance of sincerity lurked as the actual dose (cf. Bond 1965: II, 592 [No. 280, 21 January 1712]; Mee 2011: 43).

But once the door was opened to such appearances, such courtiership, the door was likewise opened to a world of flattery. Guazzo realised, after all, that the appearance of men was deceptive: 'I know in deede many which have the skil with the eyes, countenance, gesture, and other outward signes, to make men think they are verie attentive to their talke, and yet have their minds turned an other way, so that in one instant, they are both present and absent, contenting both them selves and other' (Guazzo 1967: I, 51 [Bk. 1]; 1993: I, 36–7 [1 C22]). Guazzo also echoed Plutarch on the mutability of flatterers, those counterfeits of friends, 'who resemble altogether the Fishe Polypus: for as that Fishe chaungeth colour according to the object that it incountreth, so they alter their opinions according to the appetite of the hearers' (Guazzo 1967: I, 82 [Bk. 1]; 1993: I, 57 [1 A69b]). But Guazzo was less confident than 'some famous writers' that a flatterer could be distinguished from a friend: 'yet is it in my opinion verie harde (that I may not say impossible) to attaine to that knowledge, as well for that the worlde is full of these tame beastes [flatterers], as also for that it is harde to discerne the evill which resembleth the good' (Guazzo 1967: I, 83 [Bk. 1]; 1993: I, 57 [1 A69c]). But all this was mutual: the courtierly conduct Guazzo recommended could not reliably be distinguished from the flattering conduct Guazzo found everywhere and inescapable. Civil conversation created a world of mutual flatterers as much as it created a world of mutual search for knowledge and truth.

This duality posed a dilemma: was civil conversation's mutual flattery prerequisite for the mutual search for truth? Or was there a way to remove the flattery and retain the search for truth? One contrast in Guazzo perhaps provided a hint. Annibale expressed a poor opinion of 'Rethoricians', a species of the evil-tongued who specialised in slander and the flattery of Princes (Guazzo 1967: I, 66–8, 79, 87–8 [Bk. 1]); 1993: I, 47–8 [1 A51–1 A52, 1 C54–A A54a], 55 [1 C68e], 60–1 [1 A74e–h]). On the one hand, this condemnation of 'Rethoricians' aligned civil conversation with *sermo* (and all other Renaissance rebellions against rhetoric) against the realm of oratory. On the other hand, Annibale contrasted the flatterer with the Orator: the Orator sought openly to persuade a Prince to grant him favour, while a flatterer secretly sought that favour (Guazzo 1967: I, 85 [Bk. 1]; 1993: I, 59 [1 A72b–c]). This distinction appeared to allow for a species of rhetoric that escaped corruption – one marked by open persuasion. To the extent that civil conversation was itself a species of flattery, this prescription implied that openness could also operate as an antidote to civil conversation's characteristic flaws. In Guazzo's theme of openness as a solution to the tensions of civil conversation, we see a first hint of the tradition that would proffer *publicity* as a necessary component of proper political speech.

Various corollaries arose from Guazzo's discussion of civil conversation. The first regarded the capacity and the character of opinion. We may recollect that Guazzo argued that 'the trueth is taken from the common consent and opinions of men.' This argument supposed a certain capacity to perceive the truth that adhered to such opinions. Guazzo located that capacity as a result of a particularly significant civil conversation among unlike men, 'the conversation between the learned, and the ignorant'. Annibale argued that this conversation produced a middle ground

betweene learning and ignorance ... whiche consisteth in a good opinion, that is, in being partaker of the trueth, without being able to yeelde any reason why it is so: the which cannot be called learning, because learning can give a reason of thinges: and it cannot be called ignorance, because he ought not to be tearmed ignorante, who is partaker of the trueth. (Guazzo 1967: I, 213–14 [Bk. 2]; 1993: I, 150 [2 A185b, 2A188a])

The will to ignorance or knowledge mattered most in this middle ground: 'hee ought to bee called ignorant, whose minde is repugnant to knowledge, or to the common opinion of others, or to reason . . . And contrariwise, hee is to be tearmed wise, whose mind yeeldeth to learning, opinions, and reason, though hee bee not learned' (Guazzo 1967: I, 215 [Bk. 2]; 1993: I, 151 [2 A188c]). In sum, men were capable of opinion that could conduce to truth; such truth was to be located in their common consent; such opinions arose from the civil conversation of the learned and the ignorant; the desire to learn was necessary for the constitution of capable opinion; and capable opinion could be constituted from the inarticulate assent by the half-learned to the persuasions of reason. In a few brief pages, Guazzo encapsulated a large fraction of the future history of opinion and of the entire Enlightenment project.

A second corollary concerned the status of women in the realm of civil conversation. As we have seen, there had been a steady advance in the presence, role and speech of women during the preceding century and a half of Renaissance conversation in general, and in the dialogue genre in particular. As regards the more domestic subject matter of *Civil Conversation*, Smarr notes that such works as Aonio Paleario's (1503–70) *Dell'economia o vero del governo della casa* (1555) and Girolamo Razzi Silvano's (1527–1611) *Della economica christiana, e civile . . .* (1568) provided immediate precedents for discussion of women and the household (Smarr 2005: 3–4). Yet Guazzo solidified this role: civil conversation was explicitly to be conducted *nowe with men, then with women* and the metaphoric canal boat from Padua to Venice included both men and women. Unlike politics, traditionally more exclusively masculine, the sphere of *conversatio*, of society, included women both as interlocutors in and as subjects of conversation. As in Renaissance *sermo*, women were not fully equal to men in status in civil conversation, but they *had* a status. Moreover, it was a status *as* women recognised precisely for their unlikeness to men rather than for their likeness to a presumptively male norm.

The subject of the status of women was addressed at length in the third book of Guazzo's *Civil Conversation*, within the framework of a prescription of appropriate conversation between husband

and wife. This conversation was clearly unequal, one where, as a rule, the husband spoke and the silent wife listened, so as to elicit the wifely virtues – decorum, chastity, obedience. The wife, therefore, was capable of improvement by participation in this domestic conversation – but it was a capacity whose implications were still severely circumscribed (Guazzo 1967: II, 2 [Bk. 3]; 1993: I, 178 [3 A3]; Richards 2003: 39–40). Still, wives were capable of giving counsel: 'many [husbands] have found much profite by following their wives counsayle . . . if he disclose any ill happe unto her, she lightneth his greefe, eyther by comforting him lovinglye, or by helping to beare a part of it patientlye' (Guazzo 1967: II, 27 [Bk. 3]; 1993: I, 196 [3 A49g]). Women, as wives, now were the subjects as well as the objects of conversation. Moreover, Guazzo even cited the image of woman as a model for male behaviour:

> And as women before they present themselves to the view of others, prie in their glasse, and take counsayle and assistance therof: so before we utter our wordes, we must have recourse to the inward glasse, that wee may order and place them in such sorte, that the hearers may not judge, that they take their beginning rather from the mouth, then from the heart, and that they are rather shot foorth at all adventures rashly, then uttered with reason advisedly. (Guazzo 1967: I, 149 [Bk. 2]; 1993: I, 104 [2 A75a])

Although the comparison was between female appearance and male wisdom, it was women's self-control and prudence that ultimately was presented as the object that men should imitate. That such female virtue had become the measure of men's was a remarkable development in the status of women; that this development occurred in Guazzo's work registered the importance of the tradition of civil conversation (overlapping with the tradition of *sermo* in this aspect also) as a medium for the development of that status.

To this general discussion of the status of women, one should add a particular mention of Annibale's rejection of wife-beating: 'If she commit any fault, through my fault, I am better worthy to be beaten then she, but if she do it by negligence, with what hart can I so much as touch a hayre of her head?' (Guazzo 1967: II, 40 [Bk. 3]; 1993: I, 207 [3 A79]). This passage highlights an important point: what was the alternative to civil conversation? Tyranny, willfullness, bestiality – the exercise of physical violence to achieve one's desire. Now, in one long tradition, rhetoric and conversation, speech and sociability, had always been conceived of as alternates to the sheer physicality of violence (Foley 2012, 2013). Yet this dichotomy had been primarily or essentially in the public sphere, in the relations between male heads of households. Within the private sphere, the household, men were still free to exercise tyrannical violence, without it necessarily being considered a contradiction to the exercise of persuasive words in the public sphere. But to apply civil conversation to women, to the domestic sphere, made an issue of such violence – and Guazzo, in Annibale's words, forthrightly came to the conclusion that it exempted women from the exercise of male tyranny, of male violence. Guazzo's civil conversation did not construe women as the equals of men, but it said they should be persuaded into virtue rather than beaten by men. This was the bedrock in all future innovations on the Guazzian conception of civil conversation – and exemplified those future arguments which likewise proposed a universal shift from physical violence to persuasive words.

A third, related corollary concerned another aspect of the domestic sphere: the relation of master to servant. Guazzo thought masters, although they should maintain due authority over their servants and should know how to instruct and command them, above all should behave conversationally toward them. A master should 'live gently and familiarly with them [his servants], by doing whereof he shall winne the good will of his Servauntes unto him', rather than behaving imperiously and seeking to use words to instill them with fear (Guazzo 1967: II, 978, 104–8 [Bk. 3]; 1993: I, 251–2 [3 A201, 3 A204b, 3 A205a], 256–9 [3 A215 – 3 A223cCIT]). The political model was explicit: the master should behave to his servants as the Prince should behave to his courtiers (Guazzo 1967: II, 105 [Bk. 3]; Guazzo 1993: I, 257 [3 A216c]). Finally, a hierarchical variant of the Golden Rule applied: 'the maister ought to use his servaunt familiarlye, remembring to intreate his inferiours, as hee woulde bee intreated by his Superioures' (Guazzo 1967: II, 109 [Bk. 3]; 1993: I, 260 [3 A223i]). Here, as with the treatment of women, civil conversation extended to the domestic, private sphere the mutualities of respect and non-violence expected in the public sphere. The household, in effect, was no longer to be a tyranny but an (aristocratic) republic.

Guazzo's conception of civil conversation, by yoking the two concepts that compounded the phrase, broadened the application of civil to all the areas of life previously excluded from the realm of politics, and reoriented *conversatio* to a this-worldly application whose framework was political. We may note here that the areas of life previously excluded especially and significantly included both domestic and economic affairs (Richards 2003, 20–42, 87–112). This realm of civil conversation, as we shall see, would soon acquire the sobriquets of 'sociability' and 'society' – and to these concepts would be applied these various connotations of civil conversation. Sociability and society, that is, would be primarily constituted by speech, would overlap in their associations with *sermo*, would be contrasted with the tyrannical monologies of court and solitude, would have an ambivalent relationship with sincerity and honesty, would seek alternately truth and power, would be oriented both toward an otherworldly good and a worldly politics, and would include, thematically, the domestic realm and the economic realm, women and servants, and all the diversity of mankind. Thus much Guazzo had already provided for the future.

Guazzo's *Civil Conversation* had widespread popularity in the next two generations: published in 1574, expanded in 1579, it was translated into French, English, Latin and German by the end of the century and published in thirty-four separate editions through 1631 – when new editions ceased, and direct influence presumably dwindled dramatically (Miller 2008: 47). Its impact was broader still, via a variety of intermediaries. In Italy, Flavio Querenghi (1581–1647) in *Discorsi morali politici e naturali* (1644) still argued the nature and value of civil conversation in arguments much like Guazzo's (Miller 2000: 64–5). In France, Gabriel Chappuys' (*c.*1546–1613) dedicatory epistle to his French translation of *Civil Conversation* defined conversation in Senecan terms as a shared process of self-improvement in pursuit of excellence (Chappuys 1579: sig. 2^v–3^r; Miller 2000: 55–6, 184 (notes 35–6)). In Elizabethan England, Guazzo's championing of civil conversation was generally taken to support the (courtly) critique of the court by offering an alternative venue of human interaction, egalitarian and friendly (Javitch 1971: 189–98; Olmsted 2005: 162). Yet civil conversation was also open to appropriation by the court: so Spenser in *The Faerie Queene*:

> Of Court it seemes, men Courtesie doe call,
> For that it there most vseth to abound;
> And well beseemeth that in Princes hall
> That vertue should be plentifully found,
> Which of all goodly manners is the ground,
> And roote of civill conuersation.
>> (Spenser 1909: 312 [6.1.1.1–6]; Miller 2000: 68)

Most broadly, a generation and more of works on the civil life, both theories and exemplifying histories, owed a debt to Guazzo, which debt may be traced not least by examining the careers and writings of various of Guazzo's translators (Miller 2008: 53–4).

For all these writers influenced by Guazzo, his civil conversation provided an intermediate category between the (Petrarchan) stark dichotomy between solitude and the world, between contemplation and politics. Civil conversation likewise offered an intermediate category between the speech of friends and the speech of strangers, between speech in the academy and speech in the city, a polite and friendly speech toward those with whom one must speak, even though not friends. In its provision of these intermediate categories, civil conversation flowed into both the tradition of *parlementaire* and scholarly civility and the French *salon* tradition – in alternate modes, however, where the greater courtliness, the presence of women, and greater social heterogeneity characterised the civil conversation of the *salons* in distinction to that of the *parlementaires* and the Republic of Letters (Miller 2000: 55, 57–8; Miller 2008: 52–6).

Pierre Charron's widely popular *De la sagesse* (1601) perhaps was the most important conduit of Guazzo's influence in the seventeenth century: Tuck notes that 'Pierre Charron's *Of Wisdom* . . . first appeared in French in 1601, and was re-issued at least twelve times between 1601 and 1663; it was soon translated into English, and ran through eight editions between 1608 and 1670' (Tuck 1983: 44). Charron incorporated Guazzo's thought largely undigested in his writing on man's proper behaviour toward other men (Charron n.d. [after 1612]: 334–8 [II.9]; Thweatt 1980: 28, 28 (note 27)). So, for example, we find polypian conduct once more prescribed:

> It is a great vice (whereof this our Wise-man must take heed) and a defect inconvenient both to himself and to another, to be bound and subject to certaine humours and complexions, to one only course; that is, to be a slave to himself, so to be captivated to his proper inclinations, that hee cannot be bent to any other, a testimonie of an anxious scrupulous minde, and ill bred, too amorous, and too partiall to it selfe. These kinde of people have much to endure and to contest; and contrariwise it is a great sufficiency and wisedome to accommodate himselfe to all . . . To be supple and manaible, to know how to rise and fall, to bring himself into order when there is need. The fairest mindes, and the best borne, are the more universall, the more common, applicable to all understandings, communicative and open to all people. (Charron n.d. [after 1612]: 335 [II.9])

Charron likewise echoed Guazzo on the benefit of (some) conversation:

> Let us come to the other consideration, and kind of conversation more speciall, whereof the instructions are these. The first is to seek to conferrre,

and converse with men of constancie and dexteritie; for thereby the minde is confirmed and fortified, and is elevated above it selfe, as with base and weake spirits it is debased, and utterly lost: the contagion herein is, as in the bodie, and also more. (Charron n.d. [after 1612]: 337 [II.9])

By such maxims, Charron transmitted widely the Guazzian conception of the necessity and the benefit of conversation.

The great transposition

What Charron transmitted, however, rapidly ceased to be called conversation – for we come now to the seventeenth-century migration of terms. The signification of *conversatio* – *conversazione, conversation* – had already shifted considerably during the Renaissance from *way of life* to *speech*. Durng the seventeenth century, above all in France, the definition of *speech* became primary. Furthermore – and this shift is the final sign of how closely *sermo* and *conversatio* had come to overlap with one another – modern *conversation* shifted to incorporate *sermo*. Indeed, it did so with such success that we cannot now discuss *sermo* by any word in English or French save 'conversation'.

Conversatio retained links to the old definition of conversation, but *conversatio*, by its migration from the realm of behaviour to that of speech, essentially left behind a concept without a word. This concept would be taken over by *sociability* and its cognates of *society*, *sociable*, etc. In England, Withington notes that John Barston's (c.1545–c.1612) *The Safeguard of Societie* (1576) was 'the first printed text in English to display the term "society" on its title-page'; the use of the term *society* quickly spread in England to encompass all forms of 'voluntary and purposeful association', with perhaps a particular emphasis on associations such as the Royal Society, the Society for the Reformation of Manner and the Society of Jesus, meant to promote learning and virtue (Withington 2010: 102–5, 120–1, 126, 130–1). These terms would include, as had civil conversation, the entire realm of manners, of civilisation, of behaviour among mankind with an orientation toward a later good. The transformation, indeed, would be so total that, just as we now must refer to *sermo* as 'conversation', it is now almost impossible to refer to the older signification of *conversation* without using the modern words of sociability, society, etc. One register of this transformation appears in the successive translations of More's *Utopia*. The 1551

Ralph Robynson (1520–77) translation provided this section title and description of the Utopians: 'Of theire liuinge and mutual conuersation together . . . But nowe wil I declare how the citizens use them selfes on towards another: what familiar occupieng and enterteynement there is amonge the people, and what fassion they use in the distribution of every thing' (More 1952: 86). A modern translation, *sans* section title, reads: 'Now I'd better explain their social arrangements – how society is organized, how they behave towards one another, how goods are distributed, and so on' (More 2003: 59). The replacement here of *conversation* by *society* is a miniature of the larger linguistic trend.

Conversatio and *societas* had long been approaching one another. As far back as the high Middle Ages, Aquinas had stated that man's relationship to God consisted of both *societas* and *familiaris conversatio*: 'Haec autem societas hominis ad Deum, quae est quaedum familiaris conversatio cum ipso' (Aquinas 1969: 194 [1a2ae.65.5]; Wadell 1996: 165 (note 2)). During the seventeenth century, however, this overlap thickened notably. So Ripa in his *Iconologia* (1625) used the phrase 'Conversatio est hominum societas, & grata confabulatio qua mediante invicem animi recreantur', while in 1642, Charles I of England (1600–49; r. 1625–49) likewise referred to 'the Laws of Society and civil Conversation' (Ripa 1625: 133; Miller 2000: 187 (note 84); Charles I 1642: 21; Williams 1985: 292). The replacement of *conversation* with *society* and its cognates had broad and durable precedents.

The English translation of Guazzo's *Civil Conversation* also brought the two concepts into at least loose association. While discussing conversation at length, Guazzo, rendered into English, casually stated that, 'who so leaveth the civile society [*congregazione civile*] to place himself in some solitarie desert, taketh as it were the forme of a beast, and in a certaine manner putteth upon him selfe a brutishe nature' (Guazzo 1967: I, 30 [Bk. 1]; 1993: I, 24 [1 A161]). Here 'civil society' appeared to be a synonym for 'civil conversation'; at most at no great variance in meaning. This use of 'civil society' in the 1581 English translation of Guazzo preceded by seventeen years what Colas takes to be the first appearance in English, in 1598, of the phrase 'civil society' (Colas 1997: 20) – what may be the first appearance in English of the phrase 'civil society' was within the translation of Guazzo's work on civil conversation. The shift in England from civil conversation to society had roots in Guazzo's words innovatively rendered into English.

The natural law of sociability

The seventeenth-century shift from *conversation* to *sociability* and *society* thus had a broad precedent – but it derived most of its impetus from the irruption into this constellation of concepts of the innovative vocabulary and ideas of the jurisprudential natural law tradition. This irruption proceeded from a weakness in the theory of civil conversation. What, after all, was the motivation to enage in civil conversation in the first place? Why be mannerly or polite? Guazzo had argued the necessity of civil conversation, and its advantage as a means of seeking knowledge, but these did not centrally address the question of motivation.

Now, Guazzo did provide an answer to this question – one, significantly, derived from Stoic philosophy, which was soon also to be the basis of seventeenth-century developments in natural law. Guazzo simply posited that nature, that *deus ex machina*, intended man to engage in civil conversation:

> You see then (Gentleman) that conversation is not onely profitable, but moreover necessary to the perfection of man, who must confesse that hee is lyke the Bee which cannot live alone. And therefore according to the grave opinion of the Stoikes, we must thinke that as all thinges upon the earth are made for the use of man, so man is created for the use of man, to the intent that following nature as their guide and Mistres, they have to succor one another, to communicate together common profites, in giving and receiving, uniting and binding themselves together by artes, occupations, and faculties: so that hee may repute himself an unfortunate man, which hath not the meanes by conversation to purchase his own profite and other mens: a punishement inflicted by the laws on some offendors for a kinde of torment (Guazzo 1967: I, 35 [Bk. 1]; 1993: I, 27 [1 A16y]) . . . man, being a compagnable creature, loveth naturally the conversation of other men, and doing the contrarie, he doth offend nature her self. (Guazzo 1967: I, 20 [Bk. 1]; 1993: I, 17 [1 A11c])

In effect, this was a reformulation of the Stoic concept of *oikeiosis*: in Dickey's summary, 'a doctrine that holds that as human beings have more contact with each other they begin to exhibit a willingness to negotiate and co-operate with each other in common endeavors, especially in endeavors that help preserve the material well-being of socially organized groups (e.g., families, nations and empires)' (Dickey 2004: 280; and see Brandt 2004; Brooke 2012: 37–58; Pembroke 1971). This was all very well, but it remained ungrounded.

'Nature', so put – for which the (originally Stoic [Watson 1971]) conception of *natural law*, in this context, was largely synonymous – was more a waving of hands than an answer. Guazzo's proffered answer left open how precisely nature motivated the latter-day *oikeiosis* of civil conversation.

The question was all the sharper precisely since, as noted above, civil conversation was predicated as behaviour toward dissimilar people, and it took the dissimilarity of mankind as thematic: *people differ one from another in degree, in age, in kinde, in life, in maners, and in profession*. But if people were dissimilar, how could one assume that all of them would be motivated to conduct civil conversation? The excursion into natural law begins with this sceptical challenge of the late sixteenth century. Montaigne, and perhaps more influentially his populariser Pierre Charron, had made a very powerful case that the variations of mankind argued against too facile a reliance on any local custom, law or religion as a basis of natural law. As Charron put it in *Of Wisdome*, 'Now there is not any thing in the world which is not denied and contradicted, not by one nation, but by divers: and there is not any thing so strange and unnaturall in the opinion of divers, which is not approved and authorized in many places by common use' (Charron n.d. [after 1612]: 277 [II.3]; Montaigne 2003: 526–7). This could not but apply also to the disposition toward civil conversation.

Yet Charron had not abandoned the concept of natural law. Rather, traditionally, he both affirmed the the necessity and the desirability of following natural law, and associated it with reason (Charron n.d. [after 1612]: 278 [II.3]). He then, in effect, put forth a challenge: natural law was difficult to find, but could be deduced from what indeed was universally human:

> From this general and universall alteration and corruption is it come to passe, that there is nothing of Nature knowen in us. If we must say what the laws thereof are, and how many they are, we are much hindred. The ensigne & marke of a natural law is the universitie of approbation: for that which Nature shall have truely ordeined for us, we with a common consent shall follow without doubting; and not only every nation, but every particular person. (Charron n.d. [after 1612]: 277 [II.3]; see also Thweatt 1980: 25)

Charron's link of natural law with *the universitie of approbation* would have an afterlife of much influence, notably in the thought of David Hume (1711–76) (see this book's sequel), but for now we may concentrate on its immediate effect upon the natural law tradition. Natural law now had to be based upon attributes common to 'every particular person' of mankind – and therefore so too had to be the disposition to civil conversation.

The challenge posed by scepticism would elicit widely divergent answers during the seventeenth century. Descartes, and all the rationalists allied with him, concentrated upon our knowledge of our ratiocination: *ego sum res cogitans* (Descartes 1996: 19 ['Second Meditation']; and see Schiffman 1991: 78–128). An alternate answer, however, lay in the knowledge of our passions. The Earl of Shaftesbury (1671–1713) would sum up this tradition so in 'An inquiry concerning virtue or merit': 'For let us carry scepticism ever so far, let us doubt, if we can, of everything about us, we cannot doubt of what passes within ourselves. Our passions and affections are known to us. They are certain, whatever the objects may be on which they are employed' (Shaftesbury 1999: 229). But this answer, our knowledge of our passions, led to a further debate: which passions predominated? Which were common to all mankind? What passions, precisely, sparked civil conversation?

An extended debate and series of answers came from the tradition of natural jurisprudence (Forbes 1975: 3–121; Tuck 1979) – or, more precisely, from the seventeenth-century transformation of natural jurisprudence induced, above all, by the trinity of Hugo Grotius (1583–1645), Thomas Hobbes (1588–1679) and Samuel Pufendorf (1632–94). All three of these figures were to a considerable extent reacting against the sceptics' challenge as they sought to construct a natural law that accounted for the variety of humanity (Besselink 2004; Tuck 1983; 1987: 100, 107–18; 1993: 83). They therefore focused on working out a natural law based on universal human impulses.

To do so, they seized hold of what even the sceptics conceded: that, as Seneca had put it, 'there are implanted in us love of self, a desire for existence and self-preservation, and also an abhorrence of dissolution' (Seneca 1917–25: II, 251 [82.15]). Grotius first and most influentially took this concession as the basis for working out a natural law that could indeed apply to all mankind, and from which a moral system could be elaborated:

Since God fashioned creation and willed its existence, every individual part thereof has received from Him certain natural properties whereby that existence may be preserved and each part may be guided for its own good, in conformity, one might say, with the fundamental law inherent in its origin. From this fact the old poets and philosophers have rightly deduced that love, whose primary force and action are directed to self-interest, is the first principle of the whole natural order. (Grotius 1995: 9 [2]; Hont 1987: 261 (note 26), 262; Kogel 1972: 164; Tuck 1983: 52)

Grotius thus defined his natural jurisprudence as universally valid, without dependence on the particularities of local laws or religions – although he did allow a place for the customs shared by (self-defined) civilised lands and a conception of an innate – ungrounded, unexplained – desire in mankind for society, an *appetitus socialis*.

> For by reason that Man above all other Creatures is endued not only with this *Social* Faculty of which we have spoken, but likewise with Judgment to discern Things pleasant or hurtful, and those not only present but future, and such as may prove to be so in their Consequences; it must therefore be agreeable to human Nature, that according to the Measure of our Understanding we should in these Things follow the Dictates of a right and sound Judgement, and not be corrupted either by Fear, or the Allurements of a present Pleasure, nor by carried away violently by blind Passion. And whatsoever is contrary to such a Judgement is likewise understood to be contrary to Natural Right, that is, the Laws of our Nature. (Grotius 1738: xviii; Hont 1987: 258–9, 262; Tuck 1979: 72)

This concept of a social faculty, an *appetitus socialis*, was, of course, another rendition of Stoic *oikeiosis*, broadly synonymous with the disposition to civil conversation. Now, however, a derivation of *oikeiosis* had acquired in the motivation of self-preservation the beginning of a more thorough grounding.

Hobbes followed this lead by providing an epistemology and a concept of a state of nature derived solely from universal human nature – above all, the impulse of self-preservation – without Grotian resort either to custom or to an *appetitus socialis* (Hont 1987: 256, 259–60). Hobbes conceived of his state of nature as divided sharply from *civitas*, as pertaining to a distant, primitive past disjunct from the complex modernities of the present. He therefore conceived of a consequent polarity between the state and the individual, where the binding contract of the state provided the sole means to satisfy the agonistic individuals' passionate interest in self-preservation (Hobbes 1972: 48 [11.6]; Hont 1987: 260–2; Zagorin 2009: 32–3). As a corollary, Hobbes likewise defined the questions at issue in his philosophy by repeated reference to the agonistic modes of *controversy* and *debates* – terms not idle in their implications of the proper mode of speech. So in *Leviathan* (1651):

> And therfore, as when there is a controversy in an account, the parties must by their own accord set up for right reason the reason of some arbitrator, or judge, to whose sentence they will both stand, or their controversy must either come to blows, or be undecided, for want of a right reason constituted by Nature; so is it also in all debates of what kind soever. (Hobbes 1996: 32–3 [1.5]; and see Hobbes 1969: 188–9 [2.10.8])

Moreover, Hobbes in *De Cive* (1642) simply excluded the alternative, and aspiration, of conversation as he posited a stark binary between logic and rhetoric:

> Now, *eloquence* is twofold. The one is an elegant, and cleare expression of the conceptions of the mind, and riseth partly from the contemplation of the things themselves, partly from an understanding of words taken in their own proper, and definite signification; the other is a commotion of the Passions of the minde (such as are *hope, fear, anger, pitty*) and derives from a metaphoricall use of words fitted to the Passions: That forms a speech from true Principles, this from opinions already received, what nature soever they are of. The art of that is Logick, of this Rhetorick; the end of that is truth, of this victory. (Hobbes 1983: 154 [12.12])

Oikeiosis and its derivations of civil conversation and the social faculty all faded away from this portrait of human nature and from this reliance on a conceptual vocabulary steeped in agonistic rhetoric. Hobbes thus provided a properly universal grounding for human motivation, but one which denied any disposition to civil conversation.

Pufendorf (largely in *Of the Law of Nature and Nations* (1672), but also in *Elements of Universal Jurisprudence* (1660)) synthesised the thought of his two great predecessors, grounding Grotius in the system of Hobbes. He followed Grotius in deploying the thought of Cicero and the Stoics, especially the concept of sociability, and likewise followed Grotius in the ambition of his system of natural law (Hont 1987: 259). He also followed Grotius in relying on sociability precisely because it was universal: 'I have posited the sociality of man as the foundation of universal natural law because I could discover no other principle which all men could at the recommendation of their mortal condition itself be brought to admit, whatever conviction they ultimately had about the divine' (Pufendorf 1994: 97 [*On the Law of Nature and of Nations in Eight Books*, Preface to the First Edition]). Moreover, Pufendorf was eminently Grotian in that he took the impulse to self-preservation to be the foundation of his system of sociability (Pufendorf 1729: 136–7 [2.3.15]; Tuck 1987: 105). Pufendorf's natural law, in emphatic contradistinction, thus added to Hobbes' principle of self-preservation the principle:

> 'That he should not disturb human society,' that is, 'that he should not do anything whereby society among men may be less tranquil.' . . . But since it has been shown above that nature has directly destined man to a social life . . . The preservation of social life is also deservedly laid down as a foundation for the laws of nature. (Pufendorf 1994: 84 [*Elements of Universal Jurisprudence*, II.Observation 4: 4–5])

But Pufendorf, with Hobbes, departed from Grotius in denying any *appetitus socialis*. Sociability was not in itself benevolence or altruism. It was profoundly selfish: 'Man, therefore, first embraced civil Society, not as led to it by the Biass of Nature, but as driven by the Fear of greater Evils' (Pufendorf 1729: 626 [7.1.4]; Hont 1987: 267–8). Yet that very selfishness, married to need, promoted the practice of reciprocity and the conception of human equality:

> Now since human nature belongs equally to all men, and since one cannot lead a social life with someone by whom one is not esteemed at least as a man, it follows as a precept of natural law that 'Everyone must esteem and treat other men as his natural equals, or as men in the same sense as he.' (Pufendorf 1994: 159–64 [*On the Law of Nature and of Nations in Eight Books*, 3.2], esp. 159 [3.2.1]; Hont 1987: 268)

Indeed, it was so powerful that it made the practice of mutual sociability universal in mankind – an action of natural law: 'This then will appear a fundamental Law of Nature, *Every Man ought, as far as in him lies, to promote and preserve a peaceful Sociableness with others, agreeable to the main End and Disposition of human Race in general*' (Pufendorf 1729: 137 [2.3.15]; Hont 1987: 268).

Pufendorf, however, recast Hobbes' conception of the state of nature to emphasise its diachronic status as a product of history, as much manifest in a modern kingdom as an ancient tribe: 'Both formerly, when humankind separated into distinct family groups, as well as now, when it has been divided into civil states, those who do not obey one another and have no common master among men live mutually in a natural state' (Pufendorf 1994: 143 [*On the Law of Nature and of Nations in Eight Books*, 2.2.4]; Hont 1987: 256–7). He also stipulated that the mutual need of one man for another for sheer survival made human cooperation, and the consequent instinct of *socialitas*, sociability, fundamental attributes of the human desire for self-preservation: 'Man is an Animal extremely desirous of his own Preservation, of himself expos'd to many Wants, unable to secure his own Safety and Maintenance without the Assistance of his Fellows, and capable of returning the Kindness by the Further-ance of mutual Good' (Pufendorf 1729: 136–7 [2.3.15]; Hont 1987: 264–5; cf. Seneca 1917–25: III, 397 [121.2]). Indeed, these attributes preceded the state, and they created society – Aristotelian *koinonia* – independent of the process that would create the state (Hont 1987: 264–5).[1] Such sociability was not original to mankind – but then neither was speech. The development of sociability was as natural as the development of speech (Pufendorf 1729: 139 [2.3.16]; Hont 1987: 268).

Pufendorf thus established a conception of sociability as natural law grounded in universal human nature. The universality of this natural law, however, did still require at least one predicate outside of human nature. As against Grotius, who took knowledge of *utile* to be sufficient motivation for *honestum*, Pufendorf believed that God must both give mankind reason and make mankind follow reason's strictures: 'To make these Dictates of Reason obtain the Power and the Dignity of Laws, it is necessary to call in a much higher Principle to our Assistance' (Pufendorf 1729: 143 [2.3.20]; Darwall 2012; Tuck 1987: 105–6). Pufendorf, in effect, had pushed Grotius' a priori back a level, but not eliminated it entirely: where Grotius took socia-bility as a given, Pufendorf took the will to follow reason as a given.

The root of sociability thus was still ungrounded – in the last anal-ysis, God remained the ultimate predicate. Nevertheless, Pufendorf had constructed an intellectual framework of natural law that was grounded upon the universal instinct for self-preservation, a univer-sal sociability and, by implication, a universal capacity to engage in all that followed from sociability. This most definitely included the realm of behaviour variously denominated as civil conversation and manners. As Pufendorf put it:

We cannot but think that they would so long however continue in a brutal Wildness and Disorder, till at last, either by their own Wit and Experience, or by some Hints and Instructions taken from the Conduct of mute Creatures, they should by Degrees arrive at some Method and

Elegancy of Living, and as *Virgil* says . . . [']Studious Need might beat out useful Arts[']. (Pufendorf 1729: 103 [2.2.2]; Hont 1987: 265)

The connection of sociability to behaviour thus translated into an aspect of human nature the democratising shifts implicit in Guazzo's elaboration of civil conversation. Sociability, as universal motive power, made equally universal the capacity and disposition for civil conversation and manners.

As noted above, this sociability grounded in natural law was so powerful a concept that it, and its various cognates, entirely supplanted the phrase *civil conversation*. We may locate this supplantation precisely, in the late-seventeenth-century introduction of this jurisprudential tradition into French intellectual discourse, via Jean Barbeyrac's (1674–1744) translation and popularisation of Pufendorf's works (Hochstrasser 1993: 289–90). *Honnête* conveyed some of what would be meant by *sociable* and *société*, *sociable* and *social* already had some currency in seventeenth-century French dictionaries and thought – but the great efflourescence of these cognates, and the appearance of *sociabilité*, was a phenomenon of the last decade of the seventeenth century and the first decades of the eighteenth. In these decades, the Pufendorfian-cum-Barbeyracian vocabulary naturalised itself to France – whence it spread swiftly to the rest of Europe and beyond. The French tended to appropriate the vocabulary and concepts at a quite general level rather than to engage deeply with the theoretical details of natural law – but the appropriation perhaps was all the more extensive for its lack of rigour. The result, at any rate, was that the cognates of *sociabilité* replaced the semantic field previously occupied by *civil conversation* and in so doing made that range of behaviour an attribute of all mankind, whose exercise followed inevitably from the operations of natural law (D. Gordon 1994: 51–2, 64, 74–5).

Doux commerce

We may recollect that Pufendorf had a diachronic, historicising conception of the state of nature. This opened up a new realm of inquiry: how did the impulse of sociability proceed in human history? The answer to this was that sociability found particular expression in commerce – that word previously associated, in all its connotations, with conversation – and above all in economic commerce (Clark 2007; France 1992: 97–112; Hont 1987: 266–7). Sociability, after all, in the broadest sense was the commerce of men to satisfy mutual needs; it was easy enough to take commerce in the narrower, eco-nomic sense as a prime example of such sociability. Easy, but not automatic: as Hirschman notes, 'commerce was characterized as "perpetual combat" by Jean-Baptiste Colbert (1619–83) and as "a kind of warfare" by Sir Josiah Child' (1630–99) (Clément 1869: 266; Ms. Minute Book, House of Lords Record Office, H.L. Papers (1669), no. 215, fol. 6, quoted in Letwin 1959: 28; Hirschman 1977: 79). As other forms of conduct – notably, emblematically, the duel – commerce could be conceived in agonistic terms rather than peaceful ones.

To conceive of economic commerce as a form of sociability was to make an argument that commerce indeed was peaceful in nature – that, as Jacques Savary (1622–90) put it in *Le parfait négociant* (1675), '[Divine Providence] . . . has dispersed its gifts so that men would trade together and so that the mutual need which they have to help one another would establish ties of friendship among them' (Savary 1675: 1, translated in Hirschman 1977: 59–60). Savary, of course, wrote a generation before Barbeyrac's introduction of Pufendorfian thought into France; sociability strengthened an exist-ing strand of French thought. But strengthen it did, and dramati-cally. Jean-François Melon (1675–1738) wrote in *Essai politique sur le commerce* (1734) that '[t]he spirit of conquest and the spirit of commerce are mutually exclusive in a nation'; and fourteen years later Montesquieu (1689–1755) would elaborate in *The Spirit of the Laws* (1748) that, '[t]he natural effect of commerce is to lead to peace. Two nations that trade with each other become recipro-cally dependent; if one has an interest in buying, the other has an interest in selling, and all unions are founded on mutual needs' (Melon 1966: 733, translated in Hirschman 1977: 80; Montesquieu 1989: 338 [4.20.2]; Hirschman 1977: 80). Early eighteenth-century France generally thought of economic commerce in such sociable terms. In Enlightenment Scotland, the same dichotomy would be framed as one between commercial society and the martial virtues (Berry 2013: 143–5).

But to take commerce as an example of sociability was therefore to take it as an example of sociability working in history – and commerce, in consequence, was taken to operate in history. This conception, too, already had appeared in Savary – '*This continuous exchange of all the comforts of life constitutes commerce and this commerce makes for all the gentleness* (douceur) *of life*' (Savary 1675: 1, translated in Hirschman 1977: 60) – but here also the introduction of sociability vastly strengthened this conception. Montesquieu wrote in *The Spirit of the Laws* (1748) that '[c]ommerce cures destructive prejudices, and it is an almost general rule that everywhere there are gentle mores, there is commerce and that everywhere there is commerce, there are gentle mores . . . Commerce . . . polishes and softens barbarous mores, as we see every day' (Montesquieu 1989: 338 [4.20.1]; and see France 1992: 55–9). Likewise, William Robertson (1721–93) wrote in *A View of the Progress of Society in Europe* (1769) that '[c]ommerce tends to wear off those prejudices which maintain distinction and animosity between nations. It softens and polishes the manners of men' (Robertson 1777: 97; Hirschman 1977: 61). Going backward a few years, we may find a lengthy articulation of the thesis in Hume's 'Of Refinement in the Arts' (1742):

> The more these refined arts advance, the more sociable men become: nor is it possible, that, when enriched with science, and possessed of a fund of conversation, they should be contented to remain in solitude, or live with their fellow-citizens in that distant manner, which is peculiar to ignorant and barbarous nations. They flock into cities; love to receive and communicate knowledge; to show their wit or their breeding; their taste in conversation or living, in clothes or furniture. Curiosity allures the wise; vanity the foolish; and pleasure both. Particular clubs and societies are every where formed: both sexes meet in an easy and sociable manner; and the tempers of men, as well as their behaviour, refine apace. So that, beside the improvements which they receive from knowledge and the liberal arts, it is impossible but they must feel an increase of humanity, from the very habit of conversing together, and contributing to each other's pleasure and entertainment. Thus *industry, knowledge, and humanity*, are linked together, by an indissoluble chain, and are found, from experience as well as reason, to be peculiar to the more polished, and, what are commonly denominated, the more luxurious ages. (Hume 1996: III, 297–8)

Commerce, in other words, worked in history as an operation of natural law to produce manners – decorum, courtesy, civility, civil conversation, *politesse*.

This softening operation of commerce in history would receive the sobriquet of *doux commerce*.[2] We may note first that an alternate use of the phrase, in the 1769 *Règlemens pour les exercises intérieurs du collége de Louis-le-Grand*, was more or less precisely as a synonym for *conversatio*: 'As they are to live in society upon leaving the *Collège*, the pupils will be trained at an early stage in the practice of a gentle, easy and honest intercourse (*un commerce doux, aisé et honnête*).' As Hirschman notes, the conversational etymology of *doux commerce* thus associated economic exchange with the realm of manners (Rècueil 1814: 105 [11.3], translated in Hirschman 1977: 61–2). We may note secondly that *doux commerce*'s embedment in history soon led to an explicit consideration of the role of *doux commerce* in history. Montesquieu appears to have initiated this line of analysis, although in relatively brief form: 'Therefore, one should not be surprised if our mores are less fierce than they were formerly. Commerce has spread knowledge of the mores of all nations everywhere; they have been compared to each other, and good things have resulted from this' (Montesquieu 1989: 338 [4.20.1]). Robertson recapitulated this analysis in *A View of the Progress of Society in Europe* (1769): 'The progress of commerce had considerable influence in polishing the manners of the European nations, and in establishing among them order, equal laws, and humanity' (Robertson 1840: 72 [1.10.]).

This conception of the effects of *doux commerce* overlapped with a parallel conception of the effects of private property. As Pufendorf put it in *The Whole Duty of Man* (1673), in 'the Natural State of Man, according as Men are understood to stand in respect to one another merely from that common Alliance which results from the *Likeness* of their *Natures*' (Pufendorf 1698: 207–8 [2.1.5]; Hont 1987: 264). But this likeness – this friendship of man to man – was only possible in small, simple communities, and could not be extended farther in populous, complex communities: Pufendorf added in *Elements of Universal Jurisprudence* that 'After men had multiplied, nature recommended that these things be possessed separately by individuals in shares, to the exclusion of the rest, so that the disadvantages that would arise from communion be avoided' (Pufendorf 1994: 42–3 [*Elements of Universal Jurisprudence*, 1.5.15]; Hont 1987: 272). Larger, more complex societies required an alternative system to keep the peace: the selfish sociability and mutual need of private-property owners, assured that they could keep what they produced, provided that alternative. The historical development of sociability led to the development of private property (Pufendorf 1729: 364–70 [4.4.3–8], 376 [4.4.13]; Hont 1987: 270–3).

This narrative translated the old Greek antinomy between friendship which held all things in common and familiarity based on individual property into a historical dynamic. The state of nature was one of friendship; but the development of sociability led to individual property – and the defence of property rights, in both Grotius and Pufendorf, proceeded via an extensible conception of *suum*, the preservation of one's self invoked to defend all that was one's own

(Grotius 1738: 25–6 [1.2.1]; Pufendorf 1729: 10 [1.1.16], 12–13 [1.1.20], 260 [3.5.3], 364–7 [4.4.3–5]; Buckle 1991: 29–30, 76–81, 85). The historical progression from common property to private property was thus a progression from an economic system based upon the interactions of friendship to an economic system based upon the interactions of individual selves – the entire realm of justice, of course, but also the interactions of character, individuality and familiarity (Pocock 1985, esp. 103). Natural law operating via sociability by implication associated the historical development of private property with the historical development of the post-Montaignean communication of intimacy between unlike individuals.

The development of property, of course, also led to the development of a wealthy class. The different capacities of men ensured that property would not remain divided equally, if ever it had been. As Hume wrote in the *Enquiry Concerning the Principles of Morals* (1751), 'Render possessions ever so equal, men's different degrees of art, care, and industry, will immediately break that equality. Or if you check these virtues, you reduce society to the most extreme indigence; and, instead of preventing want and beggary in a few, render it unavoidable to the whole community' (Hume 1996: IV, 256 [3.2]). Inequality of property in turn led not only to the inequalities of subjection but also to luxury: Montesquieu put it in *Spirit of the Laws* that, '*Luxury* is always proportionate to the inequality of fortunes' (Montesquieu 1989: 96 [7.1]). Such luxury made leisure possible, whether for idle amusement or for the cultivation of the self both in manners and morals. Hume estimated nicely the varying modes of leisure that luxury enabled:

> LUXURY . . . may be taken in a good as well as in a bad sense . . . To be entirely occupied with the luxury of the table, for instance, without any relish for the pleasures of ambition, study, or conversation, is a mark of stupidity, and is incompatible with any vigour of temper or genius. (Hume 1996: III, 294–5; Boyd 2008; Dickey 2004: 274–8; Hont 1987: 271–2)

Private property's nurturing of luxury among the amply propertied thus joined with *doux commerce* in fostering the development of leisure.

And leisure, *otium*, was the precondition for the exercise of conversation. Commerce, manners and conversation – *conversatio, decorum, sermo* – thus became a logical sequence. So Hume in the *Enquiry Concerning the Principles of Morals*:

> The rules of GOOD MANNERS or POLITENESS [were introduced], in order to facilitate the intercourse of minds, and an undisturbed commerce and

conversation. Among well-bred people, a mutual deference is affected; contempt of others disguised; authority concealed; attention given to each in his turn; and an easy stream of conversation maintained, without vehemence, without interruption, without eagerness for victory, and without any airs of superiority. (Hume 1996: IV, 327 [8]; Dickins 2008: 31–2)

In Hume's 'Of Essay Writing' (1742) likewise we find both the scholarly Republic of Letters and the conversational world of the Salons, the Learned World and the Conversible World, cited as examplars of these realms of *sermo* (Hume 1998: 1). The marketplace made possible the *salon*.

I have argued elsewhere that Adam Smith took economic commerce to be an exercise of prudence and interest, and that such prudence was an exercise of reason in its rhetorical mode.[3] Here I wish to emphasise that the exercise of prudence generally, and of economic prudence in particular, was in pursuit of victory (economic gain) rather than of truth.[4] Smith's economic prudence therefore derived particularly from the persuasive mode of oratory.

Oratory thus joined the intellectual complex that had already joined together the concepts of commerce and conversation. Natural law implanted the impulse toward and capacity to engage in such economic commerce within each human breast as a species of the mutual need of sociability, and this impulse and capacity now were regarded as the preconditions for manners – which was itself a precondition for the conditions of conversation (*sermo*). The world of oratory – of interest and persuasion, of power and the pursuit of victory – provided the manners and the leisure that allowed for the discussions of indefinite topics. As a matter of psychological analysis, (economic) interest united the passions and the reason; as a matter of historical analysis, (economic) interest provided the material preconditions for a leisured class whose minds were capable, in conversation, of reasoning and being reasoned with. In short, *the exercise of oratory, in the form of economic commerce, became prerequisite for the exercise of conversation.*

The motor of history: manners, virtues and liberty

Doux commerce connected manners and conversation – and this connection was now to be ramified by the extension of *doux commerce* to connect manners to virtue and liberty. This innovation was part of an elaborate response to the critique of the civil humanist school, which had always argued in favour of virtue and against luxury, that obverse of manners. One initital response to this had been evasion: Barbeyrac, underlining Pufendorf's point, had emphasised that commerce was necessary for sociability, and its attendant moral corruptions were to be censured by men of God rather than prohibited by civil law (Pufendorf 1729: 459 [5.1.1], Barbeyrac Note 1; Hont 1987: 275–6). During the eighteenth century, however, *doux commerce* theorists (I shall largely cite Shaftesbury and Hume) began to specify that commerce induced morals as well as manners – the humanitarian virtues that made the 'sociable man' who 'possesses a disposition to reach out to others in a moral sense and extend good will to them on the basis of their humanity'. There now was seen to be a progression from the cultivation of manners to the development of morals, the former prerequisite to the latter. So Hume in 'Of Refinement in the Arts': 'beside the improvements which they receive from knowledge and the liberal arts, it is impossible but they must feel an increase of humanity, from the very habit of conversing together, and contributing to each other's pleasure and entertainment. Thus *industry*, *knowledge*, and *humanity*, are linked together, by an indissoluble chain' (Hume 1996: III, 297–8; Dickey 2004: 275, 278, 280–1).

This improvement in morality affected not least the work of government: so Hume also argued in 'Of Refinement in the Arts' that:

> Laws, order, police, discipline; these can never be carried to any degree of perfection, before human reason has refined itself by exercise, and by an application to the more vulgar arts, at least of commerce and manufacture . . . Knowledge in the arts of government naturally begets mildness and moderation, by instructing men in the advantages of humane maxims above rigour and severity, which drive subjects into rebellion, and make the return to submission impracticable, by cutting off all hopes of pardon. When the tempers of men are softened as well as their knowledge improved, this humanity appears still more conspicuous, and is the chief characteristic which distinguishes a civilized age from times of barbarity and ignorance. Factions are then less inveterate, revolutions less tragical, authority less severe, and seditions less frequent. Even foreign wars abate of their cruelty; and after the field of battle, where honour and interest steel men against compassion, as well as fear, the combatants divest themselves of the brute, and resume the man. (Hume 1996: III, 299–300)

Commerce (Hume wrote in the *Treatise of Human Nature* (1738–40)) also forwarded government in that it required stability of promise (contract and the rule of law) and stability of possession (property), as the means of binding the avaricious passions and fostering the commercial (Hume 1996: II, 256 [3.2.2], 270 [3.2.3], 320 [3.2.8]; Berry 2013: 102–4). As government was the guarantor of contract, law and property, commerce not only made men governable but inclined them to desire governance.

Doux commerce promoted virtue, *doux commerce* promoted government – and, tying virtue and government together, the *doux commerce* theorists finally began to tie commerce with the subject matter of civil humanism. The development of manners now became prerequisite for the development of liberty: as Hume wrote in 'Of Refinement in the Arts,' '[i]f we consider the matter in a proper light, we shall find, that a progress in the arts is rather favourable to liberty, and has a natural tendency to preserve, if not produce a free government' (Hume 1996: III, 303). In the first place, luxury and commerce created a general opulence that fostered a middling class of tradesman the functional equivalent of the yeomen of old, who would be a new bulwark of liberty (Hume 1996: III, 304). Nor, wrote Hume, would the polish of manners erode the martial virtues: 'Nor need we fear, that men, by losing their ferocity, will lose their martial spirit, or become less undaunted and vigorous in defence of their country or their liberty. The arts have no such effect in enervating either the mind or body. On the contrary, industry, their inseparable attendant, adds new force to both' (Hume 1996: III, 300). John Millar (1735–1801) elaborated the general thesis in *An Historical View of the English Government* (1787):

> From the progress, however, of trade and manufactures, the state of a country, in this respect, is gradually changed. As the inhabitants multiply from the facility of procuring subsistence, they are collected in large bodies for the convenient exercise of their employments. Villages are enlarged into towns; and these are often swelled into populous cities. In all those places of resort, there arise large bands of labourers or artificers, who by following the same employment, and by constant intercourse, are enabled with great rapidity, to communicate all their sentiments and passions. Among these there spring up leaders, who give a tone and direction to their companions. The strong encourage the feeble; the bold animate the timid; the resolute confirm the wavering; and the movements of the whole mass proceed with the uniformity of a machine, and with a force that is often irresistible. (J. Millar 1803: 134–5 [II.3])

In a yet more optimistic rendition, Sir James Steuart (1712–80) argued that the interest of economic commerce automatically controlled tyranny: 'modern oeconomy . . . is the most effectual bridle ever was invented against the folly of despotism' (Steuart 1767: 322; Hirschman 1977: 81–93). In all these variations, however, commerce strengthened civic virtue and liberty against tyranny.

The connection of commerce to liberty now led back to the realm of conversation. Liberty, after all, promoted free inquiry, reason and the advance of arts and sciences. Shaftesbury wrote in 'Soliloquy, or Advice to an Author' (1710) that

> where persuasion was the chief means of guiding the society, where the people were to be convinced before they acted, there elocution became considerable, there orators and bards were heard, and the chief geniuses and sages of the nation betook themselves to the study of those arts by which the people were rendered more treatable in a way of reason and understanding, and more subject to be led by men of science and eruditon . . . Hence it is that those arts have been delivered to us in such perfection by free nations, who, from the nature of their government as from a proper soil, produced the generous plants, while the mightiest bodies and vastest empires, governed by force and a despotic power, could, after ages of peace and leisure, produce no other than what was deformed and barbarous of the kind. (Shaftesbury 1999: 107)

So also Jonathan Swift (1667–1745) in *Sentiments of a Church-of-England Man* (1708): 'while the rest of the known World [in antiquity] was over-run with the Arbitrary Government of single Persons, *Arts* and *Sciences* took their Rise, and flourished only in those few small Territories where the People were *free*' (Swift 2002: 179). Hume likewise wrote in 'Of the Rise and Progress of the Arts and Sciences' (1742):

> My first observation on this head is, *That it is impossible for the arts and sciences to arise, at first, among any people, unless that people enjoy the blessing of a free government* . . . Here then are the advantages of free states. Though a republic should be barbarous, it necessarily, by an infallible operation, gives rise to Law, even before mankind have made any considerable advances in the other sciences. From law arises security; from security curiosity; and from curiosity knowledge. (Hume 1996: III, 123, 126)

This realm of free inquiry, reason and the arts and sciences in turn was that of conversation. In a literary key, 'A Vindication of Montaigne's Essays' (1700) connected liberty and conversation: 'This does likewise appear, by the odd, or rather fantastical Connexion of his Discourses, wherein from one Matter he makes long Digressions upon several others. No doubt but he thought that one might take the same Liberty in his Meditations, as is assum'd in common Conversations' (Montaigne 1711: 5). In 'An Essay on Conversation,' published in the *Weekly Miscellany* in 1779, the author wrote that, 'Our great progress and improvement in arts and letters have enlarged the sphere of modern conversation to a boundless extent' (Essay 1779: 225).

We may return to Shaftesbury for the explicit link between liberty, politeness and conversation. Shaftesbury wrote in 'Sensus Communis' (1709) that liberty was prerequisite for polite, reciprocal and rational conversations: 'All politeness is owing to liberty. We polish one another and rub off our corners and rough sides by a sort of amicable collision. To restrain this is inevitably to bring a rust upon men's understandings. It is a destroying of civility, good breeding and even charity itself, under pretence of maintaining it' (Shaftesbury 1999: 31). Such polite liberty in turn interpenetrated with the realm of conversation, for politeness was the precondition for the sort of polite conversation that made conversation a pleasure:

> Men can never be better invited to the habit [of reasoning] than when they find pleasure in it. A freedom of raillery, a liberty in decent language to question everything, and an allowance of unravelling or refuting any argument without offence to the arguer, are the only terms which can render such speculative conversations any way agreeable. (Shaftesbury 1999: 33)

Such free and polite conversations allowed the possibility that the inquiry into truth might at last bear fruit: 'I will venture to make the experiment throughout and try what certain knowledge or assurance of things may be recovered in that very way by which all certainty, you thought, was lost, and an endless scepticism introduced' (Shaftesbury 1999: 39). Commerce, manners and conversation had formed one logical sequence; commerce, virtue, liberty, politeness, conversation and the conversational search for truth now formed another.

Not all Enlightenment thinkers endorsed these logical sequences. Smith noted in 'Of the Influence of Commerce on Manners' (1763) that among 'the disadvantages of a commercial spirit' was that 'The minds of men are contracted, and rendered incapable of elevation' (A. Smith 1896: 259). Rousseau restated with even greater emphasis in his *First Discourse* (1750) the old thesis that commerce qua luxury corrupted, and argued that the inevitable working of natural law framed an inevitable damnation of mankind rather than a means toward slow salvation (Rousseau 1997; Shklar 1969: 10–19, 25, 35–52, 76–7, 87ff.). Hume in 'Of the Rise and Progress of the Arts and Sciences' (in some tension with his argument in 'Of Refinement in the Arts', cited above) argued that while free states provided the root of manners, they could be maintained as well, or even better, in unfree ones (Hume 1996: III, 123, 132). Hume and other Scots generally acknowledged that conversation and its derivatives led to a hypocritical counterfeit of civility at least as much as to any virtue; so Hume's judgement in 'Of the Rise and Progress of the Arts and Sciences' that 'modern politeness . . . runs often into affectation and foppery, disguise and insincerity' (Hume 1996: III, 141; J. Davidson 2004: 95; Mee 2011: 67). Various *ancien régime* polemicists, among them Bishop Jacques-Bénigne Bossuet (1627–1704), the Chevalier de Ramsay (1686–1743) and Nicolas Delamare (1639–1723), associated sociability with a self-policing that would facilitate absolutism (D. Gordon 1994: 56–60, 72–3; and see also France 1992: 60–4). The Physiocrats took the machine-like effects of commerce and its derivative interest to lend themselves to an interpretation that precluded liberty as unnecessary, and produced a polity naturally or ideally unfree (Le Mercier 1767: 495–6; Clark 2007: 169–73; Hirschman 1977: 93–4). Indeed, a plausible corollary to the shift to the natural-law mode of jurisprudence was that coercion was necessary to make sure that all followed the law. As Pufendorf put it in *Elements of Universal Jurisprudence*:

> That obligation [of the law of nature, to cultivate a social life] has the force of a mutual agreement which, when one person departs from it, no longer binds the other person either, and grants him in addition the right to compel the former by force to furnish the things agreed upon. For one who has not treated others according to a common obligation cannot object if his own examples are inflicted upon himself and he is, besides, brought back into line by the rest by means of force. (Pufendorf 1994: 86 [*Elements of Universal Jurisprudence*, II.Observation 4.22])

These several critiques, pregnant with influence for the future, demonstrated that belief in the natural and universal operation of commerce did not necessarily coincide with a belief that commerce was beneficial or essentially linked to liberty. The link of commerce to virtue and liberty may have been a majority view, but hardly a universal one.

Yet for those who did affirm this link, these sequences provided one final corollary. If sociability made the creation of commerce, manners, virtue, liberty and conversation a dynamic within history, it was possible to foster this dynamic so as act more swiftly and surely in the future. If the past progression of society, morality and the arts had depended on the extension of commerce, then their future progression required its further extension; Hume's prediction in 'Of the Jealousy of Trade' (1742) 'that Great Britain, and all those nations, would flourish more, did their sovereigns and ministers adopt such enlarged and benevolent sentiments [fostering free trade] towards each other' implied 'flourish' in more than a narrowly economic sense (Hume 1996, III, 359–63; Dickey 2004: 277, 282–8; Hont 1987: 274). Indeed, as sociability was an inherent quality in all men, all men could acquire manners, virtue, liberty, the capacity to reason and the ability to enter into conversation. If they could acquire all these, then by implication they should – and in that implication resided several of the cultural and political projects of the Enlightenment.

Conclusion

The development of *conversatio* into *sociabilitas*, the reconception of that sociability into a prerequisite for conversation and the translation of this relationship into a historical dynamic had created a revolutionary intellectual formula. Christian Thomasius (1655–1728) summarised it concisely in the *Institutiones Jurisprudentiae Divinae* (1688):

> Human reason is formed by thought . . . But we are unable to reason except through words . . . words, however . . . stem from the imposition by men living in one and the same society . . . Let me summarise: there is no reason without conversation; conversation has no application outside society; and reason will not survive without society. (Thomasius 1717: 137–8 [52, 54], translated in Hochstrasser 2000: 119)

Inasmuch as society was centrally constituted by economic commerce, this formula also argued that the exercise of oratory (of political debate and counsel, of the faculty of prudence, of the actions of economic self-interest) had become a predicate to the exercise of conversation: the complementary nature of the two modes shifted from the realm of rhetoric to that of history.

Sociability's role as the motor of natural law now gave to conversation a universalising dynamic. The history of the conversational strand of the Enlightenment would consist in good measure in the working out of that dynamic's implications.

Notes

1. Pufendorf delays his discussion of the establishment of the state to Book 7 (Pufendorf 1729: 623–745), and he reduces the existential Hobbesian fear that motivates submission to the Leviathan to a prudent wariness that motivates the estabslishment of the state as a safeguard to society (Pufendorf 1729: 632 [7.1.8]).
2. Marx used the exact phrase; Hirschman has popularised it. Hirschman (1977: 56–63, esp. 62 (note aa)). Hirschman has established a fairly tight semantic relation between variations of *doux* and *commerce*, even where the exact phrase was absent or used with slightly different application.
3. Randall (2011c, 2016b). This argument is key to this work's narrative.
4. Smith's dialogic language of price was 'a conversation irreducibly rooted in egocentric desires', which played a crucial role in educating the prudent man toward the conversations that form judgement, conscience and wisdom. Randall 2016b [344–6]. Price thus formed the precise hinge between the realms of oratory and conversation.

Conclusion

The changed conception of conversation that emerged by *c.*1700 was about to expand its scope enormously – to the broad culture of Enlightenment Europe, to the fine arts, to philosophy and into the broad political world, both via the conception of public opinion and via the constitutional thought of James Madison (1751–1836). In the Enlightenment, the early modern conception of conversation would expand into a whole wing of Enlightenment thought. The intellectual history of the heirs of Cicero and Petrarch would become the practice of millions and the constitutional architecture of a great republic.

The widening of the conception of conversation in the Enlightenment would also have implications for the political and philosophical theories of today. The target of this book and its sequel is Habermasian theory – the combined historical-theoretical complex that roots a theory of communicative rationality in the history of an Enlightenment public sphere. The narrative of the conversable world establishes a theory of conversational rationality, of interest to philosophers and political theorists as much as to historians. All that is pregnant in the narrative presented here.

These widenings – of historical scope, of theory, of discipline – are explored fully in the sequel to this book.

Bibliography

Abizadeh, Arash (2001) 'Banishing the Particular: Rousseau on Rhetoric, *Patrie*, and the Passions', *Political Theory* 29, 4: 556–82.

Abizadeh, Arash (2007) 'On the Philosophy/Rhetoric Binaries: Or, Is Habermasian Discourse Motivationally Impotent?', *Philosophy and Social Criticism* 33, 4: 445–72.

Account of the Expedition to the Isle of Rhe (1627) Additional MS 4106, fos. 160–5. London: British Library.

Achinstein, Sharon (1994) *Milton and the Revolutionary Reader*. Princeton: Princeton University Press.

Acontius, Jacobus (1651) *Darkness Discovered. Or the Devils Secret Stratagems Laid Open*. London: Ley.

Acontius, Jacobus (1940) *Satan's Stratagems*, 2 vols, trans. Walter T. Curtis, intro. Charles D. O'Malley, Occasional Papers, English Series no. 5, parts 1 and 2. San Francisco: California State Library.

Advertizement from Caskcales in the River of Lishborne the vth of June 1589 (1589) Stowe MS 159, fos. 373–74. London: British Library.

Aelred of Rievaulx (2010) *Spiritual Friendship*, trans. Lawrence C. Braceland, SJ, ed. Marsha L. Dutton. Collegeville, MN: Liturgical Press.

Affaires and generall Businesse of Europe, The (1624) London: Nathaniel Butter, 24 February, no. 14.

Alberti, Leon Battista (1845) *Opere Volgari di Leon Batt. Alberti, Tomo III*, ed. Anicio Bonucci. Florence: Tipografia Galileiana.

Alberti, Leon Battista (1971) *The Albertis of Florence: Leon Battista Alberti's Della famiglia*, trans. Guido A. Guarino. Lewisburg: Bucknell University Press.

Allestree, Richard (1684) *The Whole Duty of Man*. London: Pawlet.

Ambrose (2001) *De officiis*, Vol. I, ed. and trans. Ivor J. Davidson. Oxford: Oxford University Press.

Amyot, Jacques (1992) *Projet d'éloquence royale, d'après le manuscrit autographe de l'auteur*, ed. Philippe-Joseph Salazar. Paris: Les Belles Lettres.

Anderson, Penelope (2012) *Friendship's Shadows: Women's Friendship and the Politics of Betrayal in England, 1640–1705*. Edinburgh: Edinburgh University Press.

Andreadis, Harriette (2006) 'Re-Configuring Early Modern Friendship: Katherine Philips and Homoerotic Desire', *Studies in English Literature, 1500–1900* 46, 3: 523–42.

Apuleius (1866) *The Works of Apuleius*, ed. Frank H. Cilley. London: Bell & Daldy.

Aquinas, Thomas (1969) *Summa theologiae. Latin Text and English Translation. Vol. 23. Virtue* (1a2ae. 55–67), trans. W. D. Hughes. [Cambridge? Eng.] Blackfriars; New York: McGraw-Hill.

Aristotle (1986) *Politics*, trans. Hippocrates G. Apostle and Lloyd P. Gerson. Grinnell, IA: Peripatetic Press.

Aristotle (2004) *Rhetoric*, trans. W. Rhys Roberts. Mineola, NY: Dover.

Aristotle (2013) *Eudemian Ethics*, trans. and ed. Brad Inwood and Raphael Woolf. Cambridge: Cambridge University Press.

Aristotle (2014) *Nicomachean Ethics*, trans. C. D. C. Reeve. Indianapolis: Hackett.

Arnauld, Antoine and Pierre Nicole (1662) *La Logique ou L'Art de Penser*. Paris: Guignart, Savreux, Lavnay.

Astell, Mary (1697) *A Serious Proposal to the Ladies for the Advancement of Their True and Greatest Interest*. London: Richard Wilkin.

Augustine (1996) *The Rule of St. Augustine, Masculine and Feminine Versions, with Introduction and Commentary*, ed. Tarsicius J. Van Bavel, OSA, trans. Raymond Canning. Kalamazoo: Cistercian Publications.

Augustine (1998) *Answer to the Pelagians, II*, trans. Roland J. Teske, ed. John E. Rotelle. Hyde Park, NY: New City Press.

Augustine (2014) *Confessions, Books 1–8*, ed. and trans. Carolyn J.-B. Hammond. Cambridge, MA and London: Harvard University Press.

Aulus Gellius (1927–8) *The Attic Nights of Aulus Gellius*, 3 vols, trans. John C. Rolfe. London: William Heinemann; New York: G. P. Putnam's Sons.

Barbaro, Francesco (2015) *The Wealth of Wives: A Fifteenth-Century Marriage Manual*, ed. and trans. Margaret L. King. Toronto and Tempe, AZ: Iter Academic Press and Arizona Center for Medieval and Renaissance Studies.

Bargagli, Girolamo (1572) *Dialogo de' giuochi che nelle vegghie sanesi si vsano di fare*. Siena: Luca Bonetti.

Bargagli, Scipione (1594) *Dell'imprese di Scipion Bargagli gentil'huomo sanese: alla prima parte, la seconda, e la terza nuovamente aggiunte*. Venice: Francesco de' Franceschi.

Bary, René (1662) *L'Esprit de cour, ou les conversations galantes*. Paris: C. de Sercy.

Bassanese, Fiora A. (1996) 'Selling the Self; or, the Epistolary Production of Renaissance Courtesans', in *Italian Women Writers from the Renaissance to the Present: Revising the Canon*, ed. Maria Ornella Marotti. University Park: Pennsylvania State University Press, pp. 69–82.

Battisti, Giuseppa Saccaro (1980) 'La donna, le donne nel *Cortegiano*', in *La corte e il cortegiano, vol. 1, La scena del testo*, ed. Carlo Ossola. Rome: Bulzoni, pp. 219–50.

Bayle, Pierre (1735) *The Dictionary Historical and Critical of Mr Peter Bayle. The Second Edition. Volume the Second*. London: Knapton et al.

Bayle, Pierre (1738) *A General Dictionary Historical and Critical. Volume VII*. London: Bettenham et al.

Beasley, Faith E. (2006) *Salons, History, and the Creation of Seventeenth-Century France: Mastering Memory*. Aldershot: Ashgate.

Behr, Francesca D'Allesandro (2007) *Feeling History: Lucan, Stoicism, and the Poetics of Passion*. Columbus: Ohio University State Press.

Bellegarde, Jean-Baptiste Morvan de (1688) *Réflexions sur ce qui peut plaire ou déplaire dans le commerce du monde*. Paris: Seneuze.

Bellegarde, Jean-Baptiste Morvan de (1707) *Reflexions upon the Politeness of Manners; with Maxims for Civil Society*. London: Newborough, Mindwinter, & Tooke.

Bellegarde, Jean-Baptiste Morvan de (1717) *Reflexions upon Ridicule*. London: Nicholason, Tooke, & Midwinter.

Bellegarde, Jean-Baptiste Morvan de (1765) *Models of Conversation for Persons of Polite Education*. London: Millar.

Benedict (1981) *The Rule of St. Benedict*, ed. Timothy Fry. Collegeville, MN: Liturgical Press.

Berry, Christopher J. (2013) *The Idea of Commercial Society in the Scottish Enlightenment*. Edinburgh: Edinburgh University Press.

Besselink, Leonard F. M. (2004) 'Cynicism, Scepticism and Stoicism: A Stoic Distinction in Grotius' Concept of Law', in *Grotius and the Stoa*, ed. Hans W. Blom and Laurens C. Winkel. Assen, Netherlands: Royal Van Gorcum, pp. 177–95.

Bevington, David M. (1961) 'The Dialogue in *Utopia*: Two Sides to the Question', *Studies in Philology* 58, 3: 496–509.

Bhaldraithe, Eoin de (1984) 'Conversatio – St. Benedict Recovers Early Christian Terminology', *Regulae Benedicti Studia* 13: 3–15.

Bibliothèque italique ou Histoire Litteraire de l'Italie. Janvier, Fevrier, Mars, Avril, 1728, Tome I. (1728) Geneva: Bosquiet.

Bodin, Jean (1967) *Six Books of the Commonwealth*, abridged and trans. M. J. Tooley. New York: Barnes & Noble.

Bond, Donald F. (ed.) (1965) *The Spectator*, 5 vols. Oxford: Clarendon Press.

Borgerhoff, E. B. O. (1968) *The Freedom of French Classicism*. New York: Russell & Russell.

Bouhours, Dominique (1675) *Remarques Nouvelles su la langue françoise*. Paris: Mabre-Cramoisy.

Bouwsma, William J. (1990) 'Changing Assumptions in Later Renaissance Culture', in *A Usable Past: Essays in European Cultural History*. Berkeley and Los Angeles: University of California Press, pp. 74–96.

Boyd, Richard (2008) 'Manners and Morals: David Hume on Civility, Commerce, and the Social Construction of Difference', in *David Hume's Political Economy*, ed. Carl Wennerlind and Margaret Schabas. New York: Routledge, pp. 65–85.

Boyer, Abel (1702) *The English Theophrastus: or, the Manners of the Age*. London: Turner & Chantry.

Bracciolini, Poggio (1978a) 'On Avarice', trans. Benjamin G. Kohl and Elizabeth B. Welles, in *The Earthly Republic: Italian Humanists on Government and Society*, ed. Benjamin G. Kohl, Elizabeth B. Welles and Ronald G. Witt. Philadelphia: University of Pennsylvania Press, pp. 241–89.

Bracciolini, Poggio (1978b) 'On Nobility', trans. David Marsh and Renée Neu Watkins, in *Humanism & Liberty: Writings on Freedom from Fifteenth-Century Florence*, ed. Renée Neu Watkins. Columbia: University of South Carolina Press, pp. 121–48.

Brandt, Reinhard (2004) 'Self-consciousness and Self-care: On the Tradition of *oikeiosis* in the Modern Age', trans. Philipp U. Beckmann, in *Grotius and the Stoa*, ed. Hans W. Blom and Laurens C. Winkel. Assen, Netherlands: Royal Van Gorcum, pp. 73–91.

Bray, Alan (2003) *The Friend*. Chicago and London: University of Chicago Press.

Brief Relation of the Late Battle between the Duke of Saxony & the Emperor on the one side & the Swede, A (1636) Additional MS 27402, fos. 73–4. London: British Library.

Broad, Jacqueline (2009) 'Mary Astell on Virtuous Friendship', *Parergon* 26, 2: 65–86.

Brooke, Christopher (2012) *Philosophic Pride: Stoicism and Political Thought from Lipsius to Rousseau*. Princeton: Princeton University Press.

Broughton, Richard (1591) *Richard Broughton to Richard Bagot, 2 July 1591*. Bagot Papers L.a.261. Folger Shakespeare Library, Washington, DC.

Bruni, Leonardo (1987) 'The Dialogues', in *The Humanism of Leonardo Bruni: Selected Texts*, trans. and ed. Gordon Griffiths, James Hankins and David Thompson. Binghamton, NY: Medieval and Renaissance Texts and Studies, pp. 63–84.

Buckle, Stephen (1991) *Natural Law and the Theory of Property: Grotius to Hume*. Oxford: Clarendon Press.

Bullard, Paddy (2012) 'Pride, Pulpit Eloquence, and the Rhetoric of Jonathan Swift', *Rhetorica* 30, 3: 252–76.

Burchell, David (2007) '"A Plain Blunt Man": Hobbes, Science, and Rhetoric Revisited', in *Science, Literature and Rhetoric in Early Modern England*, ed. Juliet Cummins and David Burchell. Aldershot: Ashgate, pp. 53–72.

Burke, Peter (1989) 'The Renaissance Dialogue', *Renaissance Studies* 3, 1: 1–12.

Burke, Peter (1993) *The Art of Conversation*. Ithaca: Cornell University Press.

Burke, Peter (1996) *The Fortunes of the* Courtier: *The European Reception of Castiglione's* Cortegiano. University Park: Pennsylvania State University Press.

Burke, Peter (1999) 'Humanism and Friendship in Sixteenth-Century Europe', in *Friendship in Medieval Europe*, ed. Julian Haseldine. Thrupp: Sutton, pp. 262–74.

Callières, François de (1692) *Des mots à la mode et des nouvelles façons de parler*. Paris: Barbin.

Callières, François de (1717) *De la Science du monde et des connaissances utiles à la conduite de la vie*. Paris: Ganeau.

Camargo, Martin (1991) *Ars Dictaminis, Ars Dictandi*. Turnhout: Brepols.

Camargo, Martin (ed.) (1995) *Medieval Rhetorics of Prose Composition. Five English Artes Dictandi and Their Tradition*. Binghamton, NY: Medieval & Renaissance Texts & Studies.

Campbell, Julie (2006) *Literary Circles and Gender in Early Modern Europe: A Cross-Cultural Approach*. Aldershot: Ashgate.

Carr, T. M., Jr (1990 *Descartes and the Resilience of Rhetoric: Varieties of Cartesian Rhetorical Theory*. Carbondale and Edwardsville: Southern Illinois University Press.

Carron, Jean-Claude (1991) 'The Persuasive Seduction: Dialogue in Sixteenth-Century France', in *Contending Kingdoms: Historical, Psychological and Feminist Approaches to the Literature of Sixteenth-Century England and France*, ed. Marie-Rose Logan and Peter L. Rudnytsky. Detroit: Wayne State University Press, pp. 90–108.

Cassian, John (1997) *John Cassian: The Conferences*, trans. Boniface Ramsey, OP. New York and Mahwah, NJ: Paulist Press.

Cassidy, Eoin G. (1999) '"He Who Has Friends Can Have No Friend": Classical and Christian Perspectives on the Limits to Friendship', in *Friendship in Medieval Europe*, ed. Julian Haseldine. Thrupp: Sutton, pp. 45–67.

Castiglione, Baldesar (1976) *The Book of the Courtier*, trans. George Bull. New York: Penguin Books.

Cereta, Laura (1997) *Collected Letters of a Renaissance Feminist*, trans. and ed. Diana Robin. Chicago and London: University of Chicago Press.

Chapelain, Jean (1880) 'A. M. de Balzac [22 March 1638]', in *Lettres de Jean Chapelain*. Tome Premier. Septembre 1632 – Décembre 1640, ed. Philippe Tamizey de Larroque. Paris: Imprimerie Nationale, pp. 215–17.

Chaplin, Gregory (2001) '"One Flesh, One Heart, One Soul": Renaissance Friendship and Miltonic Marriage', *Modern Philology* 99, 2: 266–92.

Chappuys, Gabriel (1579) [Dedicatory Epistle]. In Stefano Guazzo, *La Civile Conversation*, trans. Gabriel Chappuys. Lyon: Beraud, sigs. 2^v–7^r.

Charles I (1642) *His Maiesties declaration to all His loving Subjects. Of August 12 1642*. Cambridge: N.N.

Charron, Pierre (n.d. [after 1612]) *Of Wisdome*, trans. Samson Lennard. London: Printed [at Eliot's Court Press] for Edward Blount & Will: Aspley.

Chordas, Nina (2004) 'Dialogue, Utopia, and the Agencies of Fiction', in *Printed Voices: The Renaissance Culture of Dialogue*, ed. Dorothea Heitsch and Jean-François Vallée. Toronto: University of Toronto Press, pp. 27–41.

Churchyard, Thomas (1588) *A Sparke of Frendship and Warme Goodwill*. London: [By T. Orwin].

Cicero (1912–18) *Letters to Atticus*, 3 vols, trans. E. O. Winstedt. London: William Heinemann; New York: Macmillan.

Cicero (1927–9) *The Letters to His Friends*, 3 vols, trans. W. Glynn Williams. New York and London: G. P. Putnam's Sons and Heinemann.

Cicero (1931) *De finibus*, trans. H. Rackham. London and Cambridge, MA: William Heinemann and Harvard University Press.

Cicero (1933) *De Natura Deorum*, trans. H. Rackham, in *De Natura Deorum Academica*. London: William Heinemann; New York: G. P. Putnam's Sons, pp. 2–387.

Cicero (1967) *De oratore*, Vols I–II, trans. E. W. Sutton and H. Rackham. London and Cambridge, MA: William Heinemann and Harvard University Press.

Cicero (1971) *Orator*, in *Cicero: Brutus, Orator*, trans. H. M. Hubbell. London and Cambridge, MA: Harvard University Press, pp. 297–509.

Cicero (1989) *Tusculan Disputations*, trans. J. E. King. Cambridge, MA and London: Harvard University Press.

Cicero (1990) *Laelius, On Friendship (Laelius de Amicitia)*, in *Laelius, On Friendship (Laelius de Amicitia) & The Dream of Scipio (Somnium Scipionis)*, ed. and trans. J. G. F. Powell. Oxford: Aris & Phillips Classical Texts, pp. 1–118.

Cicero (1998) *The Republic*, in *The Republic and The Laws*, trans. Niall Rudd. Oxford: Oxford University Press, pp. 3–94.

Cicero (2000) *On Obligations (De Officiis)*, trans. P. G. Walsh. Oxford: Oxford University Press.

Cicero (2002) *Letters to Quintus and Brutus, To Octavian, Invectives, Handbooks of Electioneering*, trans. and ed. D. R. Shackleton Bailey. Cambridge, MA: Loeb Classical Library.

Clark, Henry C. (2007) *Compass of Society: Commerce and Abolutism in Old-Regime France*. Lanham, MD: Lexington Books.

Clarke, George (1594) *George Clarke to Richard Bagot, 25 October 1594*. Bagot Papers L.a.390. Folger Shakespeare Library, Washington, DC.

Classen, Albrecht and Sandidge, Marilyn (2010) 'Introduction: Friendship – The Quest for a Human Ideal and Value: From Antiquity to the Early Modern Time', in *Friendship in the Middle Ages and Early Modern Age: Explorations of a Fundamental Ethical Discourse*, ed. Albrecht Classen and Marilyn Sandidge. Berlin and New York: De Gruyter.

Clément, Pierre (1869) *Lettres, instructions et mémoires de Colbert*, Vol. VI. Paris: Imprimerie Imperiale.

Colas, Dominique (1997) *Civil Society and Fanaticism*, trans. Amy Jacobs. Stanford: Stanford University Press.

Colclough, David (2005) *Freedom of Speech in Early Stuart England*. Cambridge: Cambridge University Press.

Cole, Richard (1975 'The Reformation in Print: German Pamphlets and Propaganda', *Archiv für Reformationsgeschichte* 66: 93–102.

Collins, Raymond F. (2008) *The Power of Images in Paul.* Collegeville, MN: Liturgical Press.

Constable, Giles (1992) 'Dictators and Diplomats in the Eleventh and Twelfth Centuries: Medieval Epistolography and the Birth of Modern Bureaucracy', *Dumbarton Oaks Papers (Homo Byzantinus: Papers in Honor of Alexander Kazhdan)* 46. Cambridge, MA: Harvard University Press, pp. 37–46.

continuation of more newes from the Palatinate, A (1622) London: Bourne & Archer, 26 July.

Continuation of our Forraine Intelligence, The (1632) London: Printed [by J. Dawson?] for Nathaniel Butter and Nicolas Bourne, 8 February, no. 10.

Conwell, Joseph F. (1997) *Impelling Spirit: Revisiting a Founding Experience, 1539, Ignatius of Loyola and His Companions.* Chicago: Loyola Press.

copie of a letter wrytten by Mr Raphe Lane of the proceadinge of their Portugall voyage, The (1589) Stowe MS 159, fos. 370–1. London: British Library.

copy of a letter written by a dutyfull Servant Nobody. Sent from Bruxells to his Worthy Master Nemo, The (1621) Additional MS 34217, fos. 20–1. London: British Library.

copy of a lre sent from Manheim the 2 of June 1622, The (1622) Additional MS 34217, fo. 38v. London: British Library.

Courtin, Antoine de (1671) *Nouveau traité de la civilité que se practique en France* (Paris, 1671), trans. unknown, *The Rules of Civility.* London: J. Martyn & John Starkey.

Cox, Leonard (1532) *The art or crafte of rhetoryke.* London: Robert Redman.

Cox, Virginia (1992) *The Renaissance Dialogue: Literary Dialogue in Its Social and Political Contexts, Castiglione to Galileo.* Cambridge: Cambridge University Press.

Cox, Virginia (2000) 'Seen But Not Heard: The Role of Women Speakers in Cinquecento Literary Dialogue', in *Women in Italian Renaissance Culture and Society*, ed. Letizia Panizza. Oxford: Legenda, pp. 385–400.

Craveri, Benedetta (2005) *The Age of Conversation*, trans. Teresa Waugh. New York: New York Review of Books.

Crawford, Patricia (1995) 'Friendship and Love Between Women in Early Modern Engand', in *Venus and Mars: Engendering Love and War in Medieval and Early Modern Europe*, ed. Andrew Lynch and Philippa Maddern. Nedlands: University of Western Australia Press, pp. 47–61.

Croll, Morris W. (1969) *'Attic' & Baroque Prose Style*, ed. J. Max Patrick and Robert O. Evans with John W. Wallace. Princeton: Princeton University Press.

Crow, Thomas E. (1985) *Painters and Public Life in Eighteenth-Century Paris.* New Haven, CT: Yale University Press.

Cunningham, Mary (2003) 'Dramatic Device or Didactic Tool? The Function of Dialogue in Byzantine Preaching', in *Rhetoric in Byzantium*, ed. Elizabeth Jeffreys. Aldershot: Ashgate, pp. 101–13.

D'Aragona, Tullia (1997) *Dialogue on the infinity of love*, ed. and trans. Rinaldina Russell and Bruce Merry. Chicago and London: University of Chicago Press.

D'Aubignac, Abbé François Hédelin (1663) *Troisième Dissertation concernant le Poème dramatique en forme de remarques*. Paris: Du Brueil.

Dahl, Folke (1950) 'Amsterdam – Cradle of English Newspapers'. *The Library*, Fifth Series, 4: 166–78.

Dahl, Folke (1952) *A Bibliography of English Corantos and Periodical Newsbooks 1620–1642*. London: Bibliographical Society.

Dalton, Susan (2003) *Engendering the Republic of Letters: Reconnecting Public and Private Spheres in Eighteenth-Century Europe*. Montreal and Kingston: McGill-Queen's University Press.

Dante Alighieri (2013) *A translation of Dante's eleven letters*, trans. Charles Sterrett Latham, ed. George Rice Carpenter; (1891) Boston and New York: Houghton, Mifflin; Cambridge, MA: Riverside Press; repr. [Whitefish, MT]: Kessinger.

Darwall, Stephen (2012) 'Pufendorf on Morality, Sociability, and Moral Powers', *Journal of the History of Philosophy* 50, 2: 213–38.

Davidson, Hugh M. (1965) *Audience, Words, and Art: Studies in Seventeenth Century French Rhetoric*. Columbus: Ohio State University Press.

Davidson, Jenny (2004) *Hypocrisy and the Politics of Politeness: Manners and Morals from Locke to Austen*. Cambridge: Cambridge University Press.

Dawson, Hannah (2007) *Locke, Language and Early-Modern Philosophy*. Cambridge: Cambridge University Press.

Day, Angel (1586) *The English Secretorie*. London: Robert Waldegrave for Richard Jones.

Day, Angel (1592) *The English Secretorie*. London: Richard Jones.

Daybell, James (2007) 'Women's Letters of Recommendation: The Rhetoric of Friendship in Sixteenth-Century England', in *Rhetoric, Women and Politics in Early Modern England*, ed. Jennifer Richards and Alison Thorne. New York: Routledge, pp. 172–90.

De Pinchesne, Martin (1654) 'Au Lecteur', in Vincent Voiture, *Les Oeuvres de Monsieur de Voiture*. Paris: Courbé. Sigs. ẽʳ–õᵛ.

De Pisan, Christine (1908) *The Book of the Duke of True Lovers*, trans. Laurence Binyon and Eric R. D. MacLagan. London: Chatto & Windus.

Deakins, Roger (1980) 'The Tudor Prose Dialogue: Genre and Anti-Genre', *Studies in English Literature, 1500–1900* 20, 1: 5–23.

Della Casa, Giovanni (2013) *Galateo*, trans. and ed. M. F. Rusnak. Chicago: University of Chicago Press.

Denholm-Young, Noel (1969) 'The *Cursus* in England', in *Collected Papers of N. Denholm-Young*. Cardiff: University of Wales Press, pp. 42–73.

Descartes, René (1996) *Meditations on First Philosophy with Selections from the Objections and Replies*, revised edition, trans. and ed. John Cottingham. Cambridge: Cambridge University Press.

Dibon, Paul (1978) 'Communication in the Respublica literaria of the 17th Century', *Res Publica Litterarum* 1: 43–55.

Dickey, Laurence (2004) '*Doux commerce* and Humanitarian Values: Free Trade, Sociability and Universal Benevolence in Eighteenth-Century Thinking', in *Grotius and the Stoa*, ed. Hans W. Blom and Laurens C. Winkel. Assen, Netherlands: Royal Van Gorcum, pp. 271–317.

Dickins, Amanda (2008) 'An "Intercourse of Sentiments" and the Seductions of Virtue: The Role of Conversation in David Hume's Philosophy', in *The Concept and Practice of Conversation in the Long Eighteenth Century, 1688–1848*, ed. Katie Halsey and Jane Slinn. Newcastle: Cambridge Scholars, pp. 20–39.

Diogenes Laertius (1958) *Lives of Eminent Philosophers*, 2 vols, trans. R. D. Hicks. Cambridge, MA and London: Harvard University Press and William Heinemann.

discourse of such things as are happened in the armie, A (1569) London: By Henry Bynneman, for Lucas Haryson.

Donawerth, Jane (1997) '"As Becomes a Rational Woman to Speak": Madeleine de Scudéry's Rhetoric of Conversation', in *Listening to Their Voices: The Rhetorical Activities of Historical Women*, ed. Molly Meijer Wertheimer. Columbia: University of South Carolina Press, pp. 305–19.

Donawerth, Jane (1998) 'Conversation and the Boundaries of Public Discourse in Rhetorical Theory by Renaissance Women', *Rhetorica* 16, 2: 181–99.

Donawerth, Jane (2012) *Conversational Rhetoric: The Rise and Fall of a Women's Tradition, 1600–1900*. Carbondale and Edwardsville: Southern Illinois University Press.

Dooley, Brendan and Baron, Sabrina (eds) (2001) *The Politics of Information in Early Modern Europe*. London and New York: Routledge.

Du Bosc, Jacques (1639) *L'Honneste femme* (1632–34), trans. N.N., in *The Compleat Woman*. London: Harper & Hodgkinson.

Du Perron, Jacques Davy (1618) '[Dedicatory Epistle]', in *Laelius ou de l'Amitié*, trans. Jacques Davy du Perron. Paris: Antoine Estine.

Du Vair, Guillaume (2000) *On French Eloquence and the Reasons Why It Has Remained So Inferior*, in *Renaissance Debates on Rhetoric*, ed. and trans. Wayne A. Rebhorn. Ithaca: Cornell University Press, pp. 244–60.

Dykstal, Timothy (2001) *The Luxury of Skepticism: Politics, Philosophy, and Dialogue in the English Public Sphere 1660–1740*. Charlottesville and London: University Press of Virginia.

Ebreo, Leone (2009) *Dialogues of Love*, trans. Cosmos Damian Baich and Rossella Pescatori. Toronto: University of Toronto Press.

Eden, Kathy (2012) *The Renaissance Rediscovery of Intimacy*. Chicago and London: University of Chicago Press.

Eger, Elizabeth (2008) 'The Bluestocking Circle: Friendship, Patronage and Learning', in *Brilliant Women: 18th-Century Bluestockings*, ed. Elizabeth Eger and Lucy Peltz. New Haven, CT and London: Yale University Press, pp. 21–55.

Elyot, Thomas (1533) *Pasquil the Playne*. London: Berthelet.

Enenkel, Karl (2003) 'In Search of Fame: Self-Representation in Neo-Latin Humanism', in *Medieval and Renaissance Humanism: Rhetoric, Representation and Reform*, ed. Stephen Gersh and Bert Roest. Leiden: Brill, p. 93–113.

Erasmus, Desiderius (1965) *The Colloquies of Erasmus*, trans. Craig R. Thompson. Chicago and London: University of Chicago Press.

Erasmus, Desiderius (1974) *Institution of Christian Matrimomy*, in *Collected Works of Erasmus, Vol. 69: Spiritualia and Pastoralia*, ed. John W. O'Malley and Louis A. Perraud. Toronto: University of Toronto Press.

Erasmus, Desiderius (1985) *Collected Works of Erasmus, Vol. 25. De Conscribendis Epistolis*, trans. and annot. Charles Fantazzi, ed. J. K. Sowards. Toronto, Buffalo and London: University of Toronto Press.

Erasmus, Desiderius (1986) *Collected Works of Erasmus, Vol. 28. Literary and Educational Writings 6. Ciceronianus. Notes. Indexes*, ed. A. H. T. Levi. Toronto, Buffalo and London: University of Toronto Press.

Erasmus, Desiderius (1992) *Collected Works of Erasmus, Vol. 61. Patristic Scholarship. The Edition of St. Jerome*, ed. and trans. James F. Brady and John C. Olin. Toronto, Buffalo and London: University of Toronto Press.

Erasmus, Desiderius (1996) *In Praise of Marriage*, trans. Charles Fantazzi, in *Erasmus on Women*, ed. Erika Rummel. Toronto: University of Toronto Press, p. 57–77.

'Essay on Conversation, An' (1779) In *Weekly Miscellany* 13, 323 (6 December): 221–6.

Fader, Don (2003) 'The *Honnête homme* as Music Critic: Taste, Rhetoric, and Politesse in the 17th-Century French Reception of Italian Music', *Journal of Musicology* 20, 1: 3–44.

Fahy, Conor (2000) 'Women and Italian Cinquecento literary academies', in *Women in Italian Renaissance Culture and Society*, ed. Letizia Panizza. Oxford: Legenda, pp. 438–52.

Fantazzi, Charles (1989) 'General Introduction', in Juan Luis Vives, *De Conscribendis Epistolis*, ed. and trans. Charles Fantazzi. Leiden and New York: E. J. Brill, pp. 1–20.

Faret, Nicholas (1632) *L'honnête homme: ou, L'art de plaire à la cour* (Paris, 1630), trans. Edward Grimstone, *The Honest Man: or The Art to Please in Court*. London: Printed by Thomas Harper for Edward Blount.

Farrell, Thomas (1993) *Norms of Rhetorical Culture*. New Haven, CT and London: Yale University Press.

Fénelon, François (1722) *Dialogues sur l'éloquence* (written late 1670s, published 1718), trans. as *Dialogues concerning Eloquence*. London: Printed by T. Wood for J. Walthoe.

Finucci, Valeria (1992) *The Lady Vanishes: Subjectivity and Representation in Castiglione and Ariosto*. Stanford: Stanford University Press.

Fisher, John (1977) 'Chancery and the Emergence of Standard Written English in the Fifteenth Century', *Speculum* 52, 4: 870–99.

Flemming, Abraham (1576) *A Panoplie of Epistles*. London: [H. Middleton] for Ralph Newberie.

Foley, Megan (2012) '*Peitho* and *Bia*: The Force of Language', *symplokē* 20, 1–2: 173–81.

Foley, Megan (2013) 'Of Violence and Rhetoric: An Ethical Aporia', *Quarterly Journal of Speech* 99, 2: 191–9.

Fonte, Moderata (1997) *The Worth of Women, Wherein Is Clearly Revealed Their Nobility and Their Superiority to Men*, ed. and trans. Virginia Cox. Chicago and London: University of Chicago Press.

Forbes, Duncan (1975) *Hume's Philosophical Politics*. Cambridge: Cambridge University Press.

France, Peter (1992) *Politeness and Its Discontents: Problems in French Classical Culture*. Cambridge: Cambridge University Press.

Freccero, Carla (1992) 'Politics and Aesthetics in Castiglione's *Il Cortegiano*: Book III and the Discourse on Women', in *Creative Imitation: New Essays on Renaissance Literature in Honor of Thomas M. Greene*, ed. David Quint, Margaret W. Ferguson, G. W. Pigman III and Wayne A. Rebhorn. Binghamton, NY: Medieval & Renaissance Texts & Studies, pp. 259–79.

Frick, Carole Collier (2004) 'Francesco Barbaro's *De re uxoria*: A Silent Dialogue for a Young Medici Bride', in *Printed Voices: The Renaissance Culture of Dialogue*, ed. Dorothea Heitsch and Jean-François Vallée. Toronto: University of Toronto Press, pp. 193–205.

Fulwood, William (1568) *The Enimie of Idlenesse*. London: Henry Bynneman.

Fumaroli, Marc (1983) 'Rhetoric, Politics, and Society: From Italian Ciceronianism to French Classicism', in *Renaissance Eloquence: Studies in the Theory and Practice of Renaissance Rhetoric*, ed. James J. Murphy. Berkeley, Los Angeles and London: University of California Press, pp. 253–73.

Fumaroli, Marc (1988) 'The Republic of Letters', trans. R. Scott Walker, *Diogenes* 143: 129–52.

Fumaroli, Marc (1995) 'De l'age de l'éloquence a l'age de la conversation: la conversion de la rhétorique humaniste de la France du XVIIᵉ siècle', in *Art de la lettre, art de la conversation à l'époque classique en France, Actes du colloque de Wolfenbüttel*, October 1991, ed. Bernard Bray and Christopher Strosetzski. Paris: Klincksieck, pp. 25–45.

Furey, Constance (2003) 'The Communication of Friendship: Gasparo Contarini's Letters to Hermits at Camaldoli', *Church History* 72, 1: 71–101.

Furey, Constance (2013) 'Bound by Likeness: Vives and Erasmus on Marriage and Friendship', in *Discourses and Representations of Friendship in Early Modern Europe, 1500–1700*, ed. Daniel T. Lochman, Maritere López and Lorna Hutson. Aldershot: Ashgate, pp. 29–43.

G.B. (1591) *Newes out of France for the Gentlemen of England*. London: John Kid.

Gainsford, Thomas (1616) *The Secretaries Studie*. London: Thomas Creede for Roger Jackson.

Garrioch, David (2009) 'From Christian Friendship to Secular Sentimentality: Enlightenment Re-evalutations', in *Friendship: A History*, ed. Barbara Caine. London: Equinox, pp. 165–214.

Garver, Eugene (1987) *Machiavelli and the History of Prudence*. Madison: University of Wisconsin Press.

Gerlo, Alois (1971) 'The *Opus de conscribendis epistolis* of Erasmus and the Tradition of the Ars Epistolica', in *Classical Influences on European Culture A.D. 500–1500*, ed. R. R. Bolgar. Cambridge: Cambridge University Press, pp. 103–14.

Gibson, Jonathan (1997) 'Significant Space in Manuscript Letters', *Seventeenth Century* 12, 1: 1–9.

Gill, Amyrose McCue (2009) 'Fraught Relations in the Letters of Laura Cereta: Marriage, Friendship, and Humanist Epistolarity', *Renaissance Quarterly* 62, 4: 1098–129.

Godard, Anne (2001) *Le Dialogue à la Renaissance*. Paris: Presses Universitaires de France.

Godo, Emmanuel (2003) *Une histoire de la conversation*. Paris: Presses Universitaires de France.

Goffen, Rona (1979) '*Nostra Conversatio in Caelis Est:* Observations on the *Sacra Conversazione* in the Trecento', *Art Bulletin* 61, 2: 198–222.

Goldgar, Anne (1995) *Impolite Learning: Conduct and Community in the Republic of Letters, 1680–1750*. New Haven, CT and London Yale University Press.

Goldsmith, Elizabeth C. (1988) *Exclusive Conversations: The Art of Interaction in Seventeenth-Century France*. Philadelphia: University of Pennsylvania Press.

Goodman, Dena (1994) *The Republic of Letters: A Cultural History of the French Enlightenment*. Ithaca and London: Cornell University Press.

Gordon, Daniel (1994) *Citizens Without Sovereignty: Equality and Sociability in French Thought, 1670–1789*. Princeton: Princeton University Press.

Gordon, Pamela (1996) *Epicurus in Lycia: The Second-Century World of Diogenes of Oenoanda*. Ann Arbor: University of Michigan Press.

Grafton, Anthony (1991) 'Humanism and Political Theory', in *The Cambridge History of Political Thought 1450–1700*, ed. J. H. Burns and Mark Goldie. Cambridge: Cambridge University Press, pp. 9–29.

Gray, Hanna H. (1963) 'Renaissance Humanism: The Pursuit of Eloquence', *Journal of the History of Ideas* 24, 4: 497–514.

Grendler, Paul (1989) *Schooling in Renaissance Italy: Literacy and Learning, 1300–1600*. Baltimore and London: Johns Hopkins University Press.

Grotius, Hugo (1738) *The Rights of War and Peace*, ed. Jean Barbeyrac, trans. anon. London: Innis et al.

Grotius, Hugo (1995) *De Iure Praedae Commentarius: Commentary on the Law of Prize and Booty*, Vol. I, trans. Gwladys L. Williams and Walter H. Zeydel. Buffalo, NY: William S. Hein.

Grube, G. M. A. (ed.) (1961) *A Greek Critic: Demetrius on Style*. Toronto: University of Toronto Press.

Guazzo, Stefano (1967) *The Civile Conversation of M. Steeven Guazzo*, trans. George Pettie and Bartholomew Young, 2 vols. London: Constable [1925]; repr. New York: AMS Press.

Guazzo, Stefano (1993) *La Civil conversazione*, ed. Amedeo Quondam. Modena: Franco Cosimo Panini.

Guenther, Otto (ed.) (1895) *Corpus Scriptorum Ecclesiasticorum Latinorum, Vol. XXXV, Epistulae imporatorum pontificum aliorum etc. Part I*. Prague, Vienna and Leipzig: F. Tempsky and G. Freytag.

Guez de Balzac, Jean-Louis (1652) 'A Discourse of the Conversation of the Romans', in *The Roman. The Conversation of the Romans and Maecenas*, trans. unknown. London: Printed by T.N. for J. Holden, pp. 41–109.

Guez de Balzac, Jean-Louis (1657) *Les Entretiens de feu Monsieur de Balzac*. Paris: Courbé.

Guicciardini, Francesco (1994) *Dialogue on the Government of Florence*, ed. and trans. Alison Brown. Cambridge: Cambridge University Press.

Guy, John (1993) 'The Henrician Age', in *The Varieties of British Political Thought, 1500–1800*, ed. J. G. A. Pocock. Cambridge: Cambridge University Press, pp. 13–46.

Guy, John (1995) 'The Rhetoric of Counsel in Early Modern England', in *Tudor Political Culture*, ed. Dale Hoak. Cambridge: Cambridge University Press, pp. 292–310.

Habermas, Jürgen (1973) *Theory and Practice*, trans. John Viertel. Boston: Beacon Press.

Habermas, Jürgen (1991) *The Structural Transformation of the Public Sphere: An Inquiry into a Category of Bourgeois Society*, trans. Thomas Burger and Frederick Lawrence. Cambridge, MA: MIT Press.

Hall, Marie (1965) 'Henry Oldenburg and the Art of Scientific Communication', *British Journal for the History of Science* 2, IV, 8: 277–90.

Hanning, Robert W. and Rosand, David (1983) 'Preface', in *Castiglione: The Ideal and the Real in Renaissance Culture*, ed. Robert W. Hanning and David Rosand. New Haven, CT and London: Yale University Press, pp. vii–xvi.

Harline, Craig (1987) *Pamphlets, Printing, and Political Culture in the Early Dutch Republic*. Dordrecht: Martinus Nijhoff.

Harrán, Don (2009) 'Volume Editor's Introduction', in *Sarra Copia Sulam: Jewish Poet and Intellectual in Seventeenth-Century Venice. The Works of Sarra Copia Sulam in Verse and Prose, Along with Writings of Her Contemporaries in Her Praise, Condemnation, or Defense*, ed. and trans. Don Harrán. Chicago and London: University of Chicago Press.

Harris, William (1989) *Ancient Literacy*. Cambridge, MA: Harvard University Press.

Hart, Thomas R. (1990) 'Renaissance Dialogue into Novel: Cervantes's *Coloquio*', *MLN* 105: 191–202.

Harth, Erica (1992) *Cartesian Women: Versions and Subversions of Rational Discourse in the Old Regime*. Ithaca, NY and London: Cornell University Press.

Haskins, Charles Homer (1929) 'The Early *Artes dictandi* in Italy', in *Studies in Mediaeval Culture*. New York: Frederick Ungar, pp. 170–92.

Haskins, Ekaterina V. (2001) 'Rhetoric Between Orality and Literacy: Cultural Memory and Performance in Isocrates and Aristotle', *Quarterly Journal of Speech* 87, 2: 158–78.

Hauser, Gerard (1999) *Vernacular Voices: The Rhetorics of Publics and Public Spheres*. Columbia: University of South Carolina Press.

Heitsch Dorothea and Vallée, Jean-François (2004) 'Foreword', in *Printed Voices: The Renaissance Culture of Dialogue*, ed. Dorothea Heitsch and Jean-François Vallée. Toronto: University of Toronto Press, p. ix–xxiii.

Henderson, Judith (1983a) 'Defining the Genre of the Letter: Juan Luis Vives' *De conscribendis epistolis*', *Renaissance and Reformation*, n.s. 7, 2: 89–105.

Henderson, Judith (1983b) 'Erasmus on the Art of Letter-Writing', in *Renaissance Eloquence: Studies in the Theory and Practice of Renaissance Rhetoric*, ed. James Murphy. Berkeley: University of California Press, pp. 331–55.

Henderson, Judith (1992) 'Erasmian Ciceronians: Reformation Teachers of Letter-Writing', *Rhetorica* 10, 3: 273–302.

Herbert, Amanda E. (2014) *Female Alliances: Gender, Identity, and Friendship in Early Modern Britain*. New Haven, CT and London: Yale University Press.

Hildegard of Bingen (1994) *The Letters of Hildegard of Bingen*, trans. Joseph L. Baird and Radd K. Ehrman, Vol. I. New York and Oxford: Oxford University Press.

Hirschman, Albert (1977) *The Passions and the Interests: Political Arguments for Capitalism before Its Triumph*. Princeton: Princeton University Press.

Hobbes, Thomas (1969) *The Elements of Law*, ed. Ferdinand Tönnies and M. M. Goldsmith. London: Frank Cass.

Hobbes, Thomas (1972) *On Man*, in *Man and Citizen*, ed. Bernard Gert. Garden City, NY: Anchor Books, pp. 33–85.

Hobbes, Thomas (1983) *De Cive: The English Version*, ed. Howard Warrender. Oxford: Clarendon Press.

Hobbes, Thomas (1996) *Leviathan*, ed. Richard Tuck. Cambridge: Cambridge University Press.

Hochstrasser, T. J. (1993) 'Conscience and Reason: The Natural Law Theory of Jean Barbeyrac', *Historical Journal* 36, 2: 289–308.

Hochstrasser, T. J. (2000) *Natural Law Theories in the Early Enlightenment*. Cambridge: Cambridge University Press.

Hont, Istvan (1987) 'The Language of Sociability and Commerce: Samuel Pufendorf and the Theoretical Foundations of the "Four-Stages Theory"', in *The Languages of Political Theory in Early-Modern Europe*, ed. Anthony Pagden. Cambridge: Cambridge University Press, pp. 253–76.

Hoppenbrouwers, H. (1964) 'Conversatio. Une étude sémasiologique', *Graecitas et Latinitas Christianorum primaeva: Supplementa 1*. Nijmegen: Dekker & Van de Vegt, pp. 47–95.

Hotman, Antoine (1616) *Deux paradoxes de l'amitié et de l'avarice*, in Jean Hotman, François Hotman and Antoine Hotman, *Opuscules françoises des Hotmans*. Paris: Veuve M. Guillemot.

Howell, Wilbur Samuel (1975) *Poetics, Rhetoric, and Logic: Studies in the Basic Disciplines of Criticism*. Ithaca and London: Cornell University Press.

Huet, Pierre-Daniel (1715) *The History of Romances*, trans. Stephen Lewis. London: J. Hooke & T. Caldecott.

Hull, Suzanne W. (1982) *Chaste, Silent & Obedient: English Books for Women 1475–1640*. San Marino: Huntington Library.

Hume, David (1996) *The Philosophical Works of David Hume, Vols. I–IV*. Bristol: Thoemmes Press, 1854 repr.

Hume, David (1998) *Selected Essays*, ed. Stephen Copley and Andrew Edgar. Oxford: Oxford University Press.

Hurley, Alison E. (2006) 'A Conversation of Their Own: Watering-Place Correspondence among the Bluestockings', *Eighteenth-Century Studies* 40, 1: 1–21.

Hutter, Horst (1978) *Politics as Friendship: The Origins of Classical Notions of Politics in the Theory and Practice of Friendship*. Waterloo, ON: Wilfrid Laurier University Press.

Hyatte, Reginald (1994) *The Arts of Friendship: The Idealization of Friendship in Medieval and Early Renaissance Literature*. Leiden, New York and Cologne: E. J. Brill.

Hyatte, Reginald (1999) 'Complementary Humanistic Models of Marriage and Male *Amicitia* in Fifteenth-Century Literature', in *Friendship in Medieval Europe*, ed. Julian Haseldine. Thrupp: Sutton, pp. 251–61.

Infelise, Mario (2002) 'Roman *Avvisi*: Information and Politics in the Seventeenth Century', in *Court and Politics in Papal Rome, 1492–1700*, ed. Gianvittorio Signorotto and Maria Antonietta Visceglia. Cambridge: Cambridge University Press, pp. 212–28.

Inwood, Brad (2002) 'God and Human Knowledge in Seneca's *Natural Questions*', in *Traditions of Theology: Studies in Hellenistic Theology, Its Background and Aftermath*, ed. Dorothea Frede and André Laks. Leiden: Brill, pp. 119–57.

Jaeger, C. Stephen (1985) *The Origins of Courtliness: Civilizing Trends and the Formation of Courtly Ideals 939–1210*. Philadelphia: University of Pennsylvania Press.

James, Carolyn (2008) 'A Woman's Path to Literacy: The Letters of Margherita Datini, 1384–1410', in *Practices of Gender in Late Medieval and Early Modern Europe*, ed. Megan Cassidy-Welch and Peter Sherlock. Turnhout: Brepols, pp. 43–56.

James, Carolyn and Kent, Bill (2009) 'Renaissance Friendships: Traditional Truths, New and Dissenting Voices', in *Friendship: A History*, ed. Barbara Caine. London: Equinox, pp. 111–64.

Javitch, Daniel (1971) 'Rival Arts of Conduct in Elizabethan England: Guazzo's *Civile Conversazione* and Castiglione's *Courtier*', *Yearbook of Italian Studies* 1: 178–98.

Javitch, Daniel (1978) *Poetry and Courtliness*. Princeton: Princeton University Press.

Javitch, Daniel (1983) '*Il Cortegiano* and the Constraints of Despotism', in *Castiglione: The Ideal and the Real in Renaissance Culture*, ed. Robert W. Hanning and David Rosand. New Haven, CT and London: Yale University Press, pp. 17–28.

Jeffreys, Elizabeth (ed.) (2003) *Rhetoric in Byzantium*. Aldershot: Ashgate.

Johnson, Allison (2011) 'The "Single Lyfe" of Isabella Whitney: Love, Friendship, and the Single Woman Writer', in *Discourses and Representations of Friendship in Early Modern Europe, 1500–1700*, ed. Daniel T. Lochman, Maritere López and Lorna Hutson. Aldershot: Ashgate, pp. 117–29.

Johnson, William A. (2010) *Readers and Reading Culture in the High Roman Empire: A Study of Elite Communities*. Oxford: Oxford University Press.

Jones, Howard (1998) *Master Tully: Cicero in Tudor England*. Nieuwkoop: De Graaf.

Jordan, Constance (1990) *Renaissance Feminism: Literary Texts and Political Models*. Ithaca and London: Cornell University Press.

Jordan, Constance (1996) 'Renaissance Women Defending Women: Arguments Against Patriarchy', in *Italian Women Writers from the Renaissance to the Present: Revising the Canon*, ed. Maria Ornella Marotti. University Park: Pennsylvania State University Press, pp. 55–67.

Jornals sent from the Campe at Arques September 18 1589 (1589) Egerton MS 2598, fos. 93–94. London: British Library.

Kaiser, T. E. (1989–90) 'Rhetoric in the Service of the King: The Abbé Du Bos and the Concept of Public Judgment', *Eighteenth-Century Studies* 23, 2: 182–99.

Kalimtzis, Kostas (2000) *Aristotle on Political Enmity and Disease: An Inquiry into* Stasis. Albany, NY: State University of New York Press.

Kaufman, Peter Iver (1981) 'The Disputed Date of Erasmus' *Liber Apologeticus*', *Medievalia et Humanistica* n.s. 10: 141–57.

Kaufman, Peter Iver (1987) 'Humanist Spirituality and Ecclesial Reaction: Thomas More's "Monstra"', *Church History* 56, 1: 25–38.

Keller, Vera (2011) 'Painted Friends: Political Interest and the Transformation of International Learned Sociability' in *Friendship in the Middle Ages and Early Modern Times: Fundamentals of Medieval and Early Modern Culture*, ed. Marilyn Sandidge and Albrecht Classen. Berlin: Walter de Gruyter Press, pp. 661–92.

Kennedy, George (1994) *A New History of Classical Rhetoric*. Princeton: Princeton University Press.

Kennedy, George (1999) *Classical Rhetoric and Its Christian and Secular Tradition*. Chapel Hill: University of North Carolina Press.

Kennerly, Michele (2010) '*Sermo* and Stoic Sociality in Cicero's *De Officiis*', *Rhetorica* 28, 2: 119–37.

King, Margaret L. and Rabil, Albert Jr (1983) *Her Immaculate Hand: Selected Works by and about the Women Humanists of Quattrocento Italy*. Binghamton, NY: Medieval and Renaissance Texts and Studies.

Kinney, Arthur F. (1989) *Continental Humanist Poetics: Studies in Erasmus, Castiglione, Marguerite de Navarre, Rabelais, and Cervantes*. Amherst, MA: University of Massachusetts Press.

Klein, Lawrence E. (1994) *Shaftesbury and the Culture of Politeness: Moral Discourse and Cultural Politics in Early Eighteenth-Century England*. Cambridge: Cambridge University Press.

Klosko, George (1986) 'Rational Persuasion in Plato's Political Theory', *History of Political Thought* 7, 1: 15–31.

Knox, Dilwyn (2000) 'Civility, Courtesy and Women in the Italian Renaissance', in *Women in Italian Renaissance Culture and Society*, ed. Letizia Panizza. Oxford: Legenda pp. 2–17.

Kogel, Renée (1972) *Pierre Charron*. Geneva: Librairie Droz.

Koselleck, Reinhart (1988) *Critique and Crisis: Enlightenment and the Pathogenesis of Modern Society*, trans. unknown. Cambridge, MA: MIT Press.

Kristeller, Paul Oskar (1961) *Renaissance Thought: The Classic, Scholastic and Humanist Strains*. New York: Harper & Row.

Kristeller, Paul Oskar (1970) 'Erasmus from an Italian Perspective', *Renaissance Quarterly* 23, 1: 1–14.

Kristeller, Paul Oskar (1972) 'Italian Humanism and Byzantium', in *Renaissance Concepts of Man and other Essays*. New York: Harper & Row, pp. 64–85.

Kronick, David A. (1976) *A History of Scientific and Technical Periodicals: The Origins and Development of the Scientific and Technical Press 1665–1790*, 2nd edn. Metuchen, NJ: Scarecrow Press.

La Fevrerie (1683) 'Du style épistolaire', in *Extraordinare de Mercure Galant. Quartier de juillet 1683. Tome XXIII*. Paris: Blageart, pp. 3–67.

La Motte Aigron, Jacques de (1634) 'The Preface', in *The Letters of Mounsieur de Balzac*, trans. W. T. London: Printed by Nicholas Okes for Richard Clotterbuck, sigs. A2ʳ–a2ᵛ.

Lambert, Anne Thérèse de Marguenat de Courcelles, Marquise de (1728) *Avis d'une mère à son fils, et à sa fille*. Paris: Ganeau.

Lambert, Anne Thérèse de Marguenat de Courcelles, Marquise de (1746) *Reflexions nouvelles sur les femmes*. London: Coderc.

Lambert, Anne Thérèse de Marguenat de Courcelles, Marquise de (1748) 'Reflexions sur le goût', in *Oeuvres de Madame la Marquise de Lambert, Tome I*. Paris: Ganeau, pp. 141–6.

Lambert, Anne Thérèse de Marguenat de Courcelles, Marquise de (1780) *Essays on Friendship and Old-Age, by the Marchioness de Lambert*. Dublin: Price, Whitestone et al.

Lamy, Bernard (1676) *La Rhétorique ou l'art de parler* (Paris, 1675), trans. unknown, *The Art of Speaking*. London: Godbid & Pitt.

Langer, Ullrich (1990) *Divine and Poetic Freedom in the Renaissance: Nominalist Theology and Literature in France and Italy*. Princeton: Princeton University Press.

Langer, Ullrich (1994) *Perfect Freedom: Studies in Literature and Moral Philosophy from Boccaccio to Corneille*. Geneva: Droz.

Lanham, Carol (1975) *Salutatio Formulas in Latin Letters to 1200: Syntax, Style, and Theory*. Munich: Bei der Arbeo-Gesellschaft.

Lanser, Susan S. (1998/9) 'Befriending the Body: Female Intimacies as Class Acts', *Eighteenth-Century Studies* 32, 2: 179–98.

Latimer, Berkley Wells (1976) *Pamphleteering in France During the Wars of Religion: Aspects of Ephemeral and Occasional Publications, 1562–1598*. PhD diss., Duke University.

Le Mercier de La Rivière, Pierre-Paul (1767) *L'ordre naturel et essentiel des sociétés politiques, Tome II*. London: Nourse.

Legault, Marianne (2012) *Female Intimacies in Seventeenth-Century French Literature*, trans. Marianne Legault and Ramine Adl. Burlington, VT: Ashgate.

Lehmberg, Stanford E. (1961) 'English Humanists, the Reformation, and the Problem of Counsel', *Archiv für Reformationsgeschichte* 52: 74–90.

Letwin, William (1959) *Sir Josiah Child, Merchant Economist*. Boston: Harvard College.

Leushuis, Reinier (2004) 'The Mimesis of Marriage: Dialogue and Intimacy in Erasmus's Matrimonial Writings', *Renaissance Quarterly* 57, 4: 1278–307.

Lévy, Carlos (1993) 'La conversation à Rome à la fin de la République: des pratiques sans théorie?', *Rhetorica* 11, 4: 399–414.

Lienhard, Joseph T. (1990) 'Friendship in Paulinus of Nola and Augustine', in *Collectanea Augustiniana. Mélanges T. J. Van Bavel* [*Augustiniana* 40], ed. B. Bruning, M. Lamberigts and J. Van Houtem. Leuven: Institut Historique Augustinien, pp. 279–96.

Lievsay, John Leon (1961) *Stefano Guazzo and the English Renaissance, 1575–1675*. Chapel Hill: University of North Carolina Press.

Lipsius, Justus (1594) *Two Bookes of Constancie*, trans. John Strandling. London: Johnes.

Logan, George M. (1983) *The Meaning of More's 'Utopia'*. Princeton: Princeton University Press.

Lomas, Sophie (ed.) (1916) *Calendar of State Papers, Foreign Series, of the Reign of Elizabeth*, Vol. XIX, August 1584 – August 1585. London: His Majesty's Stationery Office.

Lucian (1798) *Toxaris*, trans. John Carr, in *Dialogues of Lucian, Vol. V.* London: Longman, pp. 476–536.

Luck, Georg (1958) 'Vir Facetus: A Renaissance Ideal', *Studies in Philology* 55, 2: 107–21.

Luxon, Thomas H. (2005) *Single Imperfection: Milton, Marriage and Friendship*. Pittsburgh: Duquesne University Press.

Lydgate, John (1897) *Fabula Duorum Mercatorum*, ed. Gustav Schleich. Strasbourg: Trübner.

McClain, Molly (2008) 'Love, Friendship, and Power: Queen Mary II's Letters to Frances Apsley', *Journal of British Studies* 47, 3: 505–27.

McConica, James K. (1969) 'Erasmus and the Grammar of Consent', *Scrinium Erasmianum*, Vol. 2. Leiden: Brill, pp. 77–99.

McEvoy, James (1999) 'The Theory of Friendship in the Latin Middle Ages: Hermeneutics, Contextulization and the Transmission and Reception of Ancient Texts and Ideas, from *c.* AD 350 to *c.* 1500', in *Friendship in Medieval Europe*, ed. Julian Haseldine. Thrupp: Sutton, pp. 3–44.

Mack, Peter (2002) *Elizabethan Rhetoric: Theory and Practice*. Cambridge: Cambridge University Press.

McLaren, A. N. (2004) *Political Culture in the Reign of Elizabeth I: Queen and Commonwealth 1558–1585*. Cambridge: Cambridge University Press.

MacLean, Ian (1977) *Woman Triumphant: Feminism in French Literature, 1610–1652*. Oxford: Oxford University Press.

Maland, David (1970) *Culture and Society in Seventeenth-Century France*. New York: Charles Scribner's Sons.

Malespini, Celio (1609) *Ducento novelle*. Venice: Al Segno dell'Italia.

Malherbe, Abraham (1988) *Ancient Epistolary Theorists*. Atlanta, GA: Scholars Press.

Mandeville, Bernard (1988) 'The Sixth Dialogue', in *The Fable of the Bees: or Private Vices, Publick Benefits*, Volume Two, ed. F. B. Kaye. Indianapolis: Liberty Fund, pp. 266–357.

Marbeck, Dr Roger (1596a) *A Breife & a true discourse of the late honourable voyage unto Spaine & of the wynninge, Tackinge & burninge of the famous towne of Cadiz*. Stowe MS 159, fos. 353–69. London: British Library.

Marbeck, Dr Roger (1596b) *Discourse of the voyage to Spain made, in 1596, under Lord Essex and Lord Howard of Effingham*. Sloane MS 226. London: British Library.

Marsh, David (1980) *Quattrocentro Dialogue: Classical Tradition and Humanist Innovation*. Cambridge, MA and London: Harvard University Press.

Marshall, John (2006) *John Locke, Toleration and Early Enlightenment Culture: Religious Intolerance and Arguments for Religious Toleration in Early Modern and 'Early Enlightenment' Europe*. Cambridge: Cambridge University Press.

Martin, John (1997) 'Inventing Sincerity, Refashioning Prudence: The Discovery of the Individual in Renaissance Europe'. *American Historical Review* 102, 5: 1309–42.

Mee, Jon (2011) *Conversable Worlds: Literature, Contention, and Community 1762 to 1830*. Oxford: Oxford University Press.

Melon, Jean-François (1966) *Essai politique sur le commerce*, in *Économistes-Financiers du XVIIIe Siècle*, ed. Eugène Daire. Paris: Guillaumin, 1843; repr. Osnabruck: Zeller, pp. 707–835.

Mercer, R. G. G. (1979) *The Teaching of Gasparino Barzizza: With Special Reference to his Place in Paduan Humanism*. London: Modern Humanities Research Association.

Méré, Antoine Gombauld, chevalier de (1682) *Lettres de Monsieur le Chevalier de Méré, Premiere Partie*. Paris: Thierry & Barbin.

Méré, Antoine Gombauld, chevalier de (1930) *Les Discours, Tome II*. Paris: Fernand Roches.

Mews Constant J. and Chiavaroli, Neville (2009) 'The Latin West', in *Friendship: A History*, ed. Barbara Caine. London: Equinox, pp. 73–110.

Millar, Fergus (1977) *The Emperor in the Roman World (31 B.C. – A.D. 337)*. Ithaca, NY: Cornell University Press.

Millar, John (1803) *An Historical View of the English Government, Vol. IV*. London: Mawman.

Miller, Peter N. (2000) *Peiresc's Europe: Learning and Virtue in the Seventeenth Century*. New Haven, CT and London: Yale University Press.

Miller, Peter N. (2001) 'Friendship and Conversation in Seventeenth-Century Venice', *Journal of Modern History* 73, 1: 1–31.

Miller, Peter N. (2008) 'The Renaissance Republic of Letters and the Genesis of Enlightenment', in *Europäische Bildungsströme. Die Viadrina ima Kontext der europäischen Gelehrtenrepublik der frühen Neuzeit (1506–1811)*, ed. Reinhard Blänkner. Berlin: Schöneiche, pp. 45–59.

Monfasani, John (1983) 'The Byzantine Rhetorical Tradition and the Renaissance', in *Renaissance Eloquence: Studies in the Theory and Practice of Renaissance Rhetoric*, ed. James J. Murphy. Berkeley, Los Angeles and London: University of California Press, pp. 174–87.

Monfasani, John (1988) 'Humanism and Rhetoric', in *Renaissance Humanism: Foundations, Forms, and Legacy*, Vol. 3, ed. Albert Rabil, Jr. Philadelphia: University of Pennsylvania Press, pp. 171–235.

Montaigne, Michel de (1711) *Essays of Michael seigneur de Montaigne*, Vol. I, trans. Charles Cotton, 4th edn. London: Brown et al.

Montaigne, Michel de (2003) *The Complete Works*, trans. Donald Frame. New York and Toronto: A. A. Knopf.

Montesquieu, Charles de Secondat, baron de (1989) *The Spirit of the Laws*, ed. and trans. Anne M. Cohler, Basia Carolyn Miller and Harold Samuel Stone. Cambridge: Cambridge University Press.

More Newes of the good successe of the Duke of Brunswick (1623) London: Printed [by Eliot's Court Press?] for Nathaniel Butter and Nicholas Bourne, 29 July, no. 42.

More, Thomas (1952) *Utopia*, trans. Ralph Robynson. Hearne's edn, 1716; repr. Cambridge: Cambridge University Press.

More, Thomas (2003) *Utopia*, trans. Paul Turner. London: Penguin Books.

Morlet-Chantalat, Chantal (1994) *La Clélie de Mademoiselle de Scudéry, de l'épopée à la gazette: un discours féminin de la gloire*. Paris: Honoré Champion.

Moss, Ann (1996) *Printed Commonplace-Books and the Structuring of Renaissance Thought*. Oxford: Clarendon Press.

Muret, Marc Antoine (1834) *M. Antonii Mureti Opera Omnia, Vol. I*, ed. Carolus Henricus Frotscher. Leipzig: Serigiana Libraria.

Murphy, James (2001a) *Rhetoric in the Middle Ages: A History of Rhetorical Theory from St. Augustine to the Renaissance*. Tempe, AZ: Arizona Center for Medieval and Renaissance Studies.

Murphy, James (ed. and trans.) (2001b) *Three Medieval Rhetorical Arts*. Tempe: Arizona Center for Medieval and Renaissance Studies.

Myers, Sylvia Harcstark (1990) *The Bluestocking Circle: Women, Friendship, and the Life of the Mind in Eighteenth-Century England*. Oxford: Clarendon Press.

Najemy, John M. (1993) *Between Friends: Discourses of Power and Desire in the Machaivelli-Vettori Letters of 1513–1515*. Princeton: Princeton University Press.

Newes from divers countries (1597) London: Valentine Sims.

Newes from Rome, Venice, and Vienna (1595) London: By John Danter for Thomas Gosson.

Newes of Europe (1624) London: Butter & Sheffard, 12 March, no. 17.

Nicole, Pierre (1677) *Essaies de morale* (Paris, 1671), trans. unknown, *Moral Essays*, Vols 1–2. London: Magnus & Bentley.

Norris, John (1687) 'A Letter concerning Friendship', in *A Collection of Miscellanies: Consisting of Poems, Essays, Discourses, and Letters, Occasionally Writeen*. Oxford: Crosley, pp. 450–5.

Novikoff, Alex J. (2013) *The Medieval Culture of Disputation: Pedagogy, Practice, and Performance*. Philadelphia: University of Pennsylvania Press.

Olmsted, Wendy (2005) 'The Gentle Doctor: Renaissance/Reformation Friendship, Rhetoric, and Emotion in Sidney's "Old Arcadia"', *Modern Philology* 103, 2: 156–86.

Ong, Walter J. (1971) 'Tudor Writings on Rhetoric, Poetic, and Literary Theory', in *Rhetoric, Romance, and Technology*. Ithaca and London: Cornell University Press, pp. 48–103.

Palmieri, Matteo (1825) *Della vita civile*. Milan: Giovanni Silvestri.

Parsons, Nicola (2009) *Reading Gossip in the Early Eighteenth-Century England*. Basingstoke: Palgrave Macmillan.

Pasquier, Nicolas (2003) *Le Gentilhomme*, ed. Denise Carabin. Paris: Honoré Champion.

Patt, William (1978) 'The Early *Ars dictaminis* as Response to a Changing Society', *Viator 9*: 133–55.

Peacham, Henry (1577) *Garden of Eloquence*. London: Jackson.

Peacham, Henry (1593) *Garden of Eloquence*. London: Jackson.

Pekacz, Jolanta T. (1999) *Conservative Tradition in Pre-Revolutionary France: Parisian Salon Women*. New York: Peter Lang.

Pellisson, Paul (1656) 'Discours sur les oeuvres de M. Sarasin', in *Les Oeuvres de Monsieur Sarasin*. Paris: Courbé, pp. 1–72.

Peltonen, Markku (2003) *The Duel in Early Modern Engand: Civility, Politeness and Honour*. Cambridge: Cambridge University Press.

Pembroke, S. G. (1971) 'Oikeiosis', in *Problems of Stoicism*, ed. A. A. Long. London: University of London, Athlone Press, pp. 114–49.

Petrarca, Francesco (1978) *The Life of Solitude*, trans. Jacob Zeitlin. Urbana: University of Illinois Press, 1924; repr. Westport, CT: Hyperion.

Petrarca, Francesco (1992) *Letters of Old Age. Rerum senilium libri I–XVIII. Volume Two, Books X–XVIII*, trans. Aldo S. Bernardo, Saul Levin and Reta A. Bernardo. Baltimore, MD and London: Johns Hopkins University Press.

Petrarca, Francesco (1997) *Le Familiari: Edizione Critica, Vol. I*, ed. Vittorio Rossi. Florence: Casa Editrice Le Lettere.

Petrarca, Francesco (2003) *The Secret, by Francesco Petrarch, with Related Documents*, trans. and ed. Carol E. Quillen. Boston and New York: Bedford/St. Martin's.

Petrarca, Francesco (2005) *Letters on Familiar Matters (Rerum familiarum libri)*, 3 vols, trans. Aldo S. Bernardo. New York: Italica Press.

Philips, Katherine (1992) *The Collected Works of Katherine Philips, The Matchless Orinda, Volume 2. The Letters*, ed. Patrick Thomas. Stump Cross: Stump Cross Books.

Phiston, William (1584) *The welspring of wittie conceites*. London: Richard Jones.

Piccolomini, Enea Silvio (1928) *Aeneae Silvii de curialium miseriis epistola*, ed. Wilfred P. Mustard. Baltimore: Johns Hopkins University Press.

Plato (1963) *The Collected Dialogues of Plato including the Letters*, ed. Edith Hamilton and Huntington Cairns. Princeton: Princeton University Press.

Plett, Heinrich (2004) *Rhetoric and Renaissance Culture*. Berlin and New York: De Gruyter.

Plutarch (1999) 'Advice to the Bride and Groom', trans. Donald Russell, in *Plutarch's Advice to the Bride and Groom and A Consolation to His Wife: English Translations, Commentary, interpretive Esays, and Bibliography*, ed. Sarah B. Pomeroy. New York and Oxford: Oxford University Press, pp. 5–13.

Plutarch (2005) 'How to Tell a Flatterer from a Friend', in *Moralia, Volume I*, trans. Frank Cole Babbitt. Cambridge, MA and London: Harvard University Press, pp. 261–395.

Pocock, J. G. A. (1985) 'The Mobility of Property and the Rise of Eighteenth-Century Sociology', in *Virtue, Commerce, and History: Essays on Political Thought and History, Chiefly in the Eighteenth Century*. Cambridge: Cambridge University Press, pp. 103–23.

Pocock, J. G. A. (2003) *The Machiavellian Moment: Florentine Political Thought and the Atlantic Republican Tradition*. Princeton and Oxford: Princeton University Press.

Pontano, Giovanni Gioviano (2008) *De Sermone. De la conversation*, trans. and ed. Florence Bistagne. Paris: Honoré Champion.

Poulett, Anthony (1593) Anthony Poulett to Sir Francis Hastings, 23 April 1593. Hastings Collection MS #10356. Henry E. Huntington Library, San Marino, CA.

Present State of the Affaires betwixt the Emperor and King of Bohemia, The (1620) [London: Edward Allde].

Prince, Michael (1996) *Philosophical Dialogue in the British Enlightenment: Theology, Aesthetics, and the Novel*. Cambridge: Cambridge University Press.

Prostko, Jack (1989) '"Natural Conversation Set in View": Shaftesbury and Moral Speech', *Eighteenth-Century Studies* 23, 1: 42–61.

Pufendorf, Samuel (1698) *The Whole Duty of Man According to the Law of Nature*, 2nd edn, trans. unknown. London: Harper.

Pufendorf, Samuel (1729) *Of the Law of Nature and Nations*, 4th edn, ed. Jean Barbeyrac, trans. Basil Kennett. London: Walthoe et al.

Pufendorf, Samuel (1994) *The Political Writings of Samuel Pufendorf*, ed. Craig L. Carr, trans. Michael J. Seidler. Oxford: Oxford University Press.

Puterbaugh, Joseph (2004) '"Truth Hath the Victory": Dialogue and Disputation in John Foxes's *Actes and Monuments*', in *Printed Voices: The Renaissance Culture of Dialogue*, ed. Dorothea Heitsch and Jean-François Vallée. Toronto: University of Toronto Press, pp. 137–56.

Quintilian (1920–2) *Institutio oratoria*, 4 vols, ed. and trans. H. E. Butler. London and New York: William Heinemann and G. P. Putnam's Sons.

Quondam, Amedeo (2007) *La Conversazione: Un modello italiano*. Rome: Donzelli.

Ramage, Edwin S. (1963) 'Urbanitas: Cicero and Quintilian, a Contrast in Attitudes', *American Journal of Philology* 84, 4: 390–414.

Randall, David (2006) 'Joseph Mead, Novellante: News, Sociability, and Credibility in Early Stuart England', *Journal of British Studies* 45, 2: 293–312.

Randall, David (2008a) *Credibility in Elizabethan and Early Stuart Military News*. London: Pickering & Chatto.

Randall, David (2008b) 'Epistolary Rhetoric, the Newspaper, and the Public Sphere', *Past and Present* 198: 3–32.

Randall, David (2008c) 'Ethos, Poetics, and the Literary Public Sphere', *Modern Language Quarterly* 69, 2: 221–43.

Randall, David (2011a) 'Empiricism, the New Rhetoric, and the Public Sphere', *Telos* 154: 51–73.

Randall, David (2011b) 'Humean Aesthetics and the Rhetorical Public Sphere', *Telos* 157: 148–63.

Randall, David (2011c) 'The Prudential Public Sphere', *Philosophy and Rhetoric* 44, 3: 205–26.

Randall, David (2016a) 'The Rhetoric of Violence, the Public Sphere, and the Second Amendment', *Philosophy and Rhetoric* 49, 2: 125–48.

Randall, David (2016b) 'Adam Smith's Mixed Prudence and the Economy of the Public Sphere', *Political Studies* 64, 2: 335–50.

Rapin, René (1672) *Réflexions sur l'usage de l'éloquence de ce temps* (Paris, 1672); trans. as *Reflections Upon the Use of the Eloquence of These Times*, trans. unknown. Oxford: Printed and sold by the booksellers there.

Rapin, René (1716) *The Whole Critical Works of Monsieur Rapin*, Vols I–II, Second Edition, trans. Basil Kennet. London: Bonwicke, Wilkin et al.

Raymond, Joad (1996) *The Invention of the Newspaper: English Newsbooks 1641–1649*. Oxford: Clarendon Press.

Raymond, Joad (1999) 'The Newspaper, Public Opinion, and the Public Sphere in the Seventeenth Century', in *News, Newspapers, and Society in Early Modern Britain*, ed. Joad Raymond. London: Frank Cass, pp. 109–40.

Rebhorn, Wayne A. (1972) 'Ottaviano's Interruption: Book IV and the Problem of Unity in Il Libro del Cortegiano', *Modern Language Notes* 87, 1: 37–59.

Rebhorn, Wayne A. (1993) 'Baldesar Castiglione, Thomas Wilson, and the Courtly Body of Renaissance Rhetoric', *Rhetorica* 11, 3: 241–74.

Rebhorn, Wayne A. (1995) *The Emperor of Men's Minds: Literature and the Renaissance Discourse of Rhetoric*. Ithaca and London: Cornell University Press.

Rècueil de lois et règlemens concernant l'instruction publique, Tome Premier (1814) Paris: Brunot-Labbe.

Recueil General des Questions Traitees dans les Conferences du Bureau d'Adresse, Tome V (1646) Paris: Loyson.

Refuge, Eustache de (1622) *A Treatise of the Court or Instructions for Courtiers. Digested into two Books*, trans. John Reynolds. London: A[ugustine] M[atthews]: for Will: Lee.

Rehg, William (1997) 'Reason and Rhetoric in Habermas's Theory of Argumentation', in *Rhetoric and Hermeneutics in Our Time: A Reader*, ed. Walter Jost and Michael Hyde. New Haven, CT and London: Yale University Press, pp. 358–77.

Relation of the Occurrances happening in the beginning and after our landing in the Isle de Ree, A (1627) HM 45148, fos. 2–20. Henry E. Huntington Library, San Marino, California.

Remer, Gary (1996) *Humanism and the Rhetoric of Toleration*. University Park: Pennsylvania State University Press.

Report of Cales (1596) Additional MS 48152, fos. 249–53. London: British Library.

Rhetorica ad Herennium (1954) trans. Harry Caplan. Cambridge, MA: Harvard University Press; London: William Heinemann.

Richards, Jennifer (2003) *Rhetoric and Courtliness in Early Modern Literature*. Cambridge: Cambridge University Press.

Richardson, Malcolm (1984) 'The *Dictamen* and Its influence on Fifteenth-Century English Prose', *Rhetorica* 2, 3: 207–26.

Richardson, Malcolm (2001) 'The Fading Influence of the Medieval *Ars Dictaminis* in England after 1400', *Rhetorica* 19, 2: 225–47.

Rigolot, François (2004) 'Problematizing Renaissance Exemplarity: The Inward Turn of Dialogue from Petrarch to Montaigne', in *Printed Voices: The Renaissance Culture of Dialogue*, ed. Dorothea Heitsch and Jean-François Vallée. Toronto: University of Toronto Press, pp. 3–24.

Rinuccini, Alamanno (1978) 'Liberty', trans. Renée Neu Watkins, in *Humanism and Liberty: Writings on Freedom from Fifteenth-Century Florence*, ed. Renée Neu Watkins. Columbia: University of South Carolina Press, pp. 193–224.

Ripa, Cesare (1625) *Iconologia*. Padua: Tozzi.

Ripa, Cesare and Orlandi, Cesare (1765) *Iconologia*, vol. II. Perugia: Costantini.

Robertson, William (1777) *The History of the Reign of the Emperor Charles V. with a View of the Progress of Society in Europe, Vol. I*. London and Edinburgh: Strahan, Cadell & Balfour.

Robertson, William (1840) *The History of the Reign of the Emperor Charles V. with a View of the Progress of Society in Europe, Vol. I*. London: Cadell.

Robiglio, Andrea A. (2006) 'Between Language and Likemindedness: Some Aspects of the Concept of *Conversatio Civilis* from Aquinas to Guazzo', in *Language and Cultural Change: Aspects of the Study and Use of Language in the Later Middle Ages and the Renaissance*, ed. Lodi Nauta. Leuven, Paris and Dudley, MA: Peeters, pp. 113–31.

Robin, Diana (2000) 'Humanism and Feminism in Laura Cereta's Public Letters', in *Women in Italian Renaissance Culture and Society*, ed. Letizia Panizza. Oxford: Legenda, pp. 368–84.

Robin, Diana (2007) *Publishing Women: Salons, the Presses, and the Counter-Reformation in Sixteenth-Century Italy*. Chicago and London: University of Chicago Press.

Roller, Matthew B. (2001) *Constructing Autocracy: Aristocrats and Emperors in Julio-Claudian Rome*. Princeton and Oxford: Princeton University Press.

Rollin, Charles (1734) *The Method of Teaching and Studying the Belles Lettres*, 4 vols, trans. unknown. London: Bettesworth & Hitch.

Rosenmeyer, Patricia (2001) *Ancient Epistolary Fictions: The Letter in Greek Literature*. Cambridge: Cambridge University Press.

Rosenthal, Margaret F. (1992) *The Honest Courtesan: Veronica Franco, Citizen and Writer in Sixteenth Century Venice*. Chicago and London: University of Chicago Press.

Roulston, Christine (1998/9) 'Separating the Inseparables: Female Friendship and Its Discontents in Eighteenth-Century France', *Eighteenth-Century Studies* 32, 2: 215–31.

Rousseau, Jean-Jacques (1997) *Discourse on the Sciences and Arts* or *First Discourse*, in *The* Discourses *and other early political writings*, ed. and trans. Victor Gourevitch. Cambridge: Cambridge University Press, pp. 3–28.

S.W. (1622) *The Appollogie of the Illustrious Prince Ernestus, Earle of Mansfield*. Heidelberg [i.e. London: Edward Allde].

Saint Simon, Louis de Rouvroy, duc de (1890) *Mémoires de Saint-Simon*. Paris: Hachette.

Salutati, Coluccio (1947) *De nobilitate legum et medicinae. De verecundia*, ed. Eugenio Garin. Florence: Vallecchi.

Savary, Jacques (1675) *Le parfait négociant, ou Instruction générale de tout ce qui regarde le commerce*. Paris: Billaine.

Sawyer, Jeffrey K. (1990) *Printed Poison. Pamphlet Propaganda, Faction Politics, and the Public Sphere in Early Seventeenth-Century France*. Berkeley and Los Angeles: University of California Press.

Schiffman, Zachary Sayre (1991) *On the Threshold of Modernity: Relativism in the French Renaissance*. Baltimore and London: Johns Hopkins University Press.

Scudéry, Madeleine de (1660) *Clélie, Histoire Romaine, Premiere Parte*. Paris: Courbé.

Scudéry, Madeleine de (1661) *Clélie, Histoire Romaine, Cinquiesme et Derniere Partie*. Paris: Courbé.

Scudéry, Madeleine de (1684) *Conversations nouvelles sur divers sujets, Tome 1*. Paris: Barbin.

Scudéry, Madeleine de (1693) *Entretiens de Morale, Dediez au Roy, Tome Premier*. Paris: L'Imprimerie Royale.

Scudéry, Madeleine de (1972) *Artamène, ou Le Grand Cyrus, Dixiesme Partie*. Paris: Courbe, 1656; repr. Geneva: Slatkine.

Scudéry, Madeleine de (2002) 'On Conversation', trans. Jane Donawerth, in *Rhetorical Theory by Women before 1900: An Anthology*, ed. Jane Donawerth. Lanham, MD: Rowman & Littlefield, pp. 84–90.

Scudéry, Madeleine de (2003) *The Story of Sapho*, trans. Karen Newman. Chicago and London: University of Chicago Press.

Scudéry, Madeleine de (2004) *Selected Letters, Orations, and Rhetorical Dialogues*, ed. and trans. Jane Donawerth and Julie Strongson. Chicago and London: University of Chicago Press.

Scudéry, Madeleine de [attributed to, and possibly written with, Georges de Scudéry] (1681) *Les Femmes Illustres of the Heroick Harrangues of the Illustrious Women*, trans. James Innes. Edinburgh: Brown, Glen & Weir.

Seddon, P. R. (ed.) (1983) *Letters of John Holles 1587–1637*, Vol. II. Nottingham: Produced for the Thoroton Society by Technical Print Services Ltd.

Seigel, Jerrold E. (1968) *Rhetoric and Philosophy in Renaissance Humanism: The Union of Eloquence and Wisdom, Petrarch to Valla*. Princeton: Princeton University Press.

Seneca (1917–25) *Ad Lucilium Epistulae Morales*, vols I–III, trans. Richard M. Gummere. Cambridge, MA: Harvard University Press; London: William Heinemann.

Seneca (1932) *Moral Essays*, Vol. II, trans. John W. Basore. London and New York: William Heinemann and G. P. Putnam's Sons.

Seneca (1935) *Moral Essays*, Vol. III, trans. John W. Basore. London: William Heinemann; Cambridge, MA: Harvard University Press.

Seneca (1971) *Naturales Quaestiones, Vol. I*, trans. Thomas H. Corcoran. Cambridge, MA: Harvard University Press; London: William Heinemann.

Shaaber, Matthias (1929) *Some Forerunners of the Newspaper in England, 1476–1622*. Philadelphia: University of Pennsylvania Press.

Shaftesbury, Anthony Ashley Cooper, Third Earl of (1999) *Characteristics of Men, Manners, Opinions, Times*, ed. Lawrence E. Klein. Cambridge: Cambridge University Press.

Shakespeare, William (2008) *The Norton Shakespeare: Based on the Oxford Edition*, 2nd edition, ed. Stephen Greenblatt et al. New York: W. W. Norton.

Shannon, Laurie (2002) *Sovereign Amity: Figures of Friendship in Shakespearean Contexts*. Chicago and London: University of Chicago Press.

Shapiro, Barbara (1983) *Probability and Certainty in Seventeenth-Century England. A Study of the Relationships Between Natural Science, Religion, History, Law, and Literature*. Princeton: Princeton University Press.

Shapiro, Barbara (2000) *A Culture of Fact: England, 1550–1720*. Ithaca, NY and London: Cornell University Press.

Shepard, Laurie (1999) *Courting Power: Persuasion and Politics in the Early Thirteenth Century*. New York and London: Garland.

Sherry, Richard (1550) *A Treatise of Schemes and Tropes*. London: John Day.

Shklar, Judith (1969) *Men and Citizens: A Study of Rousseau's Social Theory*. Cambridge: Cambridge University Press.

Skinner, Quentin (1987) 'Sir Thomas More's *Utopia* and the Language of Renaissance Humanism', in *The Languages of Political Theory in Early-Modern Europe*, ed. Anthony Pagden. Cambridge: Cambridge University Press, pp. 123–57.

Smarr, Janet Levarie (2005) *Joining the Conversation: Dialogues by Renaissance Women*. Ann Arbor: University of Michigan Press.

Smith, Adam (1896) *Lectures on Justice, Police, Revenue and Arms*, ed. Edwin Cannan. Oxford: Clarendon Press.

Smith, Christine (1992) *Architecture in the Culture of Early Humanism: Ethics, Aesthetics, and Eloquence 1400–1470*. Oxford: Oxford University Press.

Somerset, Anne (2013) *Queen Anne: The Politics of Passion*. New York: Knopf.

Sorel, Charles (1663) *Oeuvres Diverses, Ou Discours Meslez*. Paris: Campagnie des Libraires.

Southern, R. W. (1995) *Scholastic Humanism and the Unification of Europe, Volume I, Foundations*. Oxford: Blackwell.

Southern, R. W. (1990) *Saint Anselm. A Portrait in a Landscape*. Cambridge: Cambridge University Press.

Spenser, Edmund (1909) *Faerie Queene, Vol. II: Books IV–VII*, ed. J. C. Smith. Oxford: Clarendon Press.

Stadter, Philip A. (2014) *Plutarch and his Roman Readers*. Oxford: Oxford University Press.

Stephens, Mitchell (1988) *A History of News. From the Drum to the Satellite*. New York: Viking.

Steuart, James (1767) *An Inquiry into the Principles of Political Economy, Volume I*. London: Millar & Cadell.

Stirewalt, M. Luther Jr (1993) *Studies in Ancient Greek Epistolography*. Atlanta: Scholars Press.

Stowers, Stanley (1986) *Letter Writing in Greco-Roman Antiquity*. Philadelphia: Westminster Press.

Streckfuss, Richard (1998) 'News before Newspapers', *Journalism and Mass Communication Quarterly* 75, 1: 84–97.

Strosetzki, Christoph (1984) *Rhétorique de la conversation: Sa dimension littéraire et linguistique dans la societé française du XVIIe siècle*, trans. Sabine Seubert. Paris, Seattle and Tübingen: Biblio 17.

Struever, Nancy S. (1985) 'The Conversable World: Eighteenth-Century Transformations of the Relation of Rhetoric and Truth', in Brian Vickers and Nancy Struever, *Rhetoric and the Pursuit of Truth: Language Change in the Seventeenth and Eighteenth Centuries*. Los Angeles: William Andrews Clark Memorial Library, pp. 79–119.

Struever, Nancy S. (1992) *Theory as Practice: Ethical Inquiry in the Renaissance*. Chicago and London: University of Chicago Press.

Surtz, Edward (1964) 'Introduction: *Utopia* Past and Present', in Thomas More, *Utopia*, ed. Edward Surtz, *Complete Works*, IV. New Haven, CT and London: Yale University Press, pp. vii–xxx.

Swift, Jonathan (2002) *The Basic Writings of Jonathan Swift*, ed. Claude Rawson and Ian Higgins. New York: Modern Library.

Tacitus (1914) *Dialogus. Agricola. Germania*, trans. William Peterson. London: William Heinemann; New York: Macmillan.

Tasso, Torquato (1982) *Tasso's Dialogues. A Selection, with the Discourse of the Art of the Dialogue*, trans. Carnes Lord and Dain A. Trafton. Berkeley, Los Angeles and London: University of California Press.

Tateo, Francesco (1989) 'Interior Dialogue and Ideological Polemic in Petrarch's *Secretum*' (*Dialogo Interiore e polemica ideoogica nel 'Secretium' del Petrarca* (Florence: Le Monnier, 1965)), abridged in Francesco Petrarca, *Petrarch's* Secretum *with Introduction, Notes, and Critical Anthology*, trans. and ed. Davy Carozza and H. James Shey. New York: Peter Lang, pp. 251–71.

Taylor, Jeremy (1657) *A Discourse of the Nature, Offices and Measures of Friendship, with Rules of conducting it. Written in answer to a Letter from the most ingenious and vertuous M. K. P.* London: Royston.

Thomasius, Christian (1717) *Institutiones Jurisprudentiae Divinae Libri Tres*. Halle: Salfredii.

Thweatt, Vivien (1980) *La Rochefoucuald and the Seventeenth-century Concept of the Self*. Geneva: Droz.

Timmermans, Linda (1993) *L'accès des femmes à la culture (1598–1715): Un débat d'idées de Saint François de Sales à la Marquise de Lambert*. Paris: H. Champion.

Tinkler, John F. (1987) 'Renaissance Humanism and the *genera eloquentiae*', *Rhetorica* 5, 3: 279–309.

Tinkler, John F. (1988a) 'Humanism and Dialogue', *Parergon: Bulletin of the Australian and New Zealand Association for Medieval and Renaissance Studies* 6: 197–214.

Tinkler, John F. (1988b) 'Praise and Advice: Rhetorical Approaches in More's Utopia and Machiavelli's the Prince', *Sixteenth Century Journal* 19, 2: 187–207.

Tinkler, John F. (1988c) 'The Splitting of Humanism: Bentley, Swift, and the English Battle of the Books', *Journal of the History of Ideas* 49, 3: 453–72.

Tinkler, John F. (1991) 'Erasmus' Conversation with Luther', *Archiv für Reformationsgeschichte* 82: 59–81.

Todd, Janet (1980) *Women's Friendship in Literature*. New York: Columbia University Press.

Trafton, Dain A. (1983) 'Politics and the Praise of Women: Political Doctrine in the *Courtier*'s Third Book', in *Castiglione: The Ideal and the Real in Renaissance Culture*, ed. Robert W. Hanning and David Rosand. New Haven, CT and London: Yale University Press, pp. 29–44.

Triadafilopoulos, Triadafilos (1999) 'Politics, Speech, and the Art of Persuasion: Toward an Aristotelian Conception of the Public Sphere', *Journal of Politics* 61, 3: 741–57.

Trinkaus, Charles (1970) *In Our Image and Likeness: Humanity and Divinity in Italian Humanist Thought, Volume I*. Chicago and London: University of Chicago Press.

true and exact Journall or diarie of the most materiall passages happening at and after our landing at the Isle of Ree, A (1627) Additional MS 72319, fos. 1–12. London: British Library.

true relation of the affaires of Europe, A (1622) London: Printed [by Bernard Alsop?] for Nathaniel Butter and Nicholas Bourne, 4 October.

True Report of all the proceedings of Grave Mauris before the Towne of Bercke, A (1601) London: [By R. Read?] for William Jones.

true Reporte of the taking of the great towne and Castell of Polotzko, A (1579) [London].

Tuck, Richard (1979) *Natural Rights Theories: Their Origin and Development*. Cambridge: Cambridge University Press.

Tuck, Richard (1983) 'Grotius, Carneades and Hobbes', *Grotiana*, n.s., IV: 43–62.

Tuck, Richard (1987) 'The "Modern" Theory of Natural Law', in *The Langauges of Political Theory in Early-Modern Europe*, ed. Anthony Pagden. Cambridge: Cambridge University Press, pp. 99–119.

Tuck, Richard (1993) *Philosophy and Government 1572–1651*. Cambridge: Cambridge University Press.

Ultee, Maarten (1987) 'The Republic of Letters: Learned Correspondence 1680–1720', *Seventeenth Century* 2, 1: 95–112.

Valenza, Robin (2009) *Literature, Language, and the Rise of the Intellectual Disciplines in Britain, 1680–1820*. Cambridge: Cambridge University Press.

Valiavitcharska, Vessela (2013) 'The Byzantine Grammarian and Rhetorical Training', *Rhetorica* 31, 3: 237–60.

Valla, Lorenzo (1977) *On Pleasure. De voluptate*, trans. A. Kent Hieatt and Maristella Lorch. New York: Abaris Books.

Vallée, Jean-François (2004) 'The Fellowship of the Book: Printed Voices and Written Friendships in More's *Utopia*', in *Printed Voices: The Renaissance Culture of Dialogue*, ed. Dorothea Heitsch and Jean-François Vallée. Toronto: University of Toronto Press, pp. 42–62.

Van Den Hout, Michiel (1949) 'Studies in Early Greek Letter-Writing', *Mnemosyne*, ser. 4, 2: 19–41, 138–53.

Vaumorière, Pierre d'Ortigue, sieur de (1691) *L'Art de plaire dans la conversation* (Paris, 1690), trans. unknown, *The Art of Pleasing in Conversation*. London: R. Bentley.

Viala, Alain (1998) '*Les Signes Galants:* A Historical Reevaluation of Galanterie', trans. Daryl Lee, in *Exploring the Conversible World: Text and Sociability from the Classical Age to the Enlightenment*, ed. Elena Russo, Yale French Studies, No. 92, pp. 11–29.

Vickers, Brian (1988) *In Defence of Rhetoric*. Oxford: Clarendon Press.

Vives, Juan Luis (1989) *De Conscribendis Epistolis*, ed. and trans. Charles Fantazzi. Leiden and New York: E. J. Brill.

Vives, Juan Luis (2000) *The Education of a Christian Woman: A Sixteenth Century* Manual, ed. and trans. Charles Fantazzi. Chicago and London: University of Chicago Press.

Voiture, Vincent (1650) *Les Oeuvres de Monsieur de Voiture*. Paris: Courbé.

Voss, Paul (2001) *Elizabethan News Pamphlets. Shakespeare, Spenser, Marlowe and the Birth of Journalism*. Pittsburgh: Duquesne University Press.

Wadell, Paul J. CP (1996) 'Growing Together in the Divine Love: The Role of Charity in the Moral Theology of Thomas Aquinas', in *Aquinas and Empowerment: Classical Ethics for Ordinary Lives*, ed. G. Simon Harak, SJ. Washington, DC: Georgetown University Press, pp. 134–69.

Wahl, Elizabeth Susan (1999) *Invisible Relations: Representations of Female Intimacy in the Age of Enlightenment*. Stanford: Stanford University Press.

Walsingham, Francis (1589) *Francis Walsingham to anonymous, 29 June 1589*. V.b. 142, fo. 6. Folger Shakespeare Library, Washington, DC.

Warner, J. Christopher (2004) 'Thomas More's *Utopia* and the Problem of Writing a Literary History of English Renaissance Dialogue', in *Printed Voices: The Renaissance Culture of Dialogue*, ed. Dorothea Heitsch and Jean-François Vallée. Toronto: University of Toronto Press, pp. 63–76.

Warner, Lyndan (2011) *The Ideas of Man and Woman in Renaissance France: Print, Rhetoric, and Law*. Farnham: Ashgate.

Watson, Gerard (1971) 'The Natural Law and Stoicism', in *Problems of Stoicism*, ed. A. A. Long. London: University of London, Athlone Press, pp. 216–38.

Watt, Ian (1964) *The Rise of the Novel*. Berkeley and Los Angeles: University of California Press.

Welles, C. Bradford (1974) *Royal Correspondence in the Hellenistic period: A Study in Greek Epigraphy*. Chicago: Ares.

Weststeijn, Arthur (2012) *Commercial Republicanism in the Dutch Golden Age: The Political Thought of Johan and Pieter de la Court*. Leiden and Boston: Brill.

Williams, Raymond (1985) *Keywords: A Vocabulary of Culture and Society*, rev. edn. New York: Oxford University Press.

Wilson, K. J. (1985) *Incomplete Fictions: The Formation of English Renaissance Dialogue*. Washington, DC: Catholic University of America Press.

Wilson, Thomas (1553) *Arte of Rhetorique*. London: Richard Grafton.

Winn, Colette H. (ed.) (1993) *The Dialogue in Early Modern France, 1547–1630: Art and Argument*. Washington, DC: Catholic University of America Press.

Withers, Andrew (1629) *And. Withers to anonymous, 10 August 1629*. Additional MS 46189, fos. 24–5. London: British Library.

Withington, Phil (2005) *The Politics of Commonwealth: Citizens and Freemen in Early Modern England*. Cambridge: Cambridge University Press.

Withington, Phil (2010) *Society in Early Modern England: The Vernacular Origins of Some Powerful Ideas*. Cambridge: Polity Press.

Witt, Ronald (1982) 'Medieval "Ars Dictaminis" and the Beginnings of Humanism: a New Construction of the Problem', *Renaissance Quarterly* 35, 1: 1–35.

Witt, Ronald (2001) 'Medieval Italian Culture and the Origins of Humanism as a Stylistic Ideal', *Italian Humanism and Medieval Rhetoric*. Aldershot: Ashgate, I, pp. 29–70.

Witt, Ronald (2003) *In the Footsteps of the Ancients: The Origins of Humanism from Lovato to Bruni*. Boston and Leiden: Brill.

Woodbridge, Linda (1984) *Women and the English Renaissance: Literature and the Nature of Womankind, 1540–1620*. Urbana and Chicago: University of Illinois Press.

Xenophon (1979) *Memorabilia*, trans. E. C. Marchant, in *Memorabilia and Oeconomicus. Symposium and Apology*. Cambridge, MA: Harvard University Press; London: William Heinemann, pp. 3–359.

Xenophon (1994) *Oeconomicus: A Social and Historical Commentary*, trans. Sarah B. Pomeroy. Oxford: Clarendon Press.

Yadav, Alok (2004) *Before the Empire of English: Literature, Provinciality, and Nationalism in Eighteenth-Century Britain*. New York: Palgrave Macmillan.

Yeo, Richard (2009) 'John Locke on Conversation with Friends and Strangers', *Parergon* 26, 2: 11–37.

Zagorin, Perez (2009) *Hobbes and the Law of Nature*. Princeton: Princeton University Press.

Zancan, Marina (1983) 'La donna e il cerchio nel "Cortegiano" di B. Castiglione. Le funzioni del femminile nell'immagine di corte', in *Nel cerchio della luna: Figure di donna in alcuni testi del VXI secolo*, ed. Marina Zancan. Venice: Marsilio, pp. 13–56.

Zaret, David (2000) *Origins of Democratic Culture. Printing, Petitions, and the Public Sphere in Early-Modern England*. Princeton: Princeton University Press.

Index

Works, when not anonymous, are listed together with their authors.